# The Iconography
of Power

# The Iconography of Power

## The French *Nouvelle* at the End of the Middle Ages

David LaGuardia

Newark: University of Delaware Press
London: Associated University Presses

© 1999 by Associated University Presses, Inc.

All rights reserved. Authorization to photocopy items for internal or personal use, or the internal or personal use of specific clients, is granted by the copyright owner, provided that a base fee of $10.00, plus eight cents per page, per copy is paid directly to the Copyright Clearance Center, 222 Rosewood Drive, Danvers, Massachusetts 01923. [0–87413–669–5/99 $10.00 + 8¢ pp, pc.]

Other than as indicated in the foregoing, this book may not be reproduced, in whole or in part, in any form (except as permitted by Sections 107 and 108 of the U.S. Copyright Law, and except for brief quotes appearing in reviews in the public press.)

Associated University Presses
440 Forsgate Drive
Cranbury, NJ 08512

Associated University Presses
16 Barter Street
London WC1A 2AH, England

Associated University Presses
P.O. Box 338, Port Credit
Mississauga, Ontario
Canada L5G 4L8

The paper used in this publication meets the requirements
of the American National Standard for Permanence of Paper
for Printed Library Materials Z39.48–1984.

**Library of Congress Cataloging-in-Publication Data**

LaGuardia, David, 1963–.
    The iconography of power: the French nouvelle at the end of the Middle Ages / David LaGuardia.
       p. cm.
    Includes bibliographical references and index.
    ISBN 0–87413–669–5 (alk. paper)
    1. French fiction—To 1500—History and criticism. 2. Novelle—History and criticism. 3. Tales, Medieval—History and criticism. I. Title.
PQ221.L34  1999
843'.0109002—DC21                                                               98–24414
                                                                                                                  CIP

PRINTED IN THE UNITED STATES OF AMERICA

*For Juana*

# Contents

Acknowledgments
Introduction                                                                11

1. Realism and the *Nouvelle*                                               27
2. Male Homosocial Domination in the
   *Cent nouvelles nouvelles*                                               51
3. Philippe de Vigneulles and the Economy of Expenditure                    83
4. Feminist Ambivalence and Feminine Virtue
   in the *Heptaméron*                                                     113
Conclusion                                                                 146

Notes                                                                      151
Bibliography                                                               169
Index                                                                      175

# Acknowledgments

I wish to thank Lance Donaldson-Evans and Gerald Prince for their indispensable help and advice with this work; Lawrence Kritzman, whose constant encouragement and friendship helped me to complete this text; my former teachers at the University of Pennsylvania, Jean Alter, Charles Bernheimer, Frank Bowman, Kevin Brownlee, Joan DeJean, Lucienne Frappier-Mazur, and Stephen Nichols; my colleagues at Dartmouth, for their good advice; David Rollo, for his insightful and witty comments; Gary Ferguson, for his great comments on the manuscript; Walter and Constance Burke, whose generous support of research conducted by assistant professors at Dartmouth made the completion of this project possible; and, last but not least, my families on both sides of the Atlantic, for everything.

* * *

The jacket illustration is courtesy of the Hood Museum of Art, Dartmouth College, Hanover, New Hampshire, gift of Mr. and Mrs. Richard H. Rush, Class of 1937. Permission for its use is gratefully acknowledged.

# Introduction

Between 1462 and 1600, thousands of oral stories of the type known as the *nouvelle* were transcribed and published in France. Certain character types appear repeatedly in these tales: the noble husband who wants to seduce his humble neighbor's wife, or his own chambermaid; the wife who wants to slip into her neighbor's bed, or who tricks a clerk or servant into making love with her; itinerant monks who come into town to cheat its male inhabitants out of their money, to eat their food, or to rape their wives; the younger son or the bastard son of a nobleman who falls in love with the only daughter of a great house and who makes a futile attempt to win her hand; the paranoid cuckold who is hoodwinked by his clever wife and her lovers; the rogue character who robs, cheats, beats, and befouls whomever he can. Here one enters a rapacious world in which violence in one form or another (sexual, physical, political) is an integral part of the characters' activity.

A comic tradition that valorized scatological and sexual cruelty as humorous strikes our (post) politically correct sensibilities as rather distasteful. The first modern readers of the genre had similar difficulties overcoming their repugnance of its dirty details. Even as late as 1981, when the last major collection of essays on the *nouvelle* was published, V. L. Saulnier complained, "The Renaissance tale, whether French or Italian, has suffered from a false reputation for a long time. One had the impression that the tale writers of the period were principally and generally interested in exploring their taste for licentious anecdotes."

Saulnier justified the lubriciousness of the genre by appealing to an argument that had been brought to the *nouvelle*'s defense since the end of the nineteenth century: "In contrast, that which makes the *nouvelle* worth reading is its value as a microcosm."[1] That is, on the whole, the *nouvelle* was supposed to have reproduced in miniature an image of the *real* world of the period. The realism of these texts thus gave them a historical value that could be discerned within their repugnant details.[2]

This realist defense of the *nouvelle* is not satisfactory for a simple reason: the narrative practice that is characteristic of the *nouvelle* predates realism and operates according to its own logic and its own rules, which are akin to the signifying systems that dominated the visual arts of the Middle Ages. Imagine denigrating the carvings that surround the altar of Notre Dame de Paris, which depict scenes from the life of Christ, as early attempts at "realistic" sculpture, when in fact realism has little to do with the iconography of medieval art. This is essentially the reading that was imposed on the *nouvelle* until quite recently. Once this bias for realism has been recognized at least as somewhat erroneous, it becomes possible for one to perform a variety of different readings on this multifarious genre.

We will and inevitably *must* read these texts from our own point of view, which presupposes that certain theoretical concerns are relevant to the analysis of any literary artifact. Moreover, we should refrain from assigning a value judgment to their contents and from judging their mode of representation by the anachronistic code of realism. On the contrary, it is precisely what is *unreal* in these representations that may reveal the importance of this genre's explosive appearance in sixteenth-century France. The obsessive repetitions of primal scenes in which a man betrays his wife, or is betrayed by her, in which a rogue splatters eggs or feces on someone's head before his own is splattered, or in which a cuckolded gentleman castrates his wife's lover—all in the name of comedy—reveal something about the psyche of an age in which religious wars, famines, and epidemics were part of every individual's daily life. At the risk of rephrasing Saulnier's "microcosm" argument, it could be that the stylized cartoon figures who populate the *nouvelle*—the cuckold, the gallant seducer, the willing chambermaid, the rogue, the gluttonous monk—are more *real* than Emma Bovary or Eugénie Grandet in that they represent the collective imaginary of an entire people, as opposed to character types generated by a single "genius." Rather than being concerned with representing "reality," these tales seem unconsciously to affirm the *truth* of this period: to use Nietzsche's words, the perception that "life itself is violent, rapacious, exploitative, and destructive and cannot be conceived otherwise."[3]

After Freud, Marx, Nietzsche, Bataille, Bakhtin, Foucault, Irigaray, Cixous, Kristeva, and feminist criticism, we are in a unique position to understand the tragicomic obsessions of the French Renaissance, and we must interpret them from the perspectives provided by these critical discourses. In this light, for example, the *Cent nouvelles nouvelles* prove to be the homoerotic fantasies that a group of men told one another, among whom the exchange of women's bodies was the basis of power and position in a male-dominated, homosocial society. Likewise, the *Cent nouvelles nouvelles* of Philippe de Vigneulles represented an economy of expenditure, centered on the material activity of the lower body, that undermined the functioning of a restricted homosocial hierarchy. Finally, the *Heptaméron* depicted the double bind of female characters trapped in a narrative system generated by the concept of "feminine virtue," which men imposed upon women who were compelled both to defend it and to resist it. In developing these three theses, I will demonstrate that a critical reading of the *nouvelle* is important neither because the genre realistically represents everyday life in the late fifteenth and early sixteenth centuries nor because of the aesthetic value of its mode of representation. Rather, the importance of coming to terms with this noteworthy literary phenomenon (at least in terms of *quantity*) of early modern France lies in the *truths* it may reveal about this epoch to our critical eye. As Parlamente asserts in the prologue to the *Heptaméron*, "As a matter of fact, the two ladies I've mentioned [Madame the Dauphine, Madame Marguerite], along with other people of the court, made up their minds . . . that they should not write any story that was not truthful [*véritable histoire*]."[4] By telling and retelling certain kinds of stories, the writers of this period told truths about themselves that were "beyond" the realm of the real, just as, in Freud's sense, the unconscious is beyond our understanding of that which is available to our perception as the "real." Our task as readers of these texts is to reformulate these "truths" in a critical discourse that will make them clear to us in our own terms.

It may be objected that such a project is hopelessly anachronistic. Reading five-hundred-year-old texts is unavoidably anachronistic, no matter how much time and effort one spends trying to reconstruct, reconfigure, or reproduce the real world that existed at that time, which is available to us mainly in documents that we also have to interpret: court records, chronicles, civil and ecclesiastical legal texts, criminal registers, account books, memoirs, etc. The task of trying to imagine what Philippe de Vigneulles's city of Metz was *really* like in the year 1505, or what his *real* literary antecedents and models were, is a difficult one, and I admire any scholar who attempts to do so (Charles Livingston's philological comments on Philippe's text, for example, are an invaluable guide to reading it). Nevertheless, it is also possible for one to inflict an anachronistic critique on the works of imagination that have been left to us by the past, in order to understand the meaning of the recurrent images and motifs that dominate the collective imaginary of a period. The seemingly countless *nouvelles* that remain from early-modern France comprise a body of evidence that implies the existence of a "reality" constituted by redundant images. One may interpret this evidence in any number of ways—from philological, historical, psychoanalytic, feminist, Marxist, Bakhtinian, or Foucaldian perspectives, to name just a few. To claim that a Marxist reading of the *nouvelle* is anachronistic because historical materialism did not exist in the sixteenth century is tantamount to claiming that a historical reading of *The Egyptian Book of the Dead* is anachronistic because history as a rational and causal conception and analysis of human events in time did not exist in ancient Egypt.[5] While historical materialism did *not* exist in fifteenth- to sixteenth-century France, modes of production, labor, commodities, and class dominations certainly *did* exist, which means that a Marxist analysis of this period is not at all anachronistic if it remains true to the evidence at hand. For example, if sixty of the *Cent nouvelles nouvelles* are about marriage and adultery, and if the transfer of the female body from one male character to another is often accompanied by an exchange of goods, one may assume that marriage played a significant role in the economic organization of the social world that is represented in this text. Given this evidence, one could undertake a Marxist or feminist critique of the ways in which the female body became a kind of fetishized commodity in this context, without being anachronistic in the least. One could object that the real men and women living at that time could not possibly have imagined that the female body served as the material base of a male-dominated, homosocial economy. While this type of objection is valid and important, it is also clear that writers such as Marguerite de Navarre intuited the detrimental aspects of marriage as a social institution and did their best to highlight its dangers and abuses for women, even if a Marxist language for analyzing this institution was not at their disposition.

The critical terminology that I will adopt throughout the following close readings requires some explication. Chapter 1 is a brief survey of the first century of scholarly literature devoted to the French *nouvelle* of the fifteenth and sixteenth centuries. It argues that the evaluation of this genre in relation to the concept of realism, which is a critical attitude that lasted well into the 1980s, is indeed anachronistic not only because the literary codes of realism did not exist in early-modern France but also because this critical bias or value judgment (the *nouvelle* was considered inferior to the modern novel because it was less realistic) obscures the salient formal characteristics of the genre, as well as the persistent obsessions that dominate it. Throughout this chapter, the term "realism" applies to a narrative practice that was developed throughout the nineteenth century by European writers and that consisted (among other things) of precise attention to physical details and descriptions, dialectal differentiation of reported speech, extensive development of characters, penetration into their subjectivity, and so on. All of these characteristics are essentially absent from the *nouvelle*, which does not mean that it does not have its own mode and method of representation, which is much closer to the iconography of medieval painting than it is to the realistic detail of the photograph.[6]

While I will discuss my usage of the term "iconography" in greater detail in chapter 1, a few introductory remarks about the relation between iconographic images and the functioning of power in narrative are necessary here. In its most essential sense, an icon is a two-dimensional, Byzantine sacred image depicting Christ, the Virgin and Child, a saint, etc. According to Leslie Brubaker, the earliest Christian icons were meant to serve as "windows" that would compel the viewer to contemplate the sacred "prototype" that inspired the image:

> Byzantine theologians were ... careful to distinguish between an image and its prototype, and to stress that it was not the wood and paint that the faithful should venerate but rather the holy person depicted. One statement that attempted to make this distinction clear was penned by the Ecumenical Council of 787 ...: "The image resembles the prototype, not with regard to essence, but only with regard to the name and to the position of the members which can be characterized." By separating the divine essence from the image, the theologians insisted that the viewer must close the gap between the pale visual reflection of divinity and its genuine contemplation. The viewer must look through the window of the image to the holy person, rather than at the material depiction. The Byzantine beholder assumed responsibility for the proper interpretation of the sacred image.[7]

The official ecclesiastical doctrine of the icon defined it as an image that invoked a sacred name coupled with a "disposition of the members" of the represented figure, which elicited an interpretation from the viewer. In the earliest icons from Byzantium, the image communicates a coded message to the viewer via the medium of a kind of sign language: Brubaker's figure 1, the icon of Christ Pantokrator from the Monastery of St. Catherine on Mount Sinai, shows the Savior holding the Bible in his left hand, his right hand in the typical position of blessing, his ring and small fingers touching his thumb, his middle and index fingers slightly bent. In Brubaker's figure 2, St. Nicholas likewise holds a Bible in his left hand, but his right hand seems either to indicate the book or to grasp the sacred vestments that are crossed on his chest. He is surrounded by ten figures, all of whom have their right hands in different positions: with the ring finger and thumb joined and the palm facing upward; with the middle and ring fingers touching the thumb; holding a significant object (one figure appears to have a sword). The icon *signifies* or *works*, then, by means of conventional symbols or gestures that cause the viewer to interpret the image, thus forming a "prototype" in his or her mind that is the result of a process of recognition and identification. Undoubtedly, the hand positions I have just mentioned would have been recognized and understood by those initiated in the mysteries of the Orthodox religion.[8] Rabelais's parodical debate between Thaumaste and Panurge in chapter 19 of the *Pantagruel* indicates well enough that knowledge of recondite sings was part of erudition in Europe for more than a millennium. Similarly, the characters of the short narratives that dominate the end of the Middle Ages are icons in the sense that their names and gestures invite the reader to interpret their significance and to produce profane prototypes of figures who are transfixed in social power structures, just as the saints themselves were immobilized in their positions in the hierarchy of heaven. The narrative "images" of the knight, the miller, the monk, the nun, the clerk, the merchant, the wife, and the chambermaid come to life via significant details that are essentially different from realist details.[9] It is by interpreting the "disposition" of these "members" that one may form a prototype of the power-saturated social world in which these characters lived and moved as fictional subjects, independently of whether or not this world existed in actuality.

Iconography proper, as it was developed in art history by Aby Warburg and Erwin Panofsky, addresses precisely the interpretative move by which the viewer of an image identifies the name of the figure or the saint whom it represents:

> Secondary or conventional subject matter [in art] . . . is apprehended by realizing that a male figure with a knife represents St. Bartholomew, that a female figure with a peach in her hand is a personification of veracity, that a group of figures seated at a dinner table in a certain arrangement and in certain poses represents the Last Supper, or that two figures fighting each other in a certain manner represent the Combat of Vice and Virtue. In doing this we connect artistic motifs and combinations of artistic motifs (compositions) with themes or concepts. Motifs thus recognized as carriers of a secondary or conventional meaning may be called images, and combinations of images are what the ancient theorists of art called *invenzioni*; we are wont to call them stories and allegories. The identification of such images, stories and allegories is the domain of what is normally referred to as "iconography."[10]

I will use the term "iconography" throughout this text in Panofsky's sense. Moreover, one of my basic theses is the idea that the *nouvelle* literature itself is an *iconography* of power in the etymological sense of the term: the genre *writes* narrative images that contain and reveal a prototype of a social order, much in the same way that a prototypical conception of the cosmos (God-Holy Spirit-Angels-Saints) is revealed and contained in the individual depictions of its members. In the absence of this cosmological hierarchy, the sacred image would make no sense, just as the figures of the *nouvelle* would be virtually incomprehensible without the prototype of a rigid social hierarchy that we develop in our minds while reading these stories. The *nouvelle*'s characters are identified by iconographic details (much as Saint Sebastian may be identified by the arrows that pierce his flesh), which define and restrict their roles. The social world in which the characters of the *nouvelle* exist predetermines the identity of each of them, named most often only in terms of their occupation or status. The genre thus explores the implications of character displacements across a value-laden and hierarchical social grid: for example, the typical situation in which a knight attempted to seduce his chambermaid, which is described countless times in this literature, was apparently a piquant one for the audience of the period, since it figured the violation of restrictions that constituted the identity of these characters (servants could not have intimate relationships with their masters, knights could not betray their code of honor, married men could not have sex with women other than their wives).

Since the *nouvelle* is not realistic, it is not about the effect that imaginary events have on the development of characters as individual subjects, whose resultant traits are decisive for the outcome of its plot. Rather, the *nouvelle* describes the procedures by which collective social structures predetermine and constrict the actions of characters who never reach the stage of individuation that is typical of modern subjectivity and the modern novel. In other words, the genre painstakingly (if unconsciously and unintentionally) describes the ways in which power's activity or exercise—one might even say power's "being"—structures imaginary social worlds, which in turn generate characters as individual but socially determined identities. I will complement this essential thesis—fictional social hierarchies are the material form assumed by power in narrative— with a second one: narrative as technique or technology embodies, creates, transmits, and participates in these configurations of power both within the text and *as* the text. Both of these theses require some clarification.

Critical theory of the last twenty years has demonstrated that the concept of power confronts anyone who wishes to understand it with numerous intellectual dilemmas or aporias. A glance at Foucault's complex and problematic definitions, as well as the abundant secondary literature that his work has generated, reveals that his considerations, while intriguing, have hopelessly obscured any clear and straightforward understanding that one might have of power, albeit in a quite fruitful way. My purpose here is not to explicate Foucault in an attempt to clarify what so many admirable scholars have been unable to fathom. Rather, I will use a working definition of power, derived largely from *La Volonté de savoir*, *Surveiller et punir*, and *Power/Knowledge*, which has seven points:

1) Power is (something perceived by an individual subject as) an external force that incites one to act, or restricts one from acting. Power has positive as well as negative effects. It is thus not equivalent to a simple relation of domination/subordination. Every individual who lives within power relations (everyone, that is) feels compelled to act in some ways and restricted from acting in others. For example, one might assume that the Queen of tale 21 of the *Heptaméron* is in a position of power, while Rolandine is subjected to the power that the Queen possesses. The Queen must act in certain ways, however, or she will no longer be identifiable as such: she cannot simply allow Rolandine to marry the "bastard of a noble house," and she must act to interrupt this illegitimate relationship.

2) From this point of view, power is something that is exercised; it is not possessed. In my previous example, the Queen does not *have* power over Rolandine; rather, she exercises a power that is an intrinsic and constitutive element of her position as monarch. When the Queen punishes Rolandine for her relationship with the *bâtard*, she is merely assuming the role that power has assigned to the position of the monarch, and she virtually has no choice but to act as such. It is clear, however, that Rolandine cannot exercise the kind of power that is designated for the Queen, and vice versa.

3) Individuals—or characters, in the case of imaginary texts—assume given identities by performing actions that are predetermined by social configurations of power. Characters or individuals who resist the positive and negative effects of power attempt to traverse the boundaries that constitute both identity and power. In tale 21, Rolandine's resistance, made manifest in her actions, threatens her very identity as a young woman from a noble house who was a close relative of the Queen.

4) Power resides in configurations of relations among individuals and the concrete practices that define these relations. The hierarchical relationship between men and women, for example, has its basis in the perceived physical differences that traditionally distinguished male from female. For example, one essential physical difference, strength versus weakness (which is subjective and culturally determined), translates into a series of practices that are culturally contingent, depending upon what is perceived as the more physically demanding activity amidst different circumstances: men work in the fields, women in the home; men go off to sea, women work the fields and tend to the home; men go off to hunt,

women work the fields; men work in the factories, women shop and clean house; women work in the factories, men go off to war, etc. In most cultures, power has been associated with the male position in these series of practices.

While it is true that women are still socially and politically dominated by men, it is also true that the exercise of male power has its positive and negative effects: real men don't cry, don't eat quiche, are stronger than their wives, hold doors open for women, always pick up the check on dates, drink cognac and smoke cigars after dinner, etc. As trivial as these constraints may seem, they nevertheless force men to act *as* men in a configuration of power that defines dominant and subordinate positions for men and women, respectively. Rather than claiming that men have the power in a given situation and that women have none, it is perhaps more exact to say that men exercise a kind of contingent power while being subject to its constraints, at the same time that women exercise a different kind of contingent power to which they are also subject. For example, from a certain point of view, a man ceases to be a man if he does not perform certain actions (assume the role of authority in the household, adopt certain misogynistic attitudes toward women, watch sports), and the same holds true for women (a woman who is not feminine or *cocotte*, or a woman who does not assume the responsibility for raising and educating her children, for example, ceases to be a woman from a certain narrow point of view). As Parlamente says in the frame of the *Heptaméron*, tale 43:

> Women who are dominated by pleasure have no right to call themselves women. They might as well call themselves men, since it is men who regard violence and lust as something honourable. When a man kills an enemy in revenge because he has been crossed by him, his friends think he's all the more gallant. It's the same thing when a man, not content with his wife, loves a dozen other women as well. But the honour of women has a different foundation: for them the basis of honour is gentleness, patience and chastity. (397)

Both sides of this presuppositional relationship include the positive and negative effects of power: both men and women are compelled to act and to refrain from acting if they wish to be identified in gender terms. It remains true, however, that one side of this opposition is identified as dominant, the other as subordinate.

5) A special instance of the concrete practices that define a structure of power is that of marriage. According to Lévi-Strauss, the incest prohibition is the only universal of human cultures, meaning that the enforcement of exogamy and its attendant transfer of women from family to family is a concrete foundation of the relations that structure every

society.[11] Woman as the conduit through which wealth is transferred from head of family to head of family has been a constant of Western culture from its inception. Marriage thus constitutes a set of concrete practices that define the relations among individuals and even the identity of these individuals. The importance of marriage in structuring social relations, and hence as an apparatus (*dispositif*) of power, to use Foucault's term, is evident in the social hierarchies depicted in the *nouvelle*. Marriage as the cultural regulation of the biological facts of sexual difference and reproduction is a locus at which the material activities that define power relations become evident, and in which the various tensions that confront individuals as subjects of desire make themselves available for analysis. In the typical problem that is examined or parodied in the Renaissance tale—that of young men or women who are forced to marry against their will, or who are not allowed to marry the object of their desires—the positive and negative effects of power for both male and female characters stand out in stark relief.

6) Where there are relations, power is present. Any individual who attempts to enter into any kind of relation invariably feels compelled to act in certain ways, and to refrain from acting in other ways. Power thus pervades or saturates intersubjective relations, which means that the individual subject is always *within* power and *traversed* by it.

7) Power functions by means of oppositions, and where these are present, the effects of power will manifest themselves. In the *nouvelle*, the most fundamental of these distinguishes male from female. Throughout this text, I will use the terms "female," "feminine," and "feminist" in their most basic senses. The term "female" denotes the biological characteristics of characters who were born of one sex, just as the term "male" denotes those of the other sex. The term "feminine" designates the attributes of people (or in the case of literature, characters) who were engendered as women, meaning that the idea of "feminine" behaviors and activities is culturally contingent; the term "masculine" also defines the set of traits that apply to individuals engendered as men. Finally, the term "feminist" applies to acts and attitudes intended to liberate women from the position of inferiority that has been imposed upon them by social structures. The term "masculinist," in the sense of actions aimed at emancipating men from traditional gender roles, is not applicable to the context of the French *nouvelle*.

My analyses in the following chapters will concentrate on the *nouvelle* as a genre that delineates power relations and configurations, as I have just defined them, in an imaginary version of early-modern French society.[12] One might object that an analysis of power is not all that relevant to the stories of this period, since every individual alive at the time recognized and accepted the stratified social space as a given of his or her existence. In other words, the type of explication that I undertake in this text could be devalued as anachronistic, since the men and women of fifteenth- to sixteenth-century France were perhaps not conscious of the extent to which power pervaded their lives and predetermined their identities. Nevertheless, the mode of representation at work in the *nouvelle* compels the reader to explicate the process by which the genre identifies its nonindividuated characters, by means of significant details that both presuppose and outline the existence of a stratified, hierarchical, and oppositional social grid. In other words, most of the characters in these texts are nameless, except for the labels that constitute their social identity: knight, miller, monk, merchant, wife, nun, clerk, etc. When the characters are named, their proper names function as abbreviations of the attributes that define them in a social configuration: in tale 10 of the *Heptaméron*, for example, "Amadour" signifies "the younger son who, because of his virtues as a warrior, deserves to marry his beloved, Floride, the only daughter of a noble household, but he cannot marry her because he is a younger son." Similarly, the spectacular epithet that Marguerite de Navarre chose for the male protagonist of her tale 21 is overdetermined by its social connotations: throughout the tale, he is referred to as "the bastard of a noble house," and this identity limits the actions that he is allowed to perform and the relationships into which he is allowed to enter. Throughout this book, therefore, I argue essentially that the *nouvelle* is a manifestation of a fascination with power that dominated the collective imaginary of the period ("imaginary" in the sense of "the images that dominate the narrative iconography of a period," and not in the psychoanalytical sense developed by Lacan).

My purpose in this book is to describe early-modern representations of a configuration of power that is increasingly problematized in certain texts, and toward which individual characters manifest increasingly ambivalent attitudes. In other words, this book is about power and the multifarious resistance to it that is evident in a very restricted (imaginative) context. The first stage of my reading involves describing the topography of power in its most basic form: Chapter 2 examines the hyperbolic economy of male domination in *Les Cent nouvelles nouvelles*. In this male "homosocial" economy, men use women (or more specifically, the female body) as the material basis of their relationships with other men, which constitute a gender-stratified social hierarchy that does not allow women to use the male body as a medium for their relations with other women, and which attempts to keep women from recognizing the fact that their bodies are the material basis of a male economy (of course, these men and women are merely male and female characters). My reading of *Les Cent nouvelles nouvelles* thus explicates a gender-contingent social configuration that results in a given structure of power relations that has clearly discernible positive and negative effects on the characters who populate this world.

Chapter 3 considers the resistance to this male homosocial economy offered by the characters of Philippe de Vigneulles's *Cent nouvelles nouvelles*. De Vigneulles's text undermines the power structure of its predecessor by empowering female characters who resist being reduced to commodities in the sexual commerce that unites male characters. It also extends the idea of economy beyond the material basis of the female body, resulting in redistributions of wealth from privileged male characters to marginalized others. In a sense, Philippe's text enacts an inversion of this power structure that nonetheless remains merely carnivalesque in that it never seriously questions the structure's validity, just as carnival in Bakhtin's sense is merely a momentary suspension of official rules that contributes to their strength by being included within them.

Finally, chapter 4 analyzes the ambivalent feminine resistance to male homosocial power that appears in noteworthy tales of Marguerite de Navarre's *Heptaméron*. The authoritative and in some cases authoritarian female figures of this text invest a great deal of energy in maintaining a prevailing order that virtually excludes the definition and satisfaction of an authentically feminist desire. Some female characters of this work resist the gender-specific imperatives that constitute this order, only to be recuperated into its more sublimated version that appears at the end of some tales (10, 21). Other characters mount a genuine resistance to male homosocial power by creating an alternative space in which their desires may be satisfied (43, 70), only to meet with failure. From this perspective, the *Heptaméron* describes a double bind that is peculiar to subjects who have been engendered as women and that has long been of interest to feminist criticism: the collaboration of women in maintaining the place that has been determined for them by patriarchy, out of fear that transgressing this code will cause them to lose their very identity as women, as Parlamente remarked in her commentary to tale 43.

It may be that the transition from a masculine to a feminine point of view that culminates in the *Heptaméron* signifies an inchoate unraveling of identity as a function of one's social role, especially with the advent of what Foucault might have called a "humanist episteme," in which the discourse of equality circulated at least as a theory: Rabelais's description of the *abbaye de Thélème* is evidence of this development.[13] In Marguerite de Navarre's masterpiece, female characters attempt to have a say in the definition of the social role that has been assigned to them. The spiritual and intellectual difference that separates this text from the *Cent nouvelles nouvelles*, written less than a century earlier, indicates the extent to which the basis of the genre—i.e., a rigid social structure that predetermined the identities of individuals—was being undermined, at least in the theoretical discourses of the period. This type of social structure is still with us, of course, and will perhaps always be rewritten in other registers and replaced by other structures. The explosion of mercantile and marginalized activity in the text of Philippe de Vigneulles, and the valiant female characters who attempt to give a voice and a space to their desire in the *Heptaméron,* embody stages in a long genealogical movement that culminated in the egalitarian ideology of the Enlightenment, which coincided with the rise of the modern novel and the modern individual, responsible for his or her own destiny, at least in theory. The value of the *nouvelle* as a genre is to be found, therefore, in the evolving social worlds that it depicts, which occupy the threshold between the premodern and the early modern. This kind of conclusion, however, is a theoretical departure that could be based upon the research that will be carried out in the following pages, which will be focused almost exclusively on representations of power in the texts themselves.

# The Iconography of Power

# 1
## Realism and the *Nouvelle*

Like its earlier and later counterparts in Italian, Spanish, and English, the French *nouvelle* of the fifteenth and sixteenth centuries is an extraordinarily rich and varied literary artifact. The success of the genre at this time is evident from the astounding number of collections written in France.[1] Despite the enormous popularity of these short tales throughout early-modern Europe, and the large body of scholarship devoted to the genre by the earliest medievalists and their successors (from Gaston Paris to Lionello Sozzi), there has not been a significant amount of literature devoted to the *nouvelle* in the last twenty years, aside from the numerous texts dedicated to the *Heptaméron* that have appeared during the last decade. The timing of this neglect could hardly have been more unfortunate, since the succession of critical theories that began with structuralism, and which has continued through postcolonial studies and queer theory, has provided scholars with tools that facilitate the understanding of this multifarious genre. The exemplary collections of *nouvelles* of the French Renaissance must be read from some of the diverse critical perspectives that have become prominent during the last three decades.

The necessity of this task may be demonstrated by a brief history of scholarship devoted to the *nouvelle*. The first scholars to study the genre at the end of the nineteenth century attempted to give an account of its origins and dissemination on the European continent. An investigation of the Italian influences on the French *nouvelle* was an inevitable and important part of this search for literary sources. Scholars also investigated the origins of the *nouvelle* in the French narrative genres—the *lai* and the *fabliau*—that preceded its appearance in fifteenth-century France, as well as in the *exempla* literature written in Latin and translated into French. Secondly, many scholars engaged in a debate that attempted to situate and to evaluate the *nouvelle* within a literary-historical continuum that culminated in the development of modern realist narrative. Thirdly, critics dedicated themselves to formulating a definition of the genre that would delineate its formal and thematic characteristics. I will examine these aspects of the critical tradition in order to situate my own reading of the *nouvelle*, which will react in part to this lengthy (if somewhat sparse) critical tradition while borrowing its essential thesis that the *nouvelle* represents a kind of reality. In contrast, however, my own reading concentrates on the phantasmic and intersubjective social realities portrayed in these tales, and engages our own current theories and critiques of this genre in a critical dialogue.

The French *nouvelle* was "obsessed" with various images and intersubjective configurations: adultery and cuckoldry, deceit and expenditure, passion as a cause of death, the smearing of the body in food or in its own refuse. It is these "phantasmic" aspects of the *nouvelle* that merit a critical reading, rather than its possible representation of a "real" world, or its "realistic" representation of a fantastic world, and rather than the seemingly infinite task of tracing the sources and analogs of each individual anecdote.[2] Moreover, a formal analysis of these repetitions reveals narrative's role in the formation of imaginary worlds that define or are defined by given configurations of power, which in turn virtually generated the identities of the various participants in these narratives. In other words, the obsessive telling and retelling of certain types of stories in different contexts reveals what was *at stake* for the narrators and narratees, the fictional storytellers and their listeners, who formed such an integral part of almost every tale collection written from the fourteenth to the seventeenth century: by recounting these same stories repeatedly, they put into question their own identities as socialized subjects. For a critical understanding of the procedures by which each story describes the imaginary social situation of its characters, it is not so important to know *what* its historical and actual sources are, or whether or not the story corresponds to an actual reality that can be verified from other "historical" texts. From the perspective that I will adopt throughout this text, what matters in reading the *nouvelle* is the process by which the narrative properties of the genre generate rigid and strictly defined (imaginary) social hierarchies, resulting in contingent types of subjectivity, incarnated in the characters, that offer themselves to us for analysis.

This work is thus largely a reaction against the realist critique of the genre. Part of the realist thesis—best exemplified in the title of Gabriel Pérouse's important study *Nouvelles françaises du XVIe siècle: Images de la vie du temps*—is especially problematic when one is dealing with long-vanished realities that may be reconstructed only by interpreting secondary texts, which are themselves far from clear as to what "reality" may have been like at that time. Secondly, if it is true that we may not recover the real world of fifteenth- to sixteenth-century France by reading a finite series of narratives, it is also true that the obsessive repetitions present in these tales reveal certain essential or constitutive features of the period, whether or not they were recognized as such at the time. In other words, the redundant images that constitute the *nouvelle*—the violation of the represented female body, which is transported from male to male; the incessant enforced circulation of merchandise, and its reflection in hyperbolic bodily functions; the dilemma of female characters in positions of power, trapped by the double bind of the code of female virtue—reveal at least three "truths" of the period: 1) relations among men via the medium of the female body generated the power and the essential paranoia of male subjectivity (in *Les Cent nouvelles nouvelles*); 2) the bodily functions of the *nouvelle*'s characters (eating, drinking, copulation, defecation) mirrored and mocked the functioning of an increasingly powerful mercantile economy (in the tales of Philippe de Vigneulles); 3) the sixteenth-century "feminist" response to male domination became entrapped in the aporia of the code of feminine virtue, which both provoked and restricted the exploration of female desire (in the *Heptaméron*). The examination of these basic truths will demonstrate that a different kind of realism resides in the *nouvelle*'s manner of representing power configurations, which predetermine the modes of being of fictional subjects. In other words, the "reality" of given situations for the characters of these stories is constituted by social configurations of power, present in the class names and the significant objects that each employs. Each character defines him or herself in relation to these configurations, occupying a predetermined place within a given distribution of power. As Foucault remarked, these individuals passively constitute power at the same time that they are constituted by it, and contribute to its dissemination.[3] The tale collections of this period thus provide us with a clear picture of a social reality, using an "iconographic" mode of representation that is not merely a primitive or embryonic form of nineteenth-century realism, itself largely metonymic, i.e., concerned with significant details that intimate entire character descriptions.[4]

According to Lukács, the main principles of realism concern the representation of character depth: "The central aesthetic problem of realism is the adequate representation of the complete human personality.... [T]he inner life of man, its essential traits and essential conflicts can be truly portrayed only in connection with social and historical factors."[5] In contrast, the internal life of the *nouvelle*'s characters considered as conscious subjects is irrelevant in most cases since the narrative concentrates on the conflict of character types (e.g., the Miller versus the Reeve in the

*Canterbury Tales*) that generates plot developments. Stereotypical characters such as these fulfill only half of realism's formula, which requires the internal development of character. In Lukács' words, "The live portrayal of the complete human personality is possible only if the writer attempts to create types. The point in question is the organic, indissoluble connection between man as a private individual and man as a social being, as a member of a community" (8). In the *nouvelle*, in contrast, the characters are merely surface social beings, and their "private side" seems not yet to have been invented. The earlier mode of representation typical of the *nouvelle* leaves aside the depiction of psychological depth of character, to concentrate on the insignificance of the individual within the larger social scheme that forms the conceptual grid of the *nouvelles* and their imaginary world. In order to explicate this radically different mode of early-modern representation, I will examine the various trends of scholarship and the critical tools that have been applied to the *nouvelle*, so that the reader may appreciate the extent to which it has been obscured beneath an academic bias in favor of realism and its codes.

The first attempts to trace the origins of the *nouvelle* gave an "orientalist" account of the genre's emergence on the Continent. According to this theory, the short forms that preceded the *nouvelle*, such as the *exemplum*, originated in the East, specifically in India, and were brought to Europe by various means (through the Byzantine Empire, the Moorish culture in Spain, the Crusaders' contact with the Arabs in Syria, etc.). The introduction of these forms into Europe was accompanied by the narrative frame found in Boccaccio and Chaucer, which was also (assumed to have been) imported from the Orient. Joseph Bédier provides a succinct description of this theory in the introduction to his work on the *fabliau*:

> The fundamental argument of the orientalist theory is this: by following the trail of a popular tale, one regresses from age to age and from country to country until one reaches a Sanskrit text. Having reached this point, one must stop. Invincibly, we are led to India, toward the first centuries of Buddhism; at that time, there are swarms of tales. Look for them in Greece, in Rome, or at the height of the Middle Ages: Classical Antiquity, and the Christian world up through the Crusades seem to know nothing about them.[6]

Bédier's text, which was completed in 1894, was opposed to this orientalist account, which had been formulated by critics belonging to the generation of his mentor, Gaston Paris. Despite Bédier's opposition to it, this first description of the *nouvelle*'s sources provided the impetus for an enduring current in criticism.

In his study dating from 1910, for example, Werner Söderhjelm inscribes the canonical account of the genre's origins, couched in the same terms as those developed and later problematized by Gaston Paris and his followers. Some scholars of this period, such as Pietro Toldo, made the problematic assumption that earlier narrative forms were the sources of later genres if both shared common characteristics. Söderhjelm epitomizes this attitude in many passages:

> In Medieval literature which, in terms of the material it uses, corresponds to the *nouvelle*, one may distinguish three groups, of which the limits are not clearly defined. We have, first of all, the *lais*. Although they are permeated by the character of the epics of Brittany, and although they include magical and superstitious elements that are foreign to the *nouvelle* itself, the *lais* exhibit nevertheless many of the attributes that could figure in the *nouvelles* of later periods.[7]

Söderhjelm proves that the *nouvelle* is somehow related to the *lai* by citing characteristics that betray a tendency toward realism, which will become more apparent in the *nouvelle*, such as "the realist observation of details and unified composition"(2). This devotion to a continuous conception of literary history is maintained in the face of formal differences that undermine the notion of any direct influence of the *lai* upon the *nouvelle*, which Söderhjelm himself mentions in the preceding passage: the *lai* is written in poetry, while the *nouvelle* is in prose; the *lai* often represents the marvelous, while the *nouvelle* is decidedly prosaic.

When Söderhjelm shifts his attention to the thematic similarities that unite the *lai* and the *nouvelle*, his assumption that the earlier form was at the origin of the later bears more strongly the traits of the orientalist argument, stressing the historical continuity that united diverse literary phenomena, as in the following passage: "At the limits separating the *lai* from the *fabliau* we find, in the *lai* of the *Espervier*, a motif that is repeated *ad infinitum* in the *nouvelles* of later periods, which is borrowed from the cycle of oriental tales: that of the husband who comes home too early to be hoodwinked by his wife's presence of mind" (2). The salient characteristics of this first reading of the *nouvelle*'s origins are evident in these passages. Some of the genre's most common themes (such as the one in which a husband is tricked by the wiles of his adulterous wife) appear first in France in the *exemplum*, the *lai*, and the *fabliau*, and are passed on to the *nouvelle*.[8] The earlier forms, in turn, borrowed their themes and structures from oriental tales. This stage-by-stage reconstruction of a motif's dissemination in Europe is precisely the argument that Bédier reacted against in his study of the *fabliau*.[9]

The threads of this historicist argument are closely intertwined with a polemical defense of realism found in the early criticism of the *nouvelle*. When Söderhjelm shifted his attention from the *lai* to another presumed source of the *nouvelle*, the *fabliau*, he expressed the realistic aspect of his argument in terms of a literary continuum:

> There is a literary realism that has conserved its character intact across the ages. . . . This realism is apparent precisely in those traits that are characteristic of the modern novella: intimate psychological descriptions and the faithful depiction of exterior details that are closely observed. . . . [This realism] naturally finds more favorable terrain when its subject matter is borrowed from external reality, and when the narrative attempts to depict subjects drawn from this same reality. When one studies how the *nouvelle* developed in Italy and France from the $14^{th}$ to the $16^{th}$ centuries by focusing on the description of these subjects and on the presentation of a narrative situation with its origin, rising action, and dénouement, which is usually comic, but may also be tragic—it is natural for one to look for the immediate precursor of the *nouvelle* not in the *lai*, but in the *fabliau*. (3)

According to most of the critics who first studied the *nouvelle*, the two distinctive characteristics of realism mentioned in this passage—psychological insight into its characters and detailed descriptions of exterior reality—were important to the history of the genre's development and were markers of a text's value with respect to the point in time from which they considered it. To the extent that a given collection of *nouvelles* evinced these traits, it was accorded or denied value by scholarly readers, even into the second half of this century.

In the preceding passage, Söderhjelm emphasizes a point that had a noteworthy impact on subsequent criticism devoted to the *nouvelle*. He claims that the *fabliau*'s more focused concentration on the representation of a single situation (i.e., its origin, development, and dénouement) makes it a more relevant source of the *nouvelle* than the more "romantic" *lai*. Söderhjelm's claim that this type of unitary plot line is a distinctive characteristic of the genre provides early evidence of a current within the *nouvelle* literature that would receive its most extreme form in Todorov's *Grammaire du Décaméron*. The earlier critic, however, was far removed from the latter's exclusive focus on plot structure. Rather, he was of the opinion that a restricted set of semantic contents constituted the *fabliau* as a genre, insofar as it foreshadowed the coming of the *nouvelle*. In contrast to the *lai* and to fairy tales, Söderhjelm claims, "*fabliaux* derive their principal material from situations and conflicts that the public judged to be known and possible" (3). The salient points of the early criticism of the *nouvelle* converge in these passages. Söderhjelm categorizes the *lai* and the *fabliau* as precursors of the *nouvelle* because of the realistic structures that they contain. From this point of view, the formal constituents of the modern short story—psychological insights, detailed descriptions—also define the Renaissance *nouvelle*, which takes its place in a continuum of realism that stretches across the entirety of Western literary history. This conception of realism also demands a certain verisimilitude of the situations described in the stories, as well as the logical coherence of their plots.

The first scholars to study the genre include the *exemplum*, along with the *lai* and the *fabliau*, as a direct precursor of the *nouvelle* in France. The early accounts of this generic derivation employ the same conceptual terms that I have just described. Söderhjelm writes:

> I would like to speak about the earlier poetic and the later prose rewritings of collections of anecdotes and of tales of oriental origin, which were disseminated throughout Europe in a Latin form. Whether they were drawn from the book of the *Seven Sages*, or whether they came from the *Disciplina Clericalis* of Petrus Alfonsi, their purpose is moral instruction, and they highlight with peculiar insistence the didactic lesson that they wish to convey, without worrying at all about fleshing-out the characters who present this lesson, and without being preoccupied in the least about the logical or realistic development of events. The sole object of these stories is, as is the case much later in the fables of Gellert, "to present the truth in images to the feeble-minded." (7)

Dating from the twelfth century, the *Disciplina Clericalis* is one of the oldest collections of *exempla* and was widely known in Europe. The work was translated into French in the thirteenth century under the title *Le Castoiement d'un père à son fils* [A father's warnings to (or punishment of) his son], which Söderhjelm mistakenly identifies as an original French text "modeled after books of an oriental origin."[10] Söderhjelm accords little value to the *exemplum* as a genre because of its lack of realistic characteristics, while his critique provides little textual proof of the *exemplum*'s influence on the *nouvelle*.[11]

In contrast to the linear, historical readings of his contemporaries Söderhjelm and Toldo, Gaston Paris argues that the subject matter of the tales was a sort of international patrimony that had been circulating freely in Europe within a certain "oral tradition": "We believe that both of these [Nicolas de Troyes and the Italian tale writers, the *novellieri*] have a common source that is unknown to us, but which may simply be the oral tradition."[12] Paris's argument is weakened by the fact that he never defines exactly what he means by this term. Nevertheless, in his specific analyses of the collections described by Toldo, Paris provides numerous examples of possible French sources that predate the Italian analogs of the fifteenth- and sixteenth-century *nouvelle*s. He thus describes a cultural interchange in which it would be virtually impossible for one to locate a specific point as a definitive source. He characterizes this crosscultural sharing of motifs in historical terms:

> For a long time, there were more Frenchmen in Italy than there were Italians in France, and if the French certainly received much more from this other country, of which the civilization dazzled them, than they gave to it, it would not at all be surprising if the French had also taken tales or stories with them to Italy, where they would be welcomed by the *novellieri* of Naples and Milan, avid to have material for their narratives. (636)

Thus Paris formulates an account of the *nouvelle*'s origins and sources that is much more nuanced than a unidirectional historical conception of its birth and dissemination. While the efflorescence of the genre in France in the fifteenth century was certainly provoked by the *Decameron*, it is also true that the style and the subject matter of the French *nouvelle* remained within a context that was specifically French. As Paris wrote: "Of the entire movement spurred on by the *Decameron*, but which remained largely indigenous, there was not a single masterpiece comparable to that of Boccaccio" (666). While the *Cent nouvelles nouvelles* may not equal the artistic achievement of the *Decameron*, and while its very form is borrowed from this Italian model, the first book of French *nouvelles* dispenses with the frequent moral commentaries and the detailed descriptions of Boccaccio's narrative frame to concentrate on the retelling of local anecdotes, which are more like jokes than short stories and which are closer to Poggio Bracciolini's *Facetiae* than to Boccaccio's carefully crafted *novelli*. The value of the later collection, however, resides in something other than its narrative craft. These narratives depict social "realities" that we may reconstruct by examining the obsessive repetitions that constitute a type of collective imaginary of the period and by analyzing the iconographic, largely nonrealistic mode of representation at work in them.

The defense of the *nouvelle*'s realism did not meet with the almost immediate opposition that confronted the historical preconception of its origins. Once again, Werner Söderhjelm provided one of the first formal definitions of the genre, which described realism as the culmination of formal developments begun by the *nouvellistes*:

> One normally conceives of the *nouvelle* historically as a short narrative, generally in prose, which presents a situation usually taken from everyday life and restricted to a narrow context. The event that it recounts leads to an

unexpected or surprising catastrophe, which means that the dramatic element plays an essential role in the constitution of the *nouvelle*. In the beginning everything is concentrated in the effect of this point, of this final situation, and everything tends to prepare it; often the narrative is extremely short and simple, and the story is nothing more than an anecdote. Later on, and little by little, psychological depictions become more important, and the crisis is often found in the contrast of characters, represented in a striking or sudden manner. (ix-x)

Söderhjelm claims here that the situations represented in the *nouvelle* are taken from everyday life, which means that it obeys the constraints of verisimilitude and verifiability mentioned above. The *nouvelle*'s characters were no doubt well known to its potential readers and listeners since, as its name indicates, the *nouvelle* is an anecdotal bit of news that circulates orally: monks, nuns, millers, shoemakers, merchants, cart drivers, knights, servants, chambermaids, washerwomen, wives, etc. It rarely describes supernatural scenes, such as a *jongleur* playing dice in hell with Saint Peter in the *fabliau* "On Saint Peter and the Juggler," or men changing into werewolves or birds in the *Lais* of Marie de France.[13] Does this mean, however, that the genre takes a fundamental step from a more primitive mode of narrative representation toward a more highly developed and realistic mode? Certainly, the earliest *nouvelles* do not always provide more penetrating representations of psychologically complex characters when compared to their French predecessors: Marie de France's delicate portrayal of Frêne, for instance, is well beyond the subtlety of most of the *Cent nouvelles nouvelles*.

Critics throughout this century have been forced to discuss a critique whose preconceptions have had an important effect on our conception of the *nouvelle* as a genre. Both early and later readers of the *nouvelle* have continued to evaluate the genre within what they perceived as an evolutionary, historical continuum that would culminate in modern realism. The critical reactions to this "realist" position ranged from unquestioning acceptance of its premise to a categorical rejection of the notion that realism had anything to do with the tales of the Renaissance. We have already seen an exemplary treatment of this argument in the work of Werner Söderhjelm.

Another scholar who has worked extensively on the *nouvelle*, Roger Dubuis, evinced a similar adherence to the realist hypothesis in an article written almost sixty years after Söderhjelm's. Dubuis reproduced almost term for term the "canonical" account of the character and origins of the *nouvelle* found in Söderhjelm's text. Like his predecessor, Dubuis cited three genres that prepared the way for the appearance of the *nouvelle* in

France: the *lai*, the *fabliau*, and the *exemplum*.[14] Moreover, his sketch of the *exempla* contained elements of the orientalist hypothesis, as we have already seen. Some examples of Dubuis's unquestioning adherence to the realist argument are hyperbolic, as in his assessment of the *fabliau*: "It is realism that forces the authors of *fabliaux* to slide from portraiture to caricature, realism that makes them fall too often into indecency, and realism again that makes them turn their backs on didacticism" (15). Apparently, realism accomplishes all of these tasks in the *fabliau* by concentrating the *récit* on what Erich Auerbach calls "the sensory and creatural" aspects of realist narrative.[15] While the scatological humor of the *fabliau* distinguishes it from the moralistic *exemplum*, it can hardly be claimed that a supremely vulgar *fabliau*, such as *"Du con qui fu fez a la besche"* [The pussy that was made with a garden hoe],[16] is obscene because of a concern for realism, or that it is realistic because it is obscene. From these descriptions of the *nouvelle* and its supposed sources, it is evident that the exaggerated importance accorded to realism is a result more of the historical perspective from which scholars were reading the *nouvelle* than it is of the genre's formal characteristics.

The realist conception of literary history receives its most cogent expression in the work of Erich Auerbach. The French Renaissance *nouvelle* occupies its appropriate place in the enormous critical scheme developed in *Mimesis*. The chapter on what he terms "Franco-Burgundian creatural realism" evaluates the *nouvelle* of late fifteenth-century France in reference to a standard of "humanist" realism that first made its appearance in the *Decameron*. Two of the northern French collections of *nouvelle*s that I will examine here, the anonymous *Cent nouvelles nouvelles* of c. 1462 and the collection bearing the same name that was completed by Philippe de Vigneulles around 1515, exhibit some of the same formal characteristics that Auerbach critiqued in his reading of an earlier "Franco-Burgundian" *fabliau*, *Du prestre qui ot mere a force* [The priest who took a mother by force]. Auerbach judges the *fabliaux* to be more "medieval" (i.e., more crude and less realistic) than the *Decameron*, which serves as his model for the realism of the Renaissance. In contrast to this model, Auerbach judges the *fabliau* to be undeveloped and limited in scope: "The arrangement of the narrative . . . is wholly artless, even though its freshness makes it delightful. In paratactic single file, without any effort to complicate or to unravel, without any compression of what is of secondary importance, without any change of tempo, the story runs or stumbles on."[17] According to Auerbach, the realism of the *fabliaux* and of the early *nouvelle*s in northern France has little aesthetic value because it lacks the essential characteristics of modern realism, which are found in Boccaccio, and which Söderhjelm had already delineated.[18] As we have seen, the first of these is realism's "psychological" aspect, which delves into characters by delineating individually significant details. In Boccaccio's tales, Auerbach states, the characters "have a life and a character of their own, which, to be sure, is only hastily indicated but which is clearly recognizable."[19] In contrast to the mode of representation of the *fabliaux*, which is much closer to that of the *Cent nouvelles nouvelles*, Auerbach graces the "realistic" characterization of the *Decameron* with a superlative artistic value: "The gulf between the fablel [*sic*] and the art of Boccaccio by no means reveals itself only in matters of style. The characterization of the personages, the local and social setting, are at once far more sharply individualized and more extensive" (213). While it may be true that the *Decameron* is more realistic than the *Cent nouvelles nouvelles* since the settings and the characters of the former are more clearly individuated than those of the latter, it is also clear that the French text is concerned with something completely different, i.e., the description of characters who represent universal types, rather than the description of characters as subjects with unique personalities.

The second principle of realism that we have seen is the detailed description of exteriors, settings, the bodies of the characters, and dialectal differences. From this perspective, Auerbach claims that individualized characters are *better* than (stereo)typical characters, while settings that may be identified because of their detailed description in the text are better than the vague backdrops of the *fabliau* and its successors in the literature of Northern France: "Then too the setting [of the *Decameron*] is much more clearly specified than in the fablel [*sic*]. The events of the latter may occur anywhere in rural France, and its dialectal peculiarities, even if they could be more accurately identified, would be quite accidental and devoid of importance. Boccaccio's tale [Day 4, tale 2] is pronouncedly Venetian" (ibid.). Auerbach thus evaluates the French Renaissance *nouvelle* and its most immediate predecessor, the *fabliau*, in terms of the basic attributes of nineteenth-century realism. As such, his work does not consider the possibility that these later textual procedures may be irrelevant to the mode of representation employed in the tales, which should be analyzed on its own terms. His dismissal of fifteenth-century French "creatural realism" is somewhat akin to dismissing the sculptures that tell the story of Christ on the portals of the great European cathedrals because they are not chiseled according to the realistic codes developed in later centuries.

One of the most remarkable features of Auerbach's reading of the *nouvelle*, however, is his accurate perception of the genre's formal characteristics in a critique that denies them any value. The scope of his critical vision is apparent in his invention of the term "creatural realism."

In his note to the first appearance of this term in the text, the translator Willard Trask notes: "*Kreatürliches*. The word, a neologism of the 1920s, implies the suffering to which man is subject as a mortal creature" (246 n. 1). On the basis of this notion, Auerbach develops a theory of medieval and Renaissance representation that is important to my understanding of the *nouvelle*'s basic characteristics. He defines creatural realism in terms of its relationship to Christian iconography:

> The traditionalism of the serious, creatural realism of this period is explained by its origin. It stems from Christian figuralism and takes almost all its intellectual and artistic motifs from the Christian tradition. The suffering creature is present to it in the Passion of Christ, the portrayal of which becomes more and more brutal while its sensory and mystic power of suggestion grows stronger, or in the passions of the martyrs. Domestic intimacy and "serious" *intérieur* ("serious" in comparison with the *intérieur* of the farces) it derives from the Annunciation and other domestic scenes which were to be found in Scripture. (247–48)

Representations of the suffering body of Christ were thus the inspiration for narrative procedures that focused their attention on sensory perceptions in all of their crudity. Auerbach's argument suggests that even the scatological scenes of the *nouvelle* have their roots in a Christian iconography that was obsessed with the image of Christ on the cross, while the genre's concentration on domestic scenes derives from biblical representations of the Holy Family. Auerbach situates the shift from the seriousness of sacred images to the buffoonery of farce within a historical and material evolution:

> Some other points must be made in regard to the realism of the closing Middle Ages. The picture of man living in reality, which the Christian mixture of styles had produced—that is, the creatural picture—begins likewise to appear outside of the Christian sphere in its more restricted sense.... [W]e must point out that the representation of real contemporary life now turns with particular care and great art to the intimate, domestic, and everyday detail of family life. This too, as we have just observed, results from the Christian mixture of styles; it is a development for which the conceptual patterns are to be found in the motifs connected with the Virgin Mary's and Christ's birth. (248)

The third principle of realism that Söderhjelm formulated—the representation of everyday life—is here defined by Auerbach in much more compelling terms. From this perspective, the *fabliau* and the *nouvelle* are concerned with domestic details as a consequence of a medieval narrative tradition that concentrated on the minutiae of the Holy Family. In the type of degradations that Bakhtin remarks consistently in his work on Rabelais, these descriptions of the life of Christ serve as the model for parodic descriptions of the everyday lives of stereotypical characters.

While he devaluates the *fabliau* and the early French *nouvelle* because of their paratactic style, Auerbach still manages to fit these two drastically different genres into his totalizing account of Western literary history, since they both represent the everyday objects and events necessitated by the code of realism. His argument regards these genres from two distinct perspectives. On the one hand, they lack value because of their primitive treatment of specific narrative materials; on the other hand, they must be situated in their proper place in literary history because they possess the basic characteristics of realism in an embryonic form. Auerbach fails to recognize, however, that every detail of iconographic representation *signifies*: in the countless portraits of the Madonna and child, for example, which are an essential part of the medieval imaginary, the position of the infant's hand, the tilt of his head, the Madonna's attitude toward him, the objects that surround the two figures, etc.—all of these indicate the seriousness of the Savior's future mission, his mother's devotion and sacrifice for his sake, the nurturing of a divine child by an earthly mother (Mary is often depicted with milk streaming from her breast). In the *nouvelle*, therefore, the representation of a character's position in a social order by means of details (names, clothing, jewels, tools and utensils, activities) that are saturated with meaning is more important than the literal mode of representation typical of realism. It is this "iconography" of the *nouvelle*, the writing of significant images that invite the reader to interpret them, and to form the concept of a social prototype, that requires critical attention.

In the passage that follows this critique, however, Auerbach reveals his insight into the mimetic procedures at work in the *nouvelle*, at the same moment that he rejects them as valueless. Once again, he contrasts these intrinsic traits of the Renaissance *nouvelle* with the "humanistic" processes of protorealism:

> Certain it is that during the last centuries of the Middle Ages there are to be observed symptoms of fatigue and barrenness in constructive-theoretical thinking, especially insofar as it is concerned with the practical organization of life on earth, with the result that the "creatural" aspect of Christian anthropology—life's subjection to suffering and transitoriness—comes out in crass and unmitigated relief. The peculiar feature of this radically creatural picture of man, which is in particularly sharp contrast to the classico-humanistic picture, lies in the fact that it combines the highest respect for man's class

insignia with no respect whatever for man himself as soon as he is divested of them. Beneath them there is nothing but the flesh, which age and illness will ravage until death and putrefaction destroy it. It is, if you like, a radical theory of the equality of all men, not in an active and political sense but as a direct devaluation of life which affects every man individually. (249–50)

The "constructive-theoretical thinking" that Auerbach has in mind here is linked to a conception of history that accepts the rise of the bourgeoisie as a concomitant of the rise of humanism; that is, in Auerbach's opinion, the growing power of this class replaces the "barren" political system of Christian feudalism with a more egalitarian ideology. In contrast, he argues, Franco-Burgundian realism, which belongs to the old order, accepts the insignia that define class structure while situating the equality of all men and women (a concept that is a hallmark of humanist thinking) at a devalorized, corporeal level. The historicopolitical aspect of Auerbach's argument is beyond the scope of my own. In contrast, his recognition of an iconographic mode of representation at work in the *nouvelle*, which functions largely by using the names of class insignia, is crucial to the readings that follow.

At the same time that the realist conception of the *nouvelle*'s origins was being formulated, certain critics showed their dissatisfaction with its excesses. While adhering to the conventional account of the genre's ties to the rise of the bourgeoisie, some critics claimed that the tales should not be judged according to the taste of critics writing at the height of realism's vogue. For example, Karl Vossler conceived of the *nouvelle*'s basic features much in the same way as his contemporary Söderhjelm, although he was less willing to attribute its "everyday" character to a tendency toward realism:

> The essence of the *nouvelle* lies in this: as its name indicates, it [recounts] an everyday event of current interest. The fabulation of the Middle Ages gave way, and in place of the marvelous and the unlikely came forth the clammering of the middle class, the rummaging of newness, and "nouvellation" [*Fabulieren* gives way to *Novellieren*]. The assertion that we encounter so often in French and Italian *nouvellistes* to the effect that they want to report only true circumstances—whether they corresponded to [the truth] or not—is in no way a casual inspiration, but is rather founded upon a correct recognition of the *nouvelle*'s nature. . . . Of course one must guard against judging these stories on the basis of our modern conceptions of verisimilitude and actuality.[20]

The temper of Vossler's critique is admirable, since he claims that the *nouvelle* is realistic in the sense of "actual," while cautioning scholars against an evaluative examination of the genre that would be based upon modern judgments, which are predicated upon the acceptance of a realistic mode of representation as a standard. In this sense, Vossler is perhaps the first critic to question the viability of the realist position. By implying that our conception of the real and the true differs drastically from that of the early Renaissance, Vossler opens the way for a reading of these tales that would examine the distinct modes of representing "reality" typical of the writers and readers of the period. Unfortunately, the rest of Vossler's article on the origins of the *nouvelle* is limited to an exhaustive catalogue of the analogs in Italian and French tales of the period, and his conclusions adopt the realist position: "One should not forget that a similar need for a secure grounding of stories in reality [*Wirklichkeit*] took shape spontaneously within French literature itself [as in Italian literature]" (36).

By the second half of the twentieth century, the suspicion of the realist position becomes outright rejection in the work of some scholars, while others, such as Roger Dubuis, continue to accept this evaluation of the *nouvelle*. The first and most emphatic dismissal of the realist thesis is found in Janet Ferrier's discussion of the *nouvelle* as a "forerunner" of the contemporary novel. While she rejects the realist aspect of this traditional critical position, Ferrier still remains within a questionable evolutionary conception of literary history. Nevertheless, she participates in a scholarly movement that will culminate in a mode of structural analysis that conceives of the *nouvelle* as a genre that is defined by recurring formal patterns:

> These stories of the fifteenth century are cast almost without exception in a rigid and highly formal mould. Despite their prosaic backgrounds and their concern with everyday affairs they can by no means be classed as realistic literature. There is hardly a single character of the *Cent nouvelles nouvelles* who can be recalled to mind as an individual personality; all are examples of three or four unvarying types. In the same way their actions, resulting from the impact of these constant figures one upon another, fall into recurrent conventional patterns. The author's skill and originality are shown, not in a departure from these familiar patterns, but in the arrangement of the same pieces to form a new and unexpected combination. The result is a literary form as highly stylized and artificial as the courtly writings that existed side by side with it.[21]

Here Ferrier rejects the thesis that the "everyday" character of the *nouvelle* renders it realistic, and she claims that its mode of representation distinguishes it from realist works. Rather than playing a transitional role in an imagined literary continuum that evolves from the representation of nonindividuated characters to the elaboration of highly individuated ones, the *nouvelle* presents stylized characters who play predetermined roles. While critics had previously underlined the *nouvelle*'s concentration on the everyday and the natural, Ferrier highlights the artificiality of the genre. Her critique implies that a correct method of reading the tales would catalogue and recognize the recurrent patterns that define the genre, much in the same way that Propp read Russian folktales as a finite set of narrative functions. Thus Ferrier's dismissal of the conventional understanding of the genre takes part in a movement away from an "external," historicizing critique toward an "internal," structural analysis.[22]

Ferrier's rejection of the realist reading is evident in her discussion of the *Cent nouvelles nouvelles*. The first point of her argument offers an alternative conception of the work's relationship to its supposed sources. Rather than trying to establish the exact parallels existing between the *Cent nouvelles* and earlier sources, Ferrier analyzes the general, formal characteristics of the French narrative tradition to which the work may be related. This shift in methodology highlights the problems of trying to delineate the genre's sources: "The fact that the same story has been told by a writer in another period or another country does not mean that the earlier version is the true model of the later one."[23] Faced with the impossibility of discerning the exact sources of individual *nouvelles*, Ferrier develops a conception of the genre's evolution that is considerably more flexible than are preceding theories, although it retains some of the traits of the historicorealist thesis, such as its implicit acceptance of the modern novel as a standard of value toward which the *nouvelle* developed:

> The attempt to discover earlier manifestations of this variety of narrative [the *nouvelle*] takes us back to certain portions of the thirteenth-century prose romances where preoccupations and types of emphasis which were to become familiar to readers of the *Cent nouvelles nouvelles* clearly emerge. The gulf between these romances and the modern novel is so vast that from the point of view alike of structure, style and the presentation of character the two seem to stand apart as totally separate kinds of fiction. The *nouvelle*, though often regarded as yet another separate type, is in fact the vital link between the two, and to study it is to do more than to attempt the analysis of a defunct and frivolous kind of writing. (4–5)

Like the realist argument, this passage implies that the value of the *nouvelle* derives from the position it assumes in a literary evolution that culminates in the modern novel; otherwise, it is, as Ferrier remarks pointedly, a "defunct and frivolous" genre. The originality of Ferrier's thesis, however, resides in her attempt to discern the *nouvelle*'s basic characteristics within a radically different genre, the French romance. In this respect, her analysis resembles that of Gaston Paris, who suggested that the *nouvelle* owed as much to its native predecessors as it did to Boccaccio and the Italian *novellieri*. As evidence to support her claim, Ferrier cites the formal characteristics found in portions of *La Mort Artu* and the *Suite du Merlin* that prefigure the basic structure of the *nouvelle*. Her critique underlines several features of the "self-contained" stories in romance that are also constitutive of her basic definition of the *nouvelle*. "This [type of] story is above all, from the technical point of view, one of situation" (9). In other words, and as Söderhjelm had already stated, the *nouvelle* and its predecessors have nothing to do with the "fleshing out" of characters that is characteristic of realist narrative. Rather, according to Ferrier, the genre brings basic character types together in self-contained situations, which are modified by the characters' actions.[24] Thus, "the interest of the story is not so much in further psychological development as in the manner in which their predicament is intensified and finally resolved."[25] Another salient trait that the *nouvelle* derives from the self-contained stories of romance is what one might term its efficiency, i.e., all of the characters and events introduced in such a story contribute to or participate in the development of the situation that it represents: "It is significant, for example, that few characters are involved in the events of the story and none are introduced that do not have their part to play in them" (10–11). "Here are no extraneous events or marvelous adventures; nothing but the situation created by the interaction of these characters upon one another" (17).

The final element of the *nouvelle* as derived from the end of courtly romance might be characterized as the narrator's attitude toward his subject matter. According to Ferrier, the French tales of the early Renaissance are more ironic than their predecessors, perhaps because they are part of a more general literary phenomenon that is manifested in the decline of courtly idealism.[26] Whether or not this thesis concerning the origin of the *nouvelle* in the degradation of courtly romance is correct, Ferrier's approach to the notion of source and origin is quite unique in its critical context, in that she was virtually the only critic who seriously challenged the historical, realistic account of the genre.[27] Moreover, in her work, one encounters, perhaps for the first time in the literature devoted to the *nouvelle*, a critical focus that was to become the standard for scholars working in the 1960s and 1970s. In direct opposition to the fathers of medieval and Renaissance studies, Ferrier claimed that the origins of the genre were not to be found in the massive research devoted to uncovering thematic analogs in European literatures. In contrast, it was in the *form*, not in the *substance*, of preceding genres that one could discover the *nouvelle*'s true sources. This concentration on structure, and its accompanying disregard for semantic content, would become the distinguishing characteristic of the structuralist criticism of the *nouvelle* that culminated in Todorov's *Grammaire du Décaméron*.

From this brief history of criticism devoted to the *nouvelle*, one may conclude that scholarship has not yet formulated a satisfactory account of this genre. How are we to read these tales now, after structuralism and deconstruction, in a postmodern context that questions the notion of historical continuity and coherence? The following readings developed initially out of narratological analyses of the *nouvelle*. It soon became clear to me, however, that a strictly formal analysis of the type proposed by Todorov missed the essential aspects of these narratives. While performing a structuralist-narratological reading of the salient examples of the *nouvelle*, I was bothered by several nagging questions. Given Todorov's thesis that the transgression sequence is the heart of the Renaissance tale, why is it that certain kinds of transgression (adultery, robbery, the smearing of another body in filth) were more prevalent than others in the period bounded by the *Cent nouvelles nouvelles* on one end and the *Heptaméron* on the other? Is it possible for someone reading at such an enormous temporal and philosophical distance from this period to know why some transgressions were more common than others? What is the strategic importance of the difference between male and female characters in these tales? Is there a consistent difference among actions that "modify the situation," depending upon whether they are performed either by male or by female characters? By attempting to transform the study of narrative into a science that ignored semantic content, narratology neglected half of narrative's essential activity in this context, which was accomplished mainly in the semantic elements of the tales, and whose importance became apparent in these recurring questions. As Panofsky remarked so long ago in quite a different context, the analysis of artistic form without making any reference to what that form *signifies* is virtually impossible.[28] Or, in the Byzantine theological terms that we saw in the introduction, the contemplation of an icon is pointless if the viewer does not make the necessary interpretation of its features, in order to move beyond the image to the name that evokes its sacred prototype, which the viewer himself or herself must produce. Similarly, reading the *nouvelle* without trying to conceive of its prototypical world, made present in various insignias (clothing, objects, class names), is a futile exercise. In the *nouvelle*, the typical image of the knight having sex with his wife, whom he thinks to be his chambermaid, while his friend waits for his turn in the wings, would be meaningless in the absence of specific knowledge about Western codes of marital status and nobility. Even Todorov's supposedly abstract notion of "transgression" would be meaningless in this context without exact knowledge of marriage as an institution, which is unavoidably semantic in nature.

The key to answering these questions lies in an analysis of the mode of representation that is at work in the *nouvelle*. This kind of "iconographic" representation allows for the configuration of a collective imaginary (in the sense of a set of images that constitutes a collective consciousness), which is staked out using characters who have symbolic and figurative significance. This mode of representation facilitates a more succinct description of social hierarchies as systems of value than a realist code, obsessed as it is with details meant to produce what Prince (following Barthes) called a "reality effect." In the *nouvelle*'s descriptions, every detail signifies in such a way as to situate its characters in a social configuration that is saturated by judgments of value that are implicitly understood by the reader. For example, in tale 43 of the *Heptaméron*, Jambique describes the man she desires to her servant in the following manner: "'Do you see that gentleman,' she said, 'with the crimson satin doublet and the robe edged with lynx fur?" (392). The two details of the gentleman's attire signify something essential about his character, even though the text does not explain this significance in any way. The crimson satin indicates the social rank of the character, while the lynx lining of his robe reinforces these connotations of wealth with the notion of animality, ferocity, and even of heightened visual acuity, lynxes being known for their keen eyesight (later in the tale, the gentleman's desire to *see* Jambique will be his downfall). Later in the same scene, the text unmasks its descriptive procedures, when it recounts the first meeting of Jambique and her lover: "It was five or six on a winter's evening, and he could see nothing, but as he touched her clothes, he found they were of velvet—and in those days it was not every day one wore velvet, unless one was of high birth and had an important position" (393). The fabric of Jambique's dress signifies her authority and the high level of her birth, which the narrator makes explicit in this case. This type of description, which continually situates characters in terms of their birth, wealth, authority, profession, and civil or ecclesiastical status, is far from being realistic, in one sense, since it provides no clear image of the character's physical appearance: the reader cannot see the color of Jambique's hair, or how tall she is, or whether she is fair or olive complected, etc. In contrast, what mattered to the writers and readers of this period was the series of instantaneous judgments that could be made of a character on the basis of his or her position on the conceptual grid of an imaginary social order, made evident in external details.

Moreover, it could be argued that the kind of psychological descriptions that are characteristic of realism are almost completely absent from the *Cent nouvelles nouvelles* and the tales of Philippe de Vigneulles, while it is true that Marguerite de Navarre's *Heptaméron* contains a certain degree of psychological penetration into its characters (e.g., day 1, tale 10, which I will examine in depth in chapter 4).[29] The narrators of the first two collections rarely describe their characters; rather, they simply enumerate the significant external details that define them as character types: the knight is defined by his castle and his servants; the wife of a miller by the household duties that she performs; the wife of a knight by the diamond ring she wears; the monk by his habit and tonsure. These standardized descriptions identify characters by means of iconographic symbols, much in the way that the visual arts of the period represented saints and martyrs using significant objects or postures that identified them: Saint Sebastian pierced by arrows, Saint Cecilia playing her lute, Saint Denis with his head in his hand, etc.[30] Most often the characters are not described at all; rather, they are merely called into existence by class names that signify sets of features: the name "knight" evokes the attributes "is noble," "carries a sword," "lives in a castle," "has servants," etc.[31]

Almost any description from the early *nouvelles* exhibits the formal differences that distinguish a late-medieval mode of representation from the realism valued by its early critics. *Nouvelle* 99 of the *Cent nouvelles nouvelles* contains three main characters. The first of these is "an important (*gros*) merchant, a prosperous man, who was showered with wealth and riches, whose business activity consisted of transporting large quantities of merchandise across the sea to foreign countries."[32] The tale describes this unnamed character solely in terms of the activity that constitutes him as a merchant, and one is given no idea as to what his physical appearance may be (apart from the adjective "gros," which probably refers to his stature as a merchant, not to his corporeal complexion). The merchant's young wife appears in the text as follows: "She was born of respectable parents, she was wondrously beautiful, young—about fifteen years of age, or thereabouts—gentle, sweet, and very accomplished" (332). Throughout the tale, the narrator provides only subjective judgments of this female character's beauty, which provide no concrete details of her physical characteristics. Finally, the tale describes the young clerk, with whom the wife wants to have sex while her husband is away on business, as follows: "A very learned young clerk arrived in the city. He had very recently left the university of Bologna the rich where he had spent several years without returning home" (338). Once again, the text incarnates the personality of this character by naming the essential activity that constitutes the social position denominated by the term "clerk" (he studies, he has been away at the university), while his physical appearance is left to the imagination of the reader. One need only compare these descriptions with a realistic one taken from a canonical text in order to appreciate the drastically different mode of representation that is at work in the early *nouvelle*. After a long "biography" that tells of the activities that made him a rich man, *le père Grandet* is minutely brought to life by a master realist: "Physically, Grandet was five feet tall, robust, with calves that were twelve inches around, knobby knees, and large shoulders; his face was round, tanned, pock-marked; his chin was straight, and his lips offered no sinuosity at all," etc.[33] This type of description refrains from making overt value judgments, which it leaves to its reader, while the choice of details reveals clearly enough what the narrator thinks of his character (in this sense, the "pock-marked" face ["*marqué de petite vérole*"] is especially significant); in the *nouvelle*, on the contrary, the narrator makes standard judgments of beauty or worth that are presumably shared by the reader, who has a common understanding of the narrative and social codes that give meaning to the narrator's descriptions. In the *Canterbury Tales*, for example, the Miller is described as a drunkard and merry companion, with the implicit understanding that these are the normal attributes of a miller as a character type; the character of the miller in tale 3 of the *Cent nouvelles nouvelles*, which I will examine in detail, has similar attributes.

Characters are thus constituted in the early French *nouvelles* by means of iconographic details that define them within rigid social and semiotic systems, whose codes would presumably be known and understood by the readers and listeners of the period. For example, in all of the collections that I will examine, Franciscans, known as *Cordeliers*, are known to be lascivious womanizers—perhaps the long cord of their habit, which inspired their name, signified a kind of hyperbolic phallic activity to the medieval mind.[34] The manipulation of these codes is predicated upon the represented body as a basis for contact among characters who belong to diverse social categories, which are strictly distinguished from one another by means of iconographic details or by means of *names* that abbreviate sets of details. The typical story of the husband who attempts to sleep with his chambermaid (*Cent nouvelles nouvelles*, tale 9; *Heptaméron*, tale 8) exemplifies the workings of this procedure. The societies represented in these tales are stratified along class and gender lines. In most cases, the tales are about the attempts of characters to cross these boundaries, defined by a number of social conventions: the code of marriage determines who may engage in legitimate sexual relations with whom; the class code distinguishes characters into "higher" and "lower" categories; the gender code determines what kinds of relationships male and female characters may maintain with one another. Thus, in the tale of the married gentleman who attempts to sleep with his maid, the protagonist attempts to traverse several frontiers at once (those constituted by gender, class, and marital prohibitions). The social "terrain" that is mapped out in the text's iconography must be recognized by a reader who knows their significance in order for the tale to have an effect.

Characters are recognized within this system by means of identifying attributes that are present in every aspect of the text: in the modes of discourse and address employed by the characters; in the "classed" language of the narrator; in the stratified roles (wife, miller, knight, chambermaid) of each character, defined by significant objects or events (e.g., in tale 99 of the *Cent nouvelles nouvelles*, the merchant's role is defined by his treasures and his travels, the cleric's role by his education, etc.). In the variants of the "wife replaces chambermaid" story, characters who manage to escape from their social roles (and their constitutive prohibitions) by undressing both themselves and their would-be sexual partners invariably become involved in a drama of recognition and misrecognition, since cognitive processes are possible within the "society" of the *nouvelle* only by means of the external signs, such as clothes, that assign social roles, and hence identities, to each character. In *Les Cent nouvelles nouvelles*, tale 9, for example, a chambermaid who is being pursued by an amorous husband agrees to a rendez-vous with him at the request of his wife. When the time comes for the meeting, the maid's place in bed is taken by the wife herself. While the wife knows that her husband has come to commit adultery with the maid, the husband does not recognize his own wife when he makes love to her in the dark. The tables of misrecognition are turned on the wife, however: before his presumed meeting with the maid, the husband agrees to share her body with one of his friends. When the latter comes to take his place in the maid's bed after the husband has finished, the wife thinks that her husband has come back for "seconds" and does not realize that she is making love with a total stranger. In this narrative system, therefore, all bodies are equal and unrecognizable when they are lying together naked in the dark, enjoying the benefits of the irreducible difference between male and female. Tales of this type are composed fundamentally of investments and divestments of characters within a narrative economy in which value itself is accrued to a character simply by means of different types of investment: clothing or uniforms, names that designate social rank (knight, miller, cleric), symbols of class such as swords, sumptuous meals, or servants (who belong to their masters), etc. All of these markers function in much the same way as the hand positions of the earliest icons, or the swords, mitres, tonsures, types of wounds, and other objects that identified saints in medieval sculpture. The secular order that served as a "prototype" for these narrative images distinguished them from the divine order that gave meaning to the sacred images of the period. The value of these tales resides, therefore, in the iconographic mode of representation that generated the *truth* of identity for the characters of this world, which becomes apparent in the hierarchical prototype of a social world that the reader constructs as an essential part of his or her reading of the story.

In the abstract, then, the development of these tales is regulated by a narrative "grammar" that imposes rules of procedure derived from an iconographic mode of representation. Just as iconic figures are defined by the objects they bear, the clothes they wear, or the attitudes they assume, so the characters of the Renaissance *nouvelle* are defined by their uniforms, their names (which here function as abbreviations for a number of attributes and class relations), the attitudes they assume (the amorous husband, the lusty wife, the lascivious priest, the stupid woman of the lower class, the clever miller, keen for revenge, etc.). It should be noted that the significant details that define characters of this type are quite different from standard, realistic details, such as Karenin's big ears, Charles Bovary's cap (*casquette*), or le père Grandet's *petite vérole*. Moreover, the preceding scenes of the "substituted chambermaid" anecdote are *not* realistic in that they are virtually impossible in an everyday situation: how can a man *not* realize that he is making love with his own wife?[35] How can a woman not realize that she is having sex with a total stranger? These cases are possible only within an artificial system of representation within which recognition is made possible by means of insignia, and in which all bodies (of a single gender) are equal once they have been deprived of these. While the prestructuralist critics of the *nouvelle* had a subtle understanding of realism and its antecedents, they did not come to terms with the largely nonrealistic, nonhumanist mode of representation that is characteristic of the *nouvelle*, whose importance in the history of Western iconography and literature can hardly be denied. We need to examine the narrative procedures of the *nouvelle* on their own terms (insofar as this is possible), without devaluating them in reference to a totalizing, aesthetic standard, and with an emphasis on understanding the symbolic social space, saturated by power relations, that iconographic representation depicts.

In conclusion, the characters of the *nouvelle* are represented by means of attributes delineated within several categories (gender, class, wealth, profession, civil or ecclesiastical status). The tales employ these traits as iconographic markers that define the characters, mapping out a configuration of social relations that constituted a conceptual "reality" for the writers and readers of the period, which was an intellectual grid that presumably determined the *truth* of identity for real people living at the time, as well as for the characters who appear in the pages of the tales they told and wrote down.[36] The "realism" of the *nouvelle* is thus entirely different from the Balzacian variety that critics tried to impose on the genre for generations. Rather than being limited to the level of the "realistic" description of its characters' subjectivity, the *nouvelle* exhaustively catalogues the social configurations that obtain in their relations to one another, which restrict the types of subjectivity that are possible for these imaginary beings. In essence, this iconographic mapping of social space is equivalent to a delineation of power, which is itself the kind of mystical "prototype" that is immanent in the *nouvelle*'s images ("mystical" in the sense that it makes its presence felt while remaining beyond our formal intellectual grasp). The iconographic details that identify the characters of these texts are like marks that power imprints upon their bodies and that determine their identities within an intersubjective social system. Insignias generate identities predicated on configurations of power; power exists by means of producing identities that exist themselves as "bundles" of insignias imprinted on individual bodies.

Like the characters of a video game, the *nouvelle*'s characters are also identified by the kinds of "moves" they can make—the social system in this analogy constitutes the rules of the game, and each character carries the markers that fix his or her specific relation to these rules, like the various tokens that video characters acquire in their movements through an imaginary space. The *truth* of these narratives—power produces identity by imposing insignias on characters—gives these tales a value for understanding the late-medieval mind that supersedes whatever value they might have had as the "missing link" between the supposedly primitive narratives of the Middle Ages—"The realism of the Franco-Burgundian culture of the fifteenth century is, then, narrow and medieval," Auerbach writes[37]—and the enlightenment of realism.

# 2
# Male Homosocial Domination in *Les Cent nouvelles nouvelles*

Most of the anonymous *Cent nouvelles nouvelles* reflect or reconstruct the implicit rules that structure the relations of men to other men, within an imaginary patriarchy dominated by a male figure of authority. Referred to throughout the collection as "Monseigneur," the character of Duke Philippe le Bon of Burgundy as narrator imposes his taste for a particular type of story and its variants on his fellow narrators, who are named at the head of each *nouvelle*. Representations of the literal exchange of female bodies circulate among the members of this exclusively male audience. The text is thus a forum in which men come together to swap stories about the pleasure that they derive from their sexual domination of women. These insistent depictions of their sexual conquests of female characters figure an implicit masculine "desire" for other men that structures a configuration of power that becomes evident both *as* the narratives and *within* them. The iconographic details that bring the characters to life in this collection map out the terrain of a male-dominated social structure in which power is virtually constituted by the displacement of the female as fetish and as represented object within a closed circuit of male storytellers. Narrative is the conduit that allows for this circulation.

The author's dedication to the work delineates a one-sided relation of power that serves as a general frame for the tales:

> To my Very Dear and Very Respected Lord, His Lordship, Duke of Burgundy, of Brabant, etc. Because it is true that, among all worthy and profitable pastimes, the very gracious exercise of reading and studying—for which, my most respected lord, I can say without flattering you that you are

very highly endowed—are greatly and highly esteemed, I, your very obedient servant, desiring, as I ought, to realize in every way possible all your very lofty and very worthy aspirations, dare and presume to offer you the present slight work, undertaken and completed according to your request and instruction. I very humbly hope that it will be agreeable to you.[1] (15)

The writer who transcribes these quintessentially oral tales is a servant of the Duke of Burgundy, at whose request the collection was brought into being, and who is the privileged narratee to whom the other male members of his court will tell their stories. The stature of the Duke had a decisive role in the genesis of the text, and the idea of his authority is one of the keys to its interpretation.[2] As the dedication reveals, the transcription of the tales was an act of obedience on the part of a subordinate responding to an aristocratic request. In other words, both the positive and negative effects of power are evident in the moment of the text's inscription, which, as Auerbach noted, is written in an unavoidably "class-determined" language.[3] The inferior *clerc* who is its author is constrained to act as he does, while the Duke's essential fiat generates a multiplicity of narratives. The basic will of this authority figure who calls the text into being imposes a restriction upon the kinds of stories that are appropriate to the male-dominated frame within which they are told. Each tale participates in a narrative project that serves to reinforce, or perhaps even to *incarnate,* the structure within which a nobleman exercised his power.

While the hyperbole of the statement may be attributed to the stylized language common to dedications in the fifteenth century and beyond, the position of the writer with respect to his patron is obviously one of extreme inferiority.[4] The scribe's manner of designating himself thus establishes a "narrative contract" in which he is subservient to his privileged narratee.[5] The former's function here is to collect stories that reflect the preferences of the Duke, who appears himself as a narrator in the pages of the *Cent nouvelles*. Like him, the narrators of the collection are obsessed with cuckoldry, adultery, and the sharing of the female body among men, which are the "trademarks" of Philippe le Bon's narrative tastes and which betray the homosocial (if not homoerotic) basis of this male-dominated power structure—the desire of men to enter into relationships with other men, via the medium of the female body.[6] The narratee addressed throughout the work is not the Duke alone; rather, the audience for these tales is a collective one, composed of Philippe's court of gentlemen. There are several instances in which these male narratees are explicitly called upon by the narrator:

Since the donkey tales are finished now, I will compose [*je vous feray*] a story which is brief, true, and very charming, about a knight whom most of you, my good lords [*mes bons seigneurs*], already know. (286)

In a small hamlet or village of this area, rather far from the great city, there occurred a minor incident which is worthy of being heard by you, my good lords [*mes bons seigneurs*]. (306)

According to Pierre Champion's "Index des Conteurs," there are thirty-seven named narrators in the work, all of them men, as well as an unnamed narrator who recounts tales 94 and 96.[7] The audience of these tales is exclusively male. The inclusion of each narrator within this group depends as much upon his gender as it does upon the suitability of his story to the Duke's project, the goal of which is to maintain the order of rank that obtains among these men by means of an enforced circulation of a certain kind of story about male-female relations. The selection of the stories on this basis is explicitly or implicitly evident from narratorial introductions, which appraise the worth of the anecdotes that are about to be recounted.

The narrators' numerous commentaries on the tale's subject matter agree with the judgments made by the Duke himself, when he is named as the narrator of a tale. For example, in tale 9, narrated by "His Lordship (*Monseigneur*)," the story is introduced as follows:

In order to continue our project of recounting new stories which have occurred in a variety of locales, and under different circumstances, we should not remain silent about how, a short time ago, a noble knight of Burgundy, residing in one of his castles, which was both beautiful and well fortified, equipped with troops and arms (*as befitted a lord of his rank*), fell in love with one of the household's maids, more specifically, with the highest-ranking woman after madam, his own wife. (47, emphasis added)

In his biography of Philippe le Bon, Emmanuel Bourassin provides an account of the equipage that was necessary or proper to the maintenance of the Grand Duke. Philippe enjoyed the services of dozens of *écuyers,* or squires, who were in charge of his clothing, his personal appearance, his hounds and horses, the birds he shot, the weapons he owned. Many of these servants appear as narrators in the *Cent nouvelles*: the narrator of tale 13 is named as "Monseigneur de Castregat, Squire to His Lordship"; that of tale 19 as "Philipe Vignier, Squire of His Lordship"; that of tale 26 as "Monseigneur de Foquessoles, Squire of the Chamber of His Lordship," and so on. Philippe le Bon had scores of people to bake his bread, servants in charge of roasting and carving his meats, an entire army of food tasters, scribes, clowns, artisans, and painters.[8] Reading these tales against the backdrop of such a social structure, one can appreciate the assessment of the proper that the narrator who is named as the Duke himself makes in this passage. From his point of view, it was appropriate for a knight living in his own castle to be surrounded by a crowd of servants and by his own army. Moreover, the details that the Duke as narrator chooses—the castle, servants, weapons—are insignia that signify the excessive wealth of the knight. These details of the description as icon structure a social hierarchy or grid from which the represented figure of the knight derives its significance.

The army of servants that surrounded the Duke was dedicated to maintaining the royal body in a certain state of nobility. We may assume that the clerk who transcribed the tales of the *Cent nouvelles nouvelles* was one of these numerous subordinates who maintained a hierarchical order by ensuring that its highest-ranking member was presented in public by a set of hyperbolic signs. The act of collecting tales about the relationships of dominant men to subordinate women was part of a much larger social structure that signified nobility by means of significant objects that surrounded, supported, and even constituted the royal body: the Duke had to eat certain kinds of food, wear certain kinds of clothes, appear in certain attitudes in official paintings, have certain kinds of weapons, engage in certain kinds of sports, tell and listen to certain kinds of stories. The narratives of the *Cent nouvelles nouvelles* took part in an active configuration of power that was determined by the disposition of objects as icons around the figure of the royal body.

The subjectivity of the Duke as narrator is revealed in passages that declare the necessity of telling a certain kind of story. His conception of the proper is bound to the desire to maintain a male homosocial order of rank by repeatedly telling the story of the female body that serves as its material foundation. The nobleman claims that one should not allow the story he is about to tell to remain in silence; that is, the need for narrative in this context is linked to the telling of precisely *this* type of story. The authority of the Duke is apparent in this brief proclamation of his narrative preferences, since there is nothing in the tale that confirms his subjective assessment of its necessity to the entirety of the project. In the tale itself, a knight shares the sexual favors of his wife with another gentleman: for the "Monseigneur" of the *Cent nouvelles*, this exchange of the female body between at least two male characters is a privileged subject that derives its force from both of the contradictory senses of this term. Privileged information is that which must remain secret, or which is intended only for a select listening public; on the other hand, cultural practices that are reserved for the privileged few are also intended to be ostentatious, in the sense that wealth and high status must display themselves publicly by means of external signs (no one buys a Mercedes to hide it in a garage, or to prove that one has a modest income). By continually telling this type of story, the Duke shares the secret of the power that he exercises only with those who also have access to it, but he also makes a public spectacle of the fetishized sign—in this case, a certain story of mastery of the female body—that signifies his power.[9]

The other tales narrated by "Monseigneur" are consistent with this first example. Of the fourteen tales that he tells, eleven are about seduction, adultery, or cuckoldry. In seven of these, the supposed humor of the story derives from the fact that two male characters share the sexual favors of one female character. Often the two males are present at the same time during the sexual act (tales 1, 4, 7, 9, 71). Thus, the entirety of the collection is marked by the Duke's predilection for stories that depict the exploits of a specific type of male character, usually referred to as a "*bon*" or "*gentil*" *compagnon*. For example, the fourth *nouvelle*, told by "Monseigneur," begins as follows: "Le roy estant nagueres en sa ville de Tours, ung gentil compaignon escossois, archier de son corps et de sa grand garde, s'enamoura tresfort d'une tresbelle et gente damoiselle mariée et merciere" (36) [A short time ago, when the King was in the city of Tours, a Scottish gentleman, an archer in the King's troops (who was one of his body guards) fell very deeply in love with a very beautiful, kind, young married woman, who was a notions dealer (32)]. Similarly, the opening of tale 27 generalizes the role of the *gentil compagnon* in sexual adventures: "Ce n'est pas chose pou accoustumée, especialement en ce royaume, que les belles dames et damoiselles se treuvent volunties et souvent en la compaignie des gentilz compaignons" (117)[10] [It is not rare, especially in this kingdom, for lovely women and maids to find themselves—both willingly and often—in the company of noble fellows (113)]. This type of character is a clever and sometimes brutal seducer of women (such as Panurge) who does not shy away from cuckolding even his best friends; rather, the sharing of women's bodies establishes an affectionate link that unites *gentils compagnons*. In accordance with Duke Philippe's wishes, many of the narrators of the collection will employ this same formula to describe the type of male character who not only covets his neighbor's wife but also uses her body in order to enter into an institutionalized relationship with the neighbor himself.

Several of the narrators who perform within the text indicate the act of their own narration and comment upon the suitability of their stories within the context of the Duke's collection of tales. In doing so, they reveal that their authorship is subservient to the maintenance of his authority. One particularly interesting example of this phenomenon involves a narrator by the name of Monseigneur de Villiers, who recounts tale 32:

> So that I am not deprived of the most fortunate and lofty merit due those who work and labor to increase and augment the number of tales in this present book, I will briefly recount a recent adventure which will acquit me of the duty of furnishing a *nouvelle,* for which I was summoned here. (133)

The act of narrating bestowed a privilege upon those who told stories within the Duke's court. Monseigneur de Villiers's narration is ostensibly motivated by a desire to be included in the select group of those who collaborate in the Duke's enterprise. The narrator expresses this wish in economic terms: the work and labor of the narrators augments the growth of Philippe's narrative wealth. Furthermore, M. de Villiers states that he was "summoned" to give a story to the collection, and that the tale he tells "acquits" him of his duty in this respect. The legal metaphor complements the economic one that precedes it and constructs an implicit social hierarchy: the narrators of the *Cent nouvelles* are subject to the feudal authority of the Duke and are summoned to the "court" of the text to give their narrative testimony. Philippe's royal personage is constituted by a procedure of accumulation: there have to be ever more servants, weapons, food, paintings, tapestries, and women accruing around him. Similarly, each of the narrators has to contribute to the accumulation of narratives that signify a male homosocial structure, which include the female body among the material goods compiled around the figure of the sovereign. In this context, a silent narrator would be excluded from the domain of privilege, while narrative silence would interrupt the proliferation of discourse that surrounds and supports the royal body. Each narrator thus offers a narrative in which his voice is the symptom of a power that traverses his body, infecting it with positive and negative effects.

The world represented in the *Cent nouvelles nouvelles* is thus one in which a configuration of subjects (narrators) and objects (their stories) is saturated by the authority of a central figure. The dissemination of power across this grid or network—or *as* this grid or network—determines the ultimate meaning of each tale. From a close analysis of textual signs, one can profile the "society" that the operation of the text brings into being in the mind of the reader. In iconographic terms, one's contemplation of these tales as icons allows for the interpretative projection of a social prototype as an essential part of the reading process. Its narration develops within and upon the workings of power and its effects, while its structural dynamics mirror the power relations that organize a fictional society. The narrators are chosen according to the degree of their proximity, both physical and "intellectual," to the Duke of Burgundy. The stories they choose are tailored to his tastes, and the entirety of the book is offered to him in obedience. Storytelling in the work is thus an essential element of a social order based on institutionalized homosocial relations for which narratives about the seduction of women serve as a medium of exchange and an economic base, in the same way that the trade in female bodies has been seen as the foundation of male-dominated economies. Essentially, then, the *Cent nouvelles nouvelles* embody a power structure made possible by narrative technique: a gentleman had to master the art of telling a specific story about women in order to circulate in the network of relations of a male-dominated social hierarchy. The iconographic mode of representation at work in the text reveals the structure of this hierarchy, carefully presenting an array of male characters by means of significant details, while the female characters are merely accessories (or conduits, or media) of the procedures that bring men together and reinforce their ties to one another. Like the jealous husband of tale 37, the Duke and his fellow narrators and narratees compile the variations of the tale that describes the faithless wife and her innumerable seducers, which is the narrative fetish that cements their relations to one another: "He had witnessed many events, and had read and even re-read various works. But the principal end to which his erudition and study tended was an understanding of all the ways in which women can deceive their husbands" (157). In this persistent story of adultery, the exchange of the female body, and of stories that put a hyperbolic and phantasmic image of the female body into circulation, are the bases of a male imaginary that was prevalent in Western literature in works as diverse and historically distant from one another as the *Disciplina Clericalis* and Molière's *L'École des femmes*. While this system of exchange is merely a narrative one in the case of the *Cent nouvelles*, the miniature world of this text is a model for the essential exchange that constitutes the power of male domination in a patriarchal power structure (in Hartmann's sense).

The homosocial character of narrative discourse in the imaginary court of Philippe le Bon becomes evident in a close reading of almost any tale in the collection. The problematic gender relations predicated upon an economy of male domination are integral parts of the text's development, as in the opening of the first tale:

> In the town of Valenciennes, there was once a noteworthy *bourgeois*, tax-collector of Haynau in his day, who among other things was renowned for his

very large and discreet prudence. And among his other praiseworthy virtues, that of liberality was not the least, for by means of this virtue he won the grace of princes, lords, and other people from all walks of life [*et aultres gens de tous estaz*]. (*Conteurs* 21; my translation)

Named as "Monseigneur," the Duke himself, the narrator establishes an understanding with his all-male audience, emphatically represented in the text by value-saturated names that evoke a stratified social structure. The "desire" of man for man in this configuration traverses all levels of society and effaces somewhat the differences that separated nobles from the *bourgeoisie* and commoners. The suspension of this difference is precisely what will be at issue in this tale of seduction, since its two main characters are represented distinctly, one in terms of his social station (the *bourgeois*), while the other is named simply a *bon compagnon*, with all that this epithet implies. The irony of the second sentence unmasks the narrator's awareness of a habitual action that enables the gentleman to occupy a position of privilege. The *bourgeois*'s liberality enables him to win the good graces of his men friends, with the understanding that this will allow him to enjoy the sexual favors of their wives. What is really at issue in this configuration of characters is the former of these elements—the apparent end of sleeping with another man's wife serves the purpose of establishing a relation between the two men.

The *bourgeois*'s method of seduction—he seduces his neighbors' wives by seducing his neighbors first—provides a glimpse of the male homosocial desire that dominates the narrative economy of the *Cent nouvelles*:

> In order to arrive at his end, he found several subtle ways by which the good man [*bon compaignon*], the husband of the said wench, became his most intimate friend, such that very few dinners, suppers, banquets, baths and saunas [*baings et estuves*] and other such pastimes took place without his company. . . . When the bourgeois, who was as clever as a fox, had won the good graces of the good man, he wasn't at all worried about winning the love of his wife. (Ibid., my translation)

The "triangular desire" in evidence in this passage is a typical characteristic of the earliest *nouvelles*.[11] In tales of adulterous seduction, the husband is a mediator who serves as a model (the lover wants to replace him in bed), rival, and obstacle to the satisfaction of a subject (the lover) who feels desire for an object (the wife) only as part of this necessarily tripartite relation. This kind of seduction is about something other than the act itself: it figures the paradox of rivalry and desire that opposes male characters and draws them together, in a standard sequence of developments that constitutes the male homosocial economy.

As I have already noted, the trade in women's bodies is the material basis for the social relations that constitute a system of male domination. While the first point of Irigaray's thesis concerning "women on the marketplace" is essential to my understanding of the *Cent nouvelles*, its second point would be inexact if it were applied literally to the work: it is not necessarily true that a repressed homosexuality is concealed within the homosocial system of power that the text depicts.[12] What men want from their seductions of the women who "belong" to other men (or from other men's seductions of their own wives or servant girls) in the context of the *Cent nouvelles* is apparently *not* an erotic relation with other men; rather, they want sexual intercourse *with women*, and its attendant transfer of food and goods, to serve as the material basis of male-to-male relations. Transactions of the female body invariably establish a bond among two or more men. In tale 1, the wife is "bought" with a few suppers and banquets that both she and her husband enjoy. In tale 43, which is exemplary in this respect, a laborer literally sells his wife's sex for twelve measures (*rasieres*) of wheat. In other tales, the two male characters cement their friendship by agreeing to take turns *using* the body of the female for their sexual satisfaction (tales 9 and 33). This type of maneuver results in a social relation between the two males, which is not necessarily a substitute for the satisfaction of a repressed homosexual desire. The narratives that circulate in the court of Philippe de Bourgogne, and which he deems appropriate to his narrative enterprise, depict the literal pleasures that are shared by two men via the medium of the female body, providing narrators and narratees with a figurative narrative pleasure that parallels (and perhaps acts as a substitute for—there is no way to know for certain) the sexual pleasure of the tales' protagonists.

In tale 1 of the *Cent nouvelles*, the sexual relations of the female protagonist with her lover act out, in a different register, the homosocial relation established between the lover and her husband. In this sense, the text depicts an inversion of Irigaray's model: the sexual relations between the wife and her lover serve as a mirror, substitute, or support for the social relations that unite the husband and the lover. After first seducing the husband with goods, the bourgeois seduces his friend's wife with discourse, as is so often the case in the *Nouvelles*: "After a few days, he [the bourgeois] had labored so well that the brave woman was happy to listen to his case and understand his meaning. And, in order to find a suitable cure [to his disease], they needed only to find the time and the place" (*Conteurs*, 21; my translation). Later in the story, the wife is also regaled with "pâtés, tarts, spiced wine, and a surplus of God's good things, to such an extent that the arrangement [*l'appareil*] looked completely unorganized" (ibid.; my translation). Unavoidably, the husband enters the scene of his wife's seduction:

> Holding a candle in his hand, the husband approached the bed. He was on the point of stepping far enough forward to raise the cover under which his good wife, the image of moral perfection, was silently doing penance, when the burgher and his servants prevented this. The good fellow was not at all pleased. Despite all their efforts to restrain him, the husband kept his hand on the bed. But he was not the master in this house, and was not free to do his will there, and with good reason. Nonetheless, his curiosity was finally satisfied by a most ingenious and original subterfuge.
>
> The burgher gladly revealed the wife's backside, her loins and her thighs, which were fat and white, and what went with them, which was equally beautiful and well made, without revealing her face. The good fellow [*bon compagnon*], who was still holding his candle, stared, transfixed and speechless, for a while. When he did speak, it was to laud the beauty of the woman before him, his own wife. He swore heartily that he had never seen anyone whose bum [*cul*] so closely resembled that of his spouse. If he hadn't been sure that she was at home at that very moment, he would have sworn that it was his wife herself before him! (19, translation modified)

The husband asks to see the bride, since he has missed the wedding feast. This demand, which implies the rights of the "amy tresprivé" to have knowledge of his friend's secrets, unites the two men in a common desire that is *scopic* in nature.[13] The text figures this desire in the uncanny image of the candle, a kind of phallic object with a *topos* of desire burning at its tip, making vision possible. Just as the *bourgeois* has to "see" his neighbor's wife in private, so does the neighbor himself have to be shown the *bourgeois*'s new "bride" in the intimacy of the "marital" bed, where the intimate parts of her body are revealed to him as well. This scene represents the configuration that unites the two men in a reciprocal relationship founded upon an obsession with the image of the female body as a minimalist icon for sex, which haunts male consciousness in this context. Moreover, as the text's metaphors attest, cuckoldry is a travesty of marriage that reveals the essential attributes of this patriarchal institution in a grotesque form. The husband's demand to see his neighbor's new bride parodies the custom of the *chaudeau*, in which the consummation of marriage was verified by witnesses on the wedding night.[14] There is little doubt that marriage at this time was *the* male homosocial institution. In its parody of this institution, the text rearranges, supplants, and displaces its major elements, bringing them into stark relief against the dark background of adultery.[15]

The tale develops so that the two men may glimpse the object of their common desire. The woman's body, especially its "lower stratum," is the object *par excellence* of male desire in this collection. The *bourgeois*'s decision accords with the homosocial and often carnivalesque logic of this work. The husband demands to see his neighbor's wife in her most intimate place, her marital bed; accordingly, he is shown the most intimate place of his own wife's body, which is turned on its head for the occasion. He both recognizes and misrecognizes her at this instant: is the object of his desire in his neighbor's bed, i.e., is it his neighbor's bed as a metonym for his neighbor, as Irigaray might suggest? While it would be difficult to demonstrate that this scene is a phantasmic manifestation of a repressed homosexual desire, it is clear that a relationship is established between the two male characters via the uncanny vision of the object that motivates their common desire, though it is perhaps difficult to say what the *bon compagnon* wants from this situation, if it is not merely food and drink, whose importance in this context we tend to underestimate in our opulent age. Moreover, as Bakhtin remarked throughout his work on the carnivalesque, eating and drinking are essentially the same as copulation and fornication, since all of them are "located," in a sense, in the lower body. The first tale provides the most intriguing representation of the primal scene in which two men share the sexual favors of one woman, with one of the men's desire being displaced from a carnal realm to an alimentary one. The *bourgeois*'s servants beguile the neighbor into forgetting that he has recognized his wife in another man's bed:

> The woman was presently covered again, and the husband withdrew, pensive. But Lord knows that each of the servants took a turn telling him that he was mistaken, that his remarks brought dishonor down on his wife, and that the situation wasn't at all what he thought it was, as he would see. In order to restore the husband's vision, the tax-collector—who had deluded the poor martyr—instructed the servants to seat his guest at the table. Once seated, the husband amused himself by eating and drinking his fill of the remainder of the feast, of which the two who were enjoying themselves in bed at his expense had also partaken. (19; translation modified)

The consummation of the *bourgeois*'s desire coincides with the renewed culinary seduction of the husband. The scene figures an economic exchange: the husband enjoys the goods of his neighbor's table while the *bourgeois* takes possession of the other man's wife. This kind of dream displacement is typical of grotesque humor—eating and drinking serve as uncanny or carnivalesque equivalents for sex. The transfer of goods from man to man enforces a blindness to the primal scene that both fascinates and disgusts the male subject depicted in these tales, who *must* witness this scene yet is *unable* to recognize it. The obsessive retelling of this same story is necessary for the narrators and narratees of the text since it is precisely this tale that structures the life-world from which they derive their identities as males. Moreover, just as the act of seduction constitutes a social relation between the two male characters of the story, so the telling of specifically *this* kind of story, which dominates the *Cent nouvelles*, is the essential activity that produces the men of the narrative frame in a social relation.

Similarly, the third tale circumscribes its characters upon a grid of power relations stratified by social rank and by gender. The tale's opening presents these figures as empty sets to be filled by attributes that confirm the significance of its initial, abstract markers of gender and class. In other words, the tale seems to say, "I am going to draw a picture of a knight and a miller," tracing their empty forms in order to fill them in with significant insignias, transforming them into icons of their social stations: "Not very long ago, there lived, in the duchy of Burgundy, a noble knight whose name is not included in the present tale. He was married to a fair and highborn lady. Rather near the castle where this knight resided, there lived a miller, whose wife was also fair, as well as young" (26). The text names its male and female characters in distinct ways, preparing the way for their development in hierarchical terms. The names of the men situate the knight above the miller on the social scale (assuming the reader knows what a knight and a miller are), while their physical characteristics are not mentioned. In contrast, the text appraises the physical attributes of the wives, and the value of their bodies for exchange is overdetermined by a series of adjectives that exaggerate their potential erotic use-value (a female character described as a beautiful woman from this decidedly male point of view is invariably an object meant to be "used" sexually). Both women are "belles et gentes," but the knight's wife is named as a "lady" while the miller's wife is a "young woman." These nouns and adjectives place the knight's wife in a superior position with respect to her female counterpart, while the youth of the miller's wife indicates the superiority of her use-value in sexual terms: a young woman is more desirable than a mature woman throughout the *Cent nouvelles*. These seemingly visual descriptions of the characters are, in fact, not visual at all; on the contrary, the characters are evoked only in terms of two types of value, one being the hierarchical distinction between upper and lower classes, the other being the subjective evaluation of the beauty of the two women. The narrator does not see the material substance of his characters; rather, he sees only what they signify (or what they may signify) within a rigid social configuration.

The first stage of this double tale describes the scopic motivation of the knight's desire: "The knight happened to notice the wife of the said miller.... She was returning from the river with two jugs of water" (26). The two jugs, or large pitchers, that the woman is carrying are nothing like the details that are the heart of realistic description. The text immobilizes the woman as an iconographic image. She is carrying objects that signify her domestic condition and that identify her as a hierarchically determined subject: she provides for the home, she is useful to her husband while he is away from what the civil law of the period called "the domicile of the marriage."[16] The pitchers identify the social station of the wife and her limitation to this domestic realm. The exploitation of her sexual use-value occupies the story's first sequence, in which the knight seeks to capitalize on the ultimate icon of exchange-value that his penetrating gaze discerns immediately beneath the symbolic surface of her appearance. At this point, the apparently light comedy of the text is not far removed from a phantasmic male hallucination, when the knight discovers a secret of which the wife herself is not aware:[17]

> The knight saw that the miller's wife was beautiful and that she had a nice body [*en bon point*], but that she was rather lacking in intelligence. He therefore approached her, and said: "To be sure, my dear, I see that if you go even a little further, your foreparts will be in great danger of falling off. Indeed, I am such an expert in these matters that I dare say you won't have much longer before this comes to pass."

> When the simple miller's wife heard the noble knight's words, she was shocked and angry: surprised that the noble knight could possibly know that this misfortune was upon her; and angry to hear of the imminent loss of the most cherished part of her body (for it served both her and her husband better than all the others). (26; modified)

The perceptive seducer is able to see both the intimacies of her feeble mind and the supposed weakness of her most intimate body parts. As is usually the case in the *Cent nouvelles*, this fragmentation of the female body is expressed in terms of its utility to the male, in which the complicitous female takes as much pleasure as the male. Perhaps there is no better example of what MacKinnon calls the "process through which women internalize (make their own) a male image of their sexuality *as* their identity as women."[18] Here the miller's wife literally is reduced to that part of her body that is sexually useful to her husband, while this utility to the male is inscribed within an entire range of economic usefulness of the female character for the male character.

The scene follows a perspectival logic of the seen and the unseen, which decrees that certain characters (the knight) have access to information that is withheld from others (the miller's wife). This privileging of information, in the ambivalent sense that I have already indicated, gives a textual form to a particular aspect of the male homosocial domination of women. The story that circulates among many of the male narrators of these tales, serving as the basis of their relations to one another, runs as follows: intellectually deficient women will be unable to recognize the seduction imposed upon them by men; women are available to the male gaze for its pleasure, and men may take advantage of women at will; whether she realizes it or not, woman will always be ready to be seduced by an enterprising male.[19] While this story of women must remain hidden from its victims, who unconsciously internalize it as the basis of their identity, at the same time it must be told and retold by men in the company of other men. In this tale, the story of the dominating male and submissive female is complemented by the order of rank that separates high and low social orders. In the first part of the story, the knight easily takes advantage of the lowly miller's wife, not only because he is a male, but also because he is well above her on the social scale. The knight suggests a cure for her supposed malady, which succeeds because of her deficient wit: he promises that her "foreparts" will not fall if she allows him to "hammer" them on with a tool that he has at his disposal ("The knight, well schooled in courtly ways, used a special tool to hammer the foreparts of our miller's wife back on, which he did three or four times in rapid succession" [27]). The seducer takes advantage of his object without her ever being aware of it, which would be impossible if she were not downright stupid. Male homosocial domination thus assumes and requires a female blindness to its functioning, while male characters always claim that their exploitation of female characters is for the good of the latter. The frightening implication of this male imaginary is that frivolous female characters are understood to *enjoy* being virtually raped by its male characters.[20]

Unaware of her transgression, the wife tells her husband the story of her encounter with the knight. As Todorov remarked in the *Grammaire du Décaméron*, the act of telling a story within a story motivates transitions and developments in its plot.[21] The syntax of this tale is regulated entirely by the delineation of intersubjective configurations that are modified by storytelling. Each act in the tale is predicated upon acts of communication and dissimulation, which male characters employ to take advantage of female ones. By telling the story of her own seduction, the miller's wife serves as a medium for the story's transmission to her husband, which is the essential feature of homosocial relations—that is, the communication of the tale of a woman's seduction from man to man via the female body. Within the context of the *Cent nouvelles*, male characters seduce female characters for the pleasure of recounting the adventure to other men, as much as they do for the sake of the act itself. The story of one man's seduction of another man's wife has one ultimate listener: the husband himself. That this exchange of information should be accomplished despite the intentions of the male characters indicates the extent to which narrative procedures support the male homosocial imaginary of the *Cent nouvelles*.

The knight's sexual usage of the miller's wife brings him into an unspoken contract with her husband, which is made explicit at the end of the story. The exchange of information that motivates the miller's revenge—i.e., the tale of deception that his wife naïvely tells him—provokes the exchange of women between the two men, which is the essential goal of narrative in the *Cent nouvelles*. The homosocial economy inscribed *in* this narrative, or *as* this narrative, is highlighted by the details of the miller's vengeance:

> Our miller, who was a good fellow [*gentil compaignon*], often mulled over the courteous turn which the lord had done him. He behaved in such a discreet, prudent manner that the knight never realized that the miller knew of the trick which the knight had played on him. In fact, the knight assumed that the miller knew nothing about the incident. But, alas, although the miller may have behaved as if that were true, his heart and all his thoughts were bent on avenging himself, preferably in the same (or at least a similar) way; deceiving the knight's wife as the knight had deceived his. (28; modified)

Intercourse between men, in the social sense, takes place with the aid of economic substitutes, fetishes, tokens: they exchange women and goods within the stories, and stories about women in the narrative frame. Here the miller is not concerned with punishing his wife for her indiscretion, which would be the "normal" course of action from the point of view of many of the stories in the text. Rather, what interests him is the exchange of one female body for another, or the possession of the body that belongs to his neighbor as a means of avenging the possession of his own wife's body. As Georges Bataille remarked in his article on expenditure, revenge is a primitive form of exchange, and it underlies the homosocial contracts of the *Cent nouvelles*.[22] The male characters of this text and of so many others from the period often seem obsessed by vindictive exchanges, which result, paradoxically, in an economy of narrative pleasure that unites males in a common bond.

The privileged places of the body interact with valorized places in the

*Cent nouvelles* to produce a symbolic space in which the male homosocial contract works out its terms. The iconographic mode of representation that immobilized the miller's wife in mid stride with her two pitchers of water is increasingly exaggerated as the tale progresses:

> One day, it so happened that the knight rode off on his horse, taking leave of madam his wife, for at least a month, to attend to some business away from home. The miller was pleased, and in no small degree. One day, it so happened that the knight's wife wished to bathe. She had her bath [*baings*] drawn, and the tubs [*estuves*] heated in her private chamber. This event came to the attention of our miller, who was a familiar figure in her house. He therefore decided to take a fine pike (which he had been keeping alive in a ditch filled with water), and go present it to the lady at her residence. Several of her ladies-in-waiting tried to take the pike and give it to their mistress on the miller's behalf, but the miller prevented them, insisting that he wanted to give it to madam himself. He maintained that if he could not, he would take the fish home with him. Finally, because he was just like a member of the household, and a merry companion [*joieux homme*], madam had the miller escorted to her room, where she was bathing. The courteous miller presented her with his pike, for which the lady thanked him. She had the fish taken to the kitchen and prepared for supper. And while the lady was chatting with the miller, the fellow noticed a beautiful, large diamond sitting on the edge of the tub. The lady had removed the jewel before getting into the bath, for fear that the water would damage it. The miller stole the diamond so deftly that not a soul noticed. (28–29; modified)

The gaze of the vindictive miller invades the most intimate place in the lady's home, just as the clever gaze of the knight was able to penetrate the veil that covered the most intimate places of the miller's wife's body. This scene combines several *topoi* of the *nouvelle* literature, all of which signify the seductive situation. The husband's absence is an invitation to the seducer, as so often happens in this type of story. As in the first tale, the duplicitous sexual desire of the active character is expressed in the offering of food as a gift: as Bataille remarked, the offering of a gift intended to humiliate the receiver is the first stage in the process of meaningless expenditure that this tale seems to illustrate. Finally, the *estuves* and the *baing* that the wife has heated for her are places that are marked for sexual transgression in the *nouvelle*.[23] The text achieves meaning, therefore, by employing details that are laden with significance, such as the two objects that are exchanged in this scene.

The core of this sequence is the transfer of goods that is accomplished by the miller's ruse. The first French *nouvellistes* were fascinated by absurd impossibilities, such as the exchange of a fish for a diamond that is described here, both of these objects being heavy in connotations. Perhaps the imperative, "Let a fish be traded for a diamond," runs parallel to the improbable trading of wives that takes place across class barriers—improbable in the sense that the penalties for adultery at the time were extremely severe.[24] By stealing the jewel as the first step of his revenge, the miller strikes at the heart of the social division that separates the two men, which is more than apparent in the iconographic descriptions of their two wives. Both portraits signify material difference by using the detail of water. While the miller's wife has to carry her own water to her home, the knight's wife has a bath drawn for her by her maids. Whereas the miller's wife was characterized by her ability to perform work, the most noteworthy attributes of the knight's wife are those that connote leisure and wealth. The dissolution of the hierarchical barriers accomplished in this tale, which is a defining feature of "carnivalesque" comedy, complements the violation of the sacred interdiction that prohibits adultery as well as intercourse between men. It may be that the *beau brochet* itself is a marker of the sacred order that is being transgressed here, since fish undoubtedly signified not only Christ, the "fisher of men," but also the days of abstinence from meat that characterized the holiest periods of the Christian calendar.[25] In short, every detail of this passage signifies something that is well beyond the literal surface of the description, and brings into play diverse realms that are saturated by the effects of power.

When the miller steals a place in the intimacy of her home and body, he insinuates himself into the economic procedure that produces the knight's wife as a desirable commodity. The miller's surreptitious entry into a domain to which he cannot possibly have access is an anomaly in the context of the *Cent nouvelles*, much like the exchange of the fish for the diamond, and much like the forbidden erotic intercourse that is, presumably, the unconscious basis of homosocial relations. In modern Western cultures, a diamond ring is the symbol of a series of relations that are established by a marital transaction: total strangers become in-laws, two families are brought together, a man and a woman who perhaps have nothing in common become intimate relatives. The third tale of the *Cent nouvelles* underlines the fact that the diamond ring is a fetish of this type, since it magically incarnates the entire set of relations brought into being by marriage: "The knight, her husband, had presented [the diamond] to her on their wedding day, and she therefore held it most dear" (29).

As in modern engagements, the diamond is an icon that signifies the wife's relation to her husband. By stealing the diamond, and leaving a pike in its place, the miller brings about an impossible exchange whose undertones are rich yet almost incomprehensible. In the "domicile" of the woman's marriage, and in one of its most intimate places, the miller manages to steal the ultimate marker of this configuration of objects that virtually generates her identity as a married noblewoman. In its place, he puts another object that has both sacred and obscene connotations. In this privileged place, which signifies cleanliness and baptism, wealth and luxury, and finally sex and concupiscence—for a bath is all of these things to the late-medieval mind—the miller brings to market another object that signifies the sacred and the sublime: divine sustenance (the miracle of the loaves and fishes) and abstinence, and finally perhaps even sexuality and the life of the body. In other words, the characters as subjects move in a dream world defined by icons that signify across the entire spectrum of their existence and in which sex is the primal act that determines identity and meaning. The exchange of the fish for the diamond thus serves as an uncanny substructure for the superstructure in which two male characters trade their wives.

Since the miller was the only person present in the room, apart from the maids, at the time when the diamond was lost, he is immediately suspected of stealing it. He claims his innocence but assures the woman that he will find the diamond if he is left alone with her for a few moments. Once again, the woman's intellectual deficiency is assumed by the seducer: he remarks that if she were wearing the ring before taking her bath, it must have fallen into the water and become lodged in some part of her body. As in the case of the first seduction, the miller has a "tool" with which he can remove the ring from the place where he has found it. After several attempts, the ring is removed, to the delight of the knight's wife—one is reminded of MacKinnon's comments on the supposed complicity of women as the constructed objects of male desire. The functioning of the homosocial economy is contingent upon the circulation of the phallus, which the male imaginary imposes upon female characters for the sake of their own good. At this point in the tale, the seductive event becomes a story, which, like the phallus, or as a substitute for the phallus, begins its circulation among the characters:

> A short time afterwards the knight returned home and was courteously received by his wife, who welcomed him in a fitting fashion. After a short chat, which transpired in bed, madam recounted the most marvelous adventure of her diamond, how the miller had fished it from her body. Briefly stated, she gave him a full account, in minute detail, of every step of the process by which the miller undertook the quest for the diamond. The knight was none too happy at this. Instead, he thought to himself that the miller had repaid him heartily. The first time the knight and the good miller ran into

each other, the knight greeted the miller with the loud exclamation, "May God keep you, fisher after diamonds!" To this the good miller countered, "May God keep the hammerer of foreparts." "By Our Lady, you speak the truth," said the lord. "If you keep my secret, I'll keep yours." The miller was happy, and never spoke a word about the incident. Nor did the lord, at least as far as I know. (31)

Like her female counterpart, the knight's wife completes the tale of seduction's transfer from one male to another. Curiously, in the diegesis, the female characters narrate the stories that the men of the narrative frame tell one another—could this mean that the narrators of the frame are adopting what Lacan, in the *Séminaire sur <<La lettre volée>>*, called the "place of the female"?[26] Both of the women remain ignorant of the entire affair, while both of the men realize that their respective wives have been deceived. When the men finally meet, the tale of the "pecheur de diamants" is given in trade for the tale of the "recoigneur de devants," and the value of the women's bodies is replaced by the value of the transaction that has taken place between the men.

A story must be told in order for it to actualize its value, which can be measured only in its exchange. The end of the tale embodies a paradox: this story has never been told by the only persons who know all of its details, yet the narrator has just managed to tell it. This paradox is typical of the stories that male characters tell one another in this context, since the exchange of information that they cannot and must not recognize, the story of their "desire" for one another, whatever form it may take, is the foundation of the economy that their narratives put into motion. Narrative represents, embodies, and participates in power relations, and when a male character (the narrator) tells a story to another male character, he is exercising a kind of gender-contingent power within that network of relations at the same time that this narrative traverses, invades, and saturates his body with the positive and negative effects of power. In the *Cent nouvelles*, the ability to enter the domain of power by telling this kind of story is denied to female characters, since they have a voice in the tales only as media who transfer information, which they neither understand nor recognize, from male to male.

Tale 33 is perhaps the most emblematic representation of the economy of male domination in the *Cent nouvelles*. This story illustrates in a hyperbolic fashion the way in which narrative functions as a fetish that circulates among men on a metadiegetic level, resulting in a network of relations that constitutes a social structure, while the female body fulfills this same fetishistic function on the diegetic level. As in the other examples I have examined, the narrator of this tale is named as "Monseigneur," the Duke of Burgundy himself. Here there are also two male characters who maintain a relationship with one another via an exchange of the female body. The tale's opening offers a male appreciation of what is proper to a gentleman of the kind that we have already seen:

> A gentle knight from Burgundy, who was wise, valiant, and very proficient in knightly arts, in short, praiseworthy and meriting a fine reputation, was among the best known knights. He found himself so much in favor with a lovely young maiden that he was retained as her servant. After a while, he obtained from her all that she could honorably give him. Moreover, he led her to this by force of arms so that she could by no means refuse him that which several men, before and after him, were unable to obtain. A kind and gracious lord noticed this and made note of it. This lord was very shrewd. I'll say no more of his name, or his virtues. If it were in me to recount them, there's not one of you who wouldn't immediately recognize the incident on which this story is based, which I do not want. (140)

The wisdom, the bravery, and the proficiency of this gentleman consist in nothing more than his ability to conquer the resistant female body, if one judges from the story that follows this introduction. A knight's education at this time included a rigorous training in warfare, but the narrator of this passage is not referring to the knight's skills in battle when he says that the male character overcame the female character's resistance "by force of arms." The metaphors for sex in this work are military ones,[27] while the standard expression for intercourse in the collection is "to break a lance."[28] Sex for these male narrators is a joust whose end is the submission of the defeated female character. Moreover, sex for them is essentially equivalent to rape, since it is accomplished usually against the resistance of the female characters, whom they understand to want sex beyond all measure. The text later says of the female character: "You should know that this valiant woman—who had to keep her two lovers contented—was not idle, for she would have been very sorry to lose them, especially the second one, the lord, for he was cut from a better cloth, and was a better shoe to fit her foot than the first gentlemen" (140; modified). This metaphoric boasting about the receptiveness of female characters toward the male member is a commonplace of male bonding and highlights the fact that this imaginary is based upon the circulation of the phallus among phantasmic females who are produced by a male obsession with their own bodies.

The institutionalized rape of female characters that dominates this imaginary almost always implies the participation of another male character, who is a kind of wandering predator (much like the knight of tale

3) and whose gaze penetrates into the most private of situations. In this context, being "*gentil*" and "*gracieux*" also entailed being "*tresclervoyant*," which remains in English as the adjective "clairvoyant": a gentleman of a certain stature had to be able to *see* the secrets of sex that others did not want to reveal, as is the case here, or to see the secret desire for sex that constituted the essential malady of the female body, as in tale 3. The purpose of this kind of narrative is to ensure that the story detailing the virtues of the predatory and clairvoyant male character become known to all the men belonging to a certain society, as a means of constituting his public reputation. This information is privileged in the ambiguous sense indicated earlier: it must remain hidden from unauthorized eyes, yet it must be displayed to a certain public that eagerly awaits it. The male-dominated social structure is based on the necessity that male characters declare the fact of their desire to other men. This fundamental imperative is represented clearly in the narrator's description of the usurping male character's actions:

> The gentleman to whom I have referred, who noticed the love of the knight I've mentioned, asked the knight, when he saw his opportunity, if he wasn't in love with a certain young woman, that is to say, the one mentioned above. The knight replied no. The other man, the lord, who knew very well that the contrary was true, said that he knew that the knight was, indeed, in love with her. No matter what the lord said, no matter how he admonished, saying that the knight should not conceal such matters from him, and that if a similar thing happened to him (or even better), he would not conceal it, the knight wouldn't confess to him what he already knew for sure, and well. (140)

The logic that unfolds in the *Cent nouvelles* is that of a paradoxical imperative that constitutes the male homosocial contract: each individual male must *confess* the truth of male desire that all of the other participants in the contract already know to be true. Similarly, on the plane of the male narrators gathered in the Burgundian court, this story must be told and retold, even though all the men present already know what the contents of the story are, who its protagonists are, what happened to them afterward, and so on.

Similarly, once both of the male characters of this tale enter into a sexual relationship with the complicitous female character, they become obsessed with the necessity of making her *confess* that she has two lovers. Just as she first resists the sexual advances of both of the men, she later resists the desire of the male characters to incorporate her within the confessional logic of homosocial domination. When her second lover accuses her of maintaining two lovers, for example, she says to him:

"You are the only man in this world to whom I wish to give the most pleasure, and whose troubles and displeasure touch me the most" (142). When the first lover likewise accuses her of "infidelity," she responds: "You have no reason at all to suspect me any more than anyone else alive, and still I am obliged to excuse myself" (144). In essence, then, the female character's resistance to male domination is a refusal to accept the truth of the narrative account of her unbounded desire, which is forced upon her by two collaborating male characters. In other words, the female rejection of a domineering male desire is essentially a rejection of a certain narrative economy in which men share the secret of their desire. She refuses to accept the account of the relations that obtain among the characters on the basis of their desires for one another, which is imposed upon her as the *truth*.

Recognizing this resistance, the two lovers interchange the stories of their relations with the woman and plan to force her to confess to her indiscretions. Their consistent and redundant pressure upon her ultimately compels her to reveal her betrayal of the two males, which in itself is what the men desire all along. Before her confession, however, she provides physical evidence that she hopes will prove the truth of her own tale of resistance:

> The second lover sent a gentleman, a member of his intimate circle, to the woman, in order to admonish her at length about how very displeased her lover was to have a companion in serving her, hoping to fan the flames of her passion. Briefly stated, the message was that if the lady did not dismiss her other lover (the knight) he wouldn't come near her for the rest of his life. As you've heard above, she wouldn't lose him willingly. There was no male or female saint that she didn't swear by, to excuse herself for her intimate relationship with the first lover. Finally she burst out at the lord's squire, who was serving as his emissary, as if she were in a furious rage, "I'll show your master that I love him. Give me your knife." Once she had the knife, she turned around with her back to him, and lopped off all her hair, leaving not one strand. The emissary took this offering, knowing nonetheless the true details of this intrigue, and offered to do the best he could to convince his master, and to make a duty of the present, which he did. (145)

The conventional marker of the difference between male and female is sacrificed here for the sake of maintaining the appearance of virtue. Carla Freccero has argued that self-mutilation is a distinguishing mark of the female, or a kind of female signature, as we shall see in the analysis of Marguerite de Navarre's tenth tale. Similarly, François Rigolot has described this figurative sacrifice of the female body as a signifier of the sacred in the context of early modern iconography.[29] Here, the female character symbolically sacrifices herself in order to maintain the illusion of virtue, which is essentially the *truth* that the male characters require of her. This tale prefigures the infamous double bind that entraps the female characters of the *Heptaméron*, in which the male characters demand that women be absolutely virtuous at the same time that they force them to transgress the impossible code of female virtue.

The only option open to a female character in this situation is to sacrifice herself to male desire's absolute domination of her body. In doing so, she provides a fetish that the two males exchange as the basis of their relationship with one another and that enables them to impose the duplicitous truth of male domination upon the female: "The following day, or soon after, the two companions met in a room where their loyal lady was, along with several other people. Each one was sitting, and took whatever place pleased him most, the first lover next to the good lady. After a preliminary exchange of pleasantries, the fellow showed the woman the hair which she herself had sent to his companion" (146). Here, the fetishistic "merchandise" that serves as the proof of a male homosocial relationship instituted via the medium of the female body completes the cycle of its circulation among the characters. The female character still rejects the place assigned to her within this cycle until she is violently forced to recognize the truth of her demeaning position, or to recognize her demeaning position as the truth of her being, as MacKinnon might phrase this situation:

> Whatever she might have thought, she showed no sign of fright. She even said that she did not recognize the locks which he showed her, and that they certainly had nothing to do with her. . . . Once the knight saw this, he thought it was time to start his game. He pretended to want to put the lady's hood, which was on her shoulder, on top of her head, and in so doing he gave it such a knock that he threw it to the ground, leaving her ashamed and angry. Everyone present realized very well that her hair had been cut rather drastically. . . . I don't think that scarcely a woman had ever capitulated so completely as she had at that moment, first to one lover and then to the other. (146; modified)

By its nature, the male homosocial economy does violence to the female body, which it forces to surrender to its sexual (that is, in this case, military) demands. The development of the male narrative strategy is intended to uncover those parts of the female body that have suffered violence from the male, and to display them as objects of contemplation to other males. Moreover, it is precisely one of the defining iconographic attributes of the female that is the target of male violence in this tale. The story of the woman's capitulation becomes, therefore, a kind of material that circulates among the male narrators of the frame, in the same way that the female body and its fetishes pass back and forth between the male characters of the story. The tale's end describes the institutionalization of the triangular relationship that is the basis of homosocial power:

> The two companions continued in this manner with their pleasurable pastime for a long enough time without their woman's ever daring to lie to them. When one of them had his day with her, he told the other one. When one went off on a trip, and the place remained for the other lover, he made them hear his recommendations upon his departure. The two men composed fine *rondeaux* and *chansonnettes* which they had delivered back and forth to each other. These are known today [*dont il est aujourduy bruyt*], and serve as material for the affair described above, about which I'll leave off speaking, thus bring the tale to its end. (147)

Poems, songs, stories, advice that passes from man to man—the end of the tale clearly defines the material basis of the "*bruit*" that constituted the reputation of the gentleman described at the beginning of the tale. The stature and position of such a male in this imaginary society depended precisely upon the obsessive telling and retelling of this story of women, and its imposition upon women as the truth of their gendered identities, which they bear as scars and marks on their very bodies.

Similarly, tale 9 of the *Cent nouvelles*, narrated by "His Lordship," is a variant of one of the most popular tales of this period, and it appears as a *fabliau*, as well as in the *Facetiae* of Poggio Bracciolini, the tales of Philippe de Vigneulles, and the *Heptaméron*.[30] This anecdote occupies a privileged position in the imaginary of the period, given the number of times it was rewritten in vastly diverse cultural contexts. Predictably, Duke Philippe's version concentrates on the bond that unites two male characters who believe that they are sharing the body of a maiden, when in reality they both enjoy the sexual favors of the wife of one of the gentlemen. We have already seen that the opening of this tale inscribes the Duke's notion of what is proper for a knight: "A noble knight of Burgundy, residing in one of his castles, which was both beautiful and well-fortified, equipped with troops and arms (as befitted a lord of his rank), fell in love with one of the household's maids" (47). The tale details the oppressive and persistent nature of male desire in this context: "So compelling was his love that (at least to hear him tell it) his very life depended on this woman. He pursued her doggedly, entreated her constantly; he claimed that he was so smitten with love that nothing in the world mattered to him but her" (47). Perhaps the ironic tone of the narrator, which is a consistent feature of this collection, undermines the seriousness of this passage in the sense that it mocks the male protagonist at the same time that it describes his amorous plight. The female character who is the object of this character's desire reacts to his pressure by threatening to reveal his persistent advances to the mistress of the château. The communication of secret information among male characters gives form to a male economy that excludes women; in contrast, the female characters of this tale secretly communicate with one another in order to maintain the legitimacy and integrity of the household, which the male character threatens to disrupt: "In the end, the honorable damsel was obliged to inform her mistress" (47).

As in the other versions of this story, the wife and the maiden decide to play a trick on the transgressive husband: the wife instructs the maid to arrange a rendez-vous with the husband for a given evening, at which point the wife will take the maid's place. The substitution of one body for another in the darkness is a commonplace of the comic literature of this period, yet it reveals that the represented body loses its identity once it is divested of the iconographic details that define it. The tale complicates this game of misidentification by introducing a second male character, describing the friendship between the two males in a striking manner that highlights the sexual basis of homosocial relations and the gender domination that they entail:

> Toward evening on the day they had set to practice arms, a noble knight who was both a neighbor of the lord, and his very close friend, chanced to come visit him. The lord welcomed him very graciously [*il (lui) fist tresgrande et bonne chere*], as was his custom. . . . After a copious banquet, it came time to retire. After bidding goodnight to madam and her ladies, the two noblemen began to chat about a wide variety of subjects. Among other things, the guest asked his host if there was any fine place where he might chance to find a woman with whom to spend the night [literally *"pour aler courre l'aiguillette,"* a place where he might take his needle out of its sheath], being so inclined after the excellent meal he had consumed, and because of the fine weather. Because of his deep affection [*amour*] for his guest, the lord went ahead and confided to him that he had an appointment to sleep with the maid for that very night. In order to please his friend, the host said that, once he had been with her a while, he would rise stealthily, and would come and get his guest, who could then finish off the night with the damsel. (47–48)

There is, and perhaps always has been, an uncanny correspondence between sex and eating in the human imaginary. The expression *"faire bonne ou grande chère"* in Middle French signifies literally to receive one's guests well with food and drink. In the more specific context of the

*Cent nouvelles*, however, this expression most often describes a situation in which two characters dine sumptuously before going to bed together, or it may even signify a kind of foreplay.[31] Is the text implying, then, that the relationship between the two men is eroticized, and that it must be carried out by means of the fetishized female body? Whatever the case may be, the intercourse between the two men takes a material form after the women have left the scene. "The several and diverse matters" that they discuss inevitably turn toward the subject of sex, since conversations about this subject are the foundation of the relations that exist among certain types of men. As we saw in tale 33, this kind of homosocial relationship also requires that male characters share the secret of their desire with other males, while this sharing is the basis of the "love" that joins man to man. In this emblematic story, the conversation about sex is immediately translated into its physical fetish, since the narrative exchange of the secret of desire immediately becomes a literal sharing of the female body.

Another typical component of the economy of male domination is the exaggeration of male potency, coupled with an unbounded female desire for sex. The male homosocial economy entails the reduction of bodies to their most basic material level, once the iconic markers that define their identity have been stripped away. In other words, all bodies are equal in the darkness in this context:

> He [the husband] cast off his robe very quietly, and slipped into bed. Because the candle had been snuffed out, and because madam did not utter a single word, the lord assumed that he was in bed with the maid. He had not been there long before he began to perform his duty. So well did he acquit himself that three or four times cost him no effort at all. Madam was quite pleased, and soon after, thinking that that was all, she dropped off to sleep. The lord, who was in better spirits than before, saw that his wife was asleep, and remembered his promise. He got up very quietly, and went to his companion, who awaited the moment to go into battle.... The guest, more wakeful than a rat and swifter than a greyhound, left his friend and slipped into place beside madam without arousing her suspicions.... [T]he guest labored even more vigorously and more swiftly than his host (who had, nonetheless, done a good night's work). The wife was most astounded by all this. After another pleasant interlude, which madam found not at all distasteful, she once again drifted off to sleep. (48)

This male imaginary conceives of women as beings who are always ready to receive the insistent body of the male, which in itself is always ready to perform in a hyperbolic manner. Moreover, the rogue male who is always ready to seduce any available female is often defined by semes of animality, as the guest is here. The stripping away of the insignia that determine identity and class reduces the characters to a realm of animal equality, upon which the homosocial economy enacts its diverse differentiations.

There are several details of this story that distinguish it from others of the same type. The first is the female resistance to an unmeasured male desire, which takes the form of a communication among women intended to uphold the integrity of the household, based upon a rigid maintenance of female virtue. This idea of feminine communication as a means of preserving virtue in the face of masculine assaults and attacks, which is one of the major preoccupations of the *Heptaméron*, is merely sketched here as a kind of mock mirror image of the primary communications among men. When the light of day returns, and the husband returns to the room to find his wife in the maiden's bed, he is subjected to the following harangue: "You whoremonger, debaucher, coward, and pig! You thought that you were lying with my chambermaid, and so you embraced me repeatedly, to satisfy your voracious appetite. Thank the Lord, you've been tricked. At least I am the only one who can possibly possess that which belongs to me by rights, at least for now" (49; modified). The wife's last sentence aptly describes the sexual contract of marriage violated by the husband. This is one of the few stories in the *Cent nouvelles* in which the female characters give voice to a rational protest of the domineering male order and its attendant violations. The *Heptaméron*, in contrast, concentrates largely on the affirmation of this feminine voice, which remains trapped in the double bind of a male-imposed code of feminine virtue.

Secondly, the transaction of the female body in tale 9 only succeeds partly in establishing an institutionalized relation between the two men. The essential element of the male homosocial economy of the *Cent nouvelles nouvelles* is the exchange of the female body, which is later rendered in a narrative account of this transaction. While both of these take place in tale 9, it is clear that the relationship between the two men never assumes the form of a regular trade in the female body, as it does in tale 33: "The lord sought out his guest, and recounted his adventure in detail, and made two requests of his visitor. The first was that he carefully guard the secret of this most unpleasant incident. The second was that the guest never again return to a place where he would see the wife" (49). While the cycle of male domination is complete, it is clear that the relation between these best of man friends is interrupted at this point. Nevertheless, the sharing of this sexual "mystery," which the Duke imparts here to his narratees, performs the essential function that is at the root of the narrative economy of the work: the circulation of a sexual secret based on the material transfer of the female body, and which is, paradoxically, always already known to everyone.

The stories of the *Cent nouvelles* almost invariably exhibit the characteristics of the male homosocial economy that I have described, independently of the types of characters that they represent. The numerous characters in the work who were members of holy orders, for example, were forbidden the pleasures of the flesh, as is well known (it is also well known that monks and nuns were notorious gluttons and profligates in the upside-down comic imagination of the Middle Ages). Within the context of the *Cent nouvelles*, this kind of prohibition functions invariably as an incentive. An interdiction of any kind signifies one thing to the *homme rusé* who appears in these pages: how is it possible to overcome this prohibition by means of some subterfuge? Monks, being men, are no different from the amorous knights and merchants with whom we are familiar, except in terms of the symbols with which they are represented on the page (a sword signifies a knight; a tonsure signifies a monk, a lock of long hair signifies a woman, even when it is cut off, as in tale 33). The opening of tale 15 plays on the conventional, carnivalesque understanding of the religious:

> In fair Brabant, in close proximity to a monastery of white monks, there stands a nunnery of devout and charitable sisters. The story does not state the name of the nunnery, nor the particular persuasion to which the sisters belong. These two houses were such close neighbors that, to use the common expression, one was the grange and the other held the threshers. For (thanks be to God) the nuns were so charitable that they excluded few monks from the amorous distribution of feminine favors, provided, of course, that the monks were worthy of them. But to get to the heart of this story, in the white monks' cloister, there lived a young, handsome monk, who fell so passionately in love with one of the neighboring nuns that it made him quite irrational. (67)

The cliché of the religious as profligates is expressed here in terms of a proverbial expression (*"la grange et les bateurs"*), which the tale uses to invoke a familiar *topos* that will have predictable consequences. Just as marriage in itself, in this context, does not prohibit adultery—on the contrary, the logic of the *Cent nouvelles* presupposes that adultery will take place within the marital situation—so the religious vocations in themselves present no obstacle to sexual satisfaction. In *nouvelle* 15, a more specific prohibition is added to the religious one: "Although this nun was certainly a courtly sister, she responded to his advances in a very harsh and bitter manner, for she had heard about his tool's reputation"

(67). The nun is well aware of the "equipment" this particular monk has and of his ability in using it ("Word has it that you are so poorly endowed that if you were to put your instrument in a certain place, I would hardly know that it's there" [67]). The prospective lover is inadequate to the task, and the impediment he has to overcome is the nun's knowledge of presumably private information. As in the third tale, one of the characters is able to penetrate the boundaries of secrecy that would normally surround the body of another character. In this case, however, the order of rank is inverted, and the value of male supremacy's marker is placed in doubt by the nun, who takes the place of the male in the signifying chain of the narrative.

That the tale focuses on the genitals raises once again the issue of fetishism; although the terms are rearranged, the fetishistic structure remains the same. As is well known, Freud claimed that the sight of the female genitals provoked a fear of castration in the boy, who then provided a substitute for the penis that the woman lacked. Here the monk's reaction is a variation of this intersubjective configuration: faced with his fear of the "castrating" female, he tries to supplement the lack of his own body. After hearing the monk's repeated pleas, the nun finally agrees to a rendez-vous, at which she will have sex with him if she finds that he is properly "equipped." At this meeting, one of his fellow monks, a certain Conrad ("who was [Lord knows!] most generously endowed" [68]) will act as the substitute:

> If the truth be told, I am not endowed with as thick a lance as I would like, nor is it as thick a lance as this sister would like to meet in battle. I therefore beg you [Conrad], from the bottom of my heart, to come with me on the night that I am supposed to meet her. You will be doing me the greatest favor that ever one man did for another. I know what she plans to do. Once I am there, she wants to feel, to touch the lance with which I plan to do battle. At the fateful moment, this is what you must do. You will stand behind me—but without uttering a word—and you will take my place by thrusting your stout staff into her hand. Once this is done, she will certainly open her gate, and you will leave. I'll enter, and as for the rest, just leave it to me. (68)

The dynamics of this scene are quite different from the others that I have examined. In the other examples, the body of the woman was rendered desirable by the fact of her marriage, or by the relation she maintained with a man; her body had value largely because it was his property (or because he had acquired rights to its possession, as in tales 9 and 33), and it came to be the substitute of that man's position in a network of power relations. From this point of view, the woman's innate "lack" was supplemented by an abstract substitute that signified the presence of maleness, in some way. Here, the monk assumes the role that is usually forced upon women, Lacan's "position of the female" in the closed network in which the phallus circulates. Rather than trying to establish a relation with another man via the female body, he attempts to bring about a relation with a woman by substituting the icon of male power in the place of his own lack.

The fragmentation of the represented body of tale 15 does not result in the relation of two men, as would usually be the case; rather, if any one of the characters becomes a fetish here, it is Conrad, who is insignificant except for his one salient feature. Here we witness a kind of antifetishism: the nun is in a position from which she may exercise a certain kind of male power, rather than being the victim of a seducer who tries to get beyond her to the man for whom she acts as a substitute. For her, any man will apparently do, as long as he bears a sufficiently exaggerated token of masculinity, just as the desirability of most of the female characters in the tales is motivated by the presence of a male marker that supplements their supposed lack. The monk situates himself in the place of the female when confronted with this masculinized nun: he attempts to make himself acceptable to her by supplementing his body with a hyperbolic, albeit empty, male icon (empty in the sense that in this case it cannot stand for the economic advantage that marriage usually bestows upon female characters).

The would-be lover's ruse does not succeed, which reveals something about the nature of fetishism in this male-dominated, narrative setting. One could argue that, in the *Cent nouvelles*, as in Freud's text, fetishism is inherently masculine, or is necessary only to a certain kind of (neurotic?) male sexuality. Consequently, any attempt to place women in a position from which they would attempt to have access to power by appropriating a fetish would be anomalous in this narrative system, since it is male characters who access a kind of power (i.e., they enter into relationships with other male characters) by appropriating the female body as a fetish for male-to-male relationships. The end of tale 15 illustrates the impossibility of female fetishism when it becomes evident that the fetish may signify maleness only with the body of the female as the arena of its operation:

> "By my faith," said she, "you'll not be entered in my register until I've thoroughly inspected you, to know what kind of equipment you bear. Come closer now and show what stuff you're made of."
>
> "Most willingly," said he.

Whereupon Brother Conrad stepped forward to play his part. He placed his staff, a fine, powerful one, both stout and long, in the hand of the nun. As soon as she felt it, as if Nature had endowed her with the power to recognize it, she exclaimed: "No, no, that's not it at all! I recognize this one very well. It's Brother Conrad's staff. There's not a single nun in this convent who doesn't know it intimately. There's no way you can fool me. Be off, now, and seek adventure elsewhere." (68, modified)

The rapacious designs of the seductive characters represented in this text are always based upon a fetishizing gaze that sees without being seen but that is afflicted with a fundamental blindness: it cannot see the fact that it desires its object because the fetish is present. In tale 15, however, it is clear that this typically male blindness and insight loses its effect among a community of unmarried yet sexually active female characters, who recognize and desire the materiality of the male marker without being interested in whatever economic configuration it might represent. In this kind of inverted, nonsymbolic, perhaps *female* social order, the rapacious gaze of the fetishizing male does not and cannot function in the same manner as it usually does. The nun recognizes the substitution by means of an innate knowledge that is twofold: she recognizes the monk's attempt to provide himself with the penis that he lacks because this maneuver is continually imposed upon women in the fetishistic economy created by men (one might say, with MacKinnon, that desire for the phallus that they don't have is the identity that patriarchy imposes upon women). Secondly, she recognizes the object that is supremely emblematic of this economy's functioning: the exchange of women is predicated upon the circulation of the phallus. Thus, while fetishism "works" when the substitute supplements a woman's lack, it cannot have the same effect when it is meant to supplement a man's lack. In a narrative system that privileges a male-dominated exchange of secret information, and represents the unconscious exchange of fetishes that is typical of a certain kind of male sexuality, the inadequate male has no place and is relegated to failure.

In conclusion, the *Cent nouvelles nouvelles* are narrative permutations generated on the basis of a specific structure of power, defined by the difference that separates male and female characters in a stratified economic situation. The inherent inequalities of this structure, as well as the various movements of the characters across its grid, are contingent upon a given notion of sex and sexuality within this complex of relations. The bodies of these characters are almost invariably fragmented and fetishized, with certain body parts functioning as icons of the difference between male and female. The male marker signifies power and desire in this context, and the male characters are almost always roaming this imaginary space, looking for areas in which they may usurp or possess the "goods" of other men. In contrast, the female body is reduced to an icon from which the male characters intuit the prototype of a male homosocial economy. In other words, the male characters of this work perceive a value in the fetishized female body by virtue of her institutionalized relation to other males. In each of the tales, the characters are merely rearranged in reference to this grid of relations, which is graphed out by means of iconographic details. In extreme cases, the male may be placed in the position of the female. At any event, this rearrangement of the characters' positions does not change the underlying configuration that determines the ultimate meaning of each tale.

The *Cent nouvelles* are thus representations of a configuration of power based upon a specific conception of gender difference. In this context, a particular story of women is passed from man to man as the foundation of male homosocial relations: woman is an object to be possessed, or to be exchanged for other goods. She is valuable only insofar as she embodies the wealth of another man; she is desirable only insofar as her body is supplemented by the male marker, which signifies the set of relations and exchanges among men that constitute power. The absolute male domination of women in this context was predicated upon a fundamental fetishism of woman as commodity within a male homosocial economy, at least as it is figured in the narratives of this work. The male figures who populate the text are both the subjects of this story of women, in the sense that it is *they* who tell it, while they are subject to it in the sense that they are ruled absolutely by it. In other words, the positive and negative effects of power make themselves known by the persistence of these tales that traverse, envelop, and saturate the fictional male body. This story is in fact the phantasm of a fetishistic male sexuality that dominates the male imaginary of the West to this day. Its obsessive retelling in early-modern Europe, which preceded centuries in which it was repressed and sublimated, makes of this period a key moment in its long dissemination among us.

# 3
# Philippe de Vigneulles and the Economy of Expenditure

The homosocial contract of the *Cent nouvelles nouvelles* configures a network of relations among men that constitutes (the basis of) their power. These economic relations depend upon the exchange of a specific merchandise: a phantasmic story of women that circulates among them and that has several salient characteristics that are reiterated countless times in the text. According to this male fantasy of the female, woman immediately becomes the object of an indefatigable male desire as soon as she enters his field of vision. A married woman is the property of her husband, and as such she must be guarded (watched, surveiled) within the domicile of her marriage. Any woman who is in a man's control in some way (by virtue of her marriage or intimate relationship with him) is always open to the advances of a seducing male character. Men enter into transactional relationships with other men when they engage in the trade of the female body. The *Cent nouvelles* thus incarnate a gender-contingent configuration of power to which the characters have different degrees of access (i.e., different rights to occupy certain positions within a network of relations), depending upon their sex. As subjects of power, male characters are relatively free to circulate and to change positions in the social hierarchy (at least with respect to their female counterparts), while female characters are forced to act as objects of desire, or as commodities to be exchanged in an imaginary society that restricts their movements. On the metadiegetic level of this text, male characters learn the craft of narrative as a means of assuring themselves a place in the power structure. The homosocial trade in female bodies in the diegesis parallels the exchange of stories that forms the text itself. These narratives thus structure the imaginary of a given social order of power, which defines the subjectivity of a certain category (male nobles) of fictional beings.

The *Cent nouvelles nouvelles* of Philippe de Vigneulles represent a different perspective on this set of power relations. Many of these tales bring to life various forces that undermine the hegemony of the male-dominated, homosocial power of the first *Cent nouvelles*. What counts in Philippe's tales is not the restriction of wealth to a group of individuals belonging to a single gender. On the contrary, they seem to value expenditures and exchanges for their own sake. The text judges certain characters—rogues, thieves, pardoners, and especially adulterous wives and profligate women—on the basis of whether or not they provoke exchanges, especially of the hyperbolic kind to which Bataille referred in his discussion of expenditure (*dépense*). In those few tales in which the female body is exchanged, as in tale 38, the work pays little attention to the homosocial relation that this transaction establishes between the male characters involved in the deal. The fact of the exchange itself is significant in this context, rather than its implications for a social structure based upon male homosocial relations. Many of Philippe's characters, especially the female ones, resist exchanges that would appear "normal" in the context of the *Cent nouvelles*—e.g., the food traded for the female body in tale 1—by enacting a carnivalesque and at times scatological inversion of homosocial expenditure. In place of the female body that he hoped to receive for his efforts, the seducing character may find the undesirable end products of a process of consumption (garbage or excrement), as in tale 81. In some examples, such as tale 91, female characters take control of the economic functioning of entire communities, propelling themselves and the characters who surround them into the domain of nonproductive expenditure. Other *nouvelles* valorize marginal figures who disrupt the "normal" modes of commerce that subtend given hierarchies. The outrageous protagonists of tales 20 and 59, for example, seem essentially to *incarnate* or to represent (in the sense that figures in a parade represent certain qualities, attributes, or abstract notions, such as Lady Liberty) the notion of expenditure, which functions as a guiding principle throughout the text. In general, therefore, the work is dominated by an economy of corporeal excess, focused on the activities of what Bakhtin calls "the lower material bodily stratum," which undermines the strict hierarchy of Vigneulles's French model and develops its own procedures in a carnivalesque time that seemingly suspends the rigors of hierarchical difference.

A genealogy performed on narratives of this time, however, offers us a rather ambiguous picture of what might be perceived as a shift in power structures from the first to the second of these two texts. As we glimpsed in the analysis of *nouvelle* 15 of the *Cent nouvelles*, a single work of this period may offer alternative models of power at the same time that it embodies a stereotypical, male-dominated social hierarchy. Thus, while the narratives of fifteenth- and sixteenth-century France may depict shifting power relations within imaginary domains—from male to female, from feudal to mercantile, from carnival to tragic, from collective to individual—they also demonstrate increasingly ambivalent (both conservative and subversive) attitudes toward existing social hierarchies. The tales of Philippe de Vigneulles, for example, depict popular forces that enact momentary inversions of a given organization of power, while the work never seriously questions the legitimacy of such a stratified social system, nor is there any particular reason why it should. In contrast, in the culminating work of the *nouvelle* literature of the period, the *Heptaméron*, the major female characters (Floride, Rolandine, Jambique) maintain an irreducibly ambivalent relationship to the fictional societies in which they live, since all of them represent a conscious interrogation of the problems women faced while entrusted with the exercise of an essentially male power, disseminated through the concept of feminine virtue, in a context dominated by men. Before turning to Marguerite de Navarre's subtle critique, I will first examine Philippe de Vigneulles's seemingly unbounded affirmation of a social order turned upside-down, which stands the world of male homosocial domination on its head during the carnivalesque moment of the text and applauds the action of subversive female characters, along with other rogues and profligates.

Tale 38 of Philippe's collection introduces us to the various modes of resistance to homosocial power present in the work. The *nouvelle*'s opening paragraphs situate Philippe's city of Metz amid a proliferation of economic exchanges provoked by war. The narrator frames a male character's desire to appropriate the female body in a symbolic context defined by conflict and commerce:

Now we will speak a little bit about women, elegant ones as well as simple ones, and first of all about a smart woman who was duped in the manner that you will hear about. This woman was a fabric merchant in Metz, but you will help me to keep her name a secret.

This happened during the wars between the Duke René of Lorraine and the city of Metz, which took place during the year 1490. As everyone knows, during that war there were many different kinds of soldiers from different countries in the city, among whom there was one who was in love with the bourgeoise about whom we are speaking. This man maneuvered so well and so diligently that he won her good graces and her love.[1]

A single detail of these opening paragraphs indicates one of the major differences that will distinguish Philippe's *nouvelles* from their predecessors. Like most of the characters described in this collection, the female protagonist is named in reference to her professional activity, which represents an extraordinary shift in perspective from the *Cent nouvelles nouvelles*, especially given the fact that she is a female character performing an official function in a public space. According to Livingston, Philippe de Vigneulles himself was a "shoe maker and fabric merchant" (15). His work describes a range of professions that goes well beyond the limited spectrum of knights and squires found in the *Cent nouvelles*. One need consider only a partial list of these professions to grasp the extent of the work's involvement with the economic activity of the period: "red neck" or "country bumpkin" (*rusticque*), valet (tale 23), silversmith, cart driver, laborer (tale 26), merchant (tale 27), justice officer (*sergent*) (tale 30), *quetteurs* (the itinerant priests who sell bogus relics in tales 33–37), notary (tale 36), fabric merchant (tale 38), "salesman" or "reseller"(*cosson, revendeur*) (tale 45), *marowier* ("that is, one who works the land and the plow") (tale 52), cobbler, stable hand (tale 57), shepherd (tale 69), ambulant blacksmiths or makers of pots and pans (*chaudronniers*) (tale 71), weaver (tale 72), cutler (tale 81), and so on.

The anecdote of tale 38 is typical of Renaissance narrative, as Livingston informs us: "The theme of the gallant man who takes the place of another man (usually the husband) was widely disseminated in the short tales, to which each author added his own details" (176). The *topos* of the replaced lover in this example includes details of economic exchange that are typical of this work: buying and selling is the context for seduction, while the figurative cuckolding of the replaced lover is framed by an economic subtext that is almost always a constitutive element of the cuckold tale. The seducer first sees the bourgeoise while she is at work: "Our good man [*compagnon*] found his friend [*s'amye*] the bourgeoise in her boutique selling fabric to another soldier, and spoke German to the said merchant woman as she sold the fabric" (177). The usurping lover pretends that he does not speak French, thus the saleswoman and her lover speak openly (in French) of the rendez-vous they have planned for that evening, where the substitution occurs. After their amorous exercise is complete, the usurper quietly steals a gold ring from her finger, "which she tolerated, thinking that this man was her lover [*amy*]" (178).

In this tale, however, there is no relationship between the two men, and the fact that they share the sexual favors of the same woman does not constitute a contract that unites them. In contrast, what matters here is the idea of exchange and the role it plays in identifying the characters. The usurping lover steals a gold ring from the bourgeoise, which is a common motif in tales from this period. In an earlier example (*Cent nouvelles,* 62), the ring symbolized the exchange of a woman between two men, and the price that had to be paid to her husband for the usage of her body; here the ring allows the soldier to identify himself later to the merchant. While male homosocial domination was clearly at issue in the example from the *Cent nouvelles,* Philippe's *nouvelle* valorizes exchange in itself, especially when it is enacted by a marginalized character who usurps a place for himself in a business context. The *dénouement* of the tale highlights these economic aspects of the narrative:

> When the next day came, the other man, who had not been recognized, did not forget to return [to the shop] to see his lady, and he went back to bargain for some fabric. While bargaining, he showed [her] the little ring that he had taken from the finger of the bourgeoise when he went to bed with her, as we said above. She recognized the ring and was totally ashamed when she saw it. At any rate, the merry companion spoke frankly with her, and they haggled over the matter to such an extent that in the end they liked each other better. In this way, the fellow conquered a woman in love. (178)

In bargaining for the material that she sells, it is clear that the soldier is also bargaining for her body. The story focuses upon the trick by which an individual increases his store of goods by means of his intelligence. This example inscribes the female body as commodity in an economy that valorizes exchange but which is not necessarily dominated by male homosocial relations. The two male characters do not exchange information that they keep secret from the female character as the basis of the relation that unites them. The key movement of the tale is the transfer of the woman's body from one man to another, but this transaction does *not* function as the foundation of a social contract, as it had in the earlier examples, since the first lover simply disappears after the introduction of the second one. The object that brings about the bourgeoise's recognition of the usurping lover is symbolic of this process: this "little gold ring (*annelet d'or*)," as it is named earlier in the tale, signifies the wealth and position of this bourgeoise within a social economy whose stratifications are based upon the appropriation and loss of merchandise. While a gold ring is undoubtedly the icon *par excellence* of marriage, the text makes no mention whatsoever of the woman's marital status, a detail that could not be passed over in silence in the earlier tales. What is at issue in this tale, therefore, is the way in which the appropriation of wealth defines the rank and value of each character, in some cases independently of their gender. A single fact highlights the difference between this tale and the earlier examples from the *Cent nouvelles*: what the usurping lover desires here is *not* the institution of a relation with another male; rather, he desires the wealth of the female character, symbolized by the gold ring, and incarnated in her flesh, which is thus relieved of its fetishistic value, in a sense, since the first male character does not use the female character's body merely as a medium to enter into a relation with the second male character. The usurping lover wants to have sex with the merchant for the sake of the act itself, and not for the sake of what the act may signify, i.e., the homosocial relation. Perhaps this first example from Philippe's text represents a kind of "flattening" of narrative icons, since the process by which the tale might have signified the prototype of a social world seems to be negated in it. While it depicts a general mercantile order, the tale seems to concentrate on the logical consequences of its own procedures. While one male character "conquers" a female character who belonged to another male, the tale concentrates more on this transaction itself, than on the institutional consequences of such an exchange between men.

Beyond this general suspension of the male homosocial model, a more direct resistance is apparent in other tales of Philippe's collection. In what one might term "corporeal sequences," the represented body of the characters is subjected to at least two types of transformations: it can be marked by a substance, usually filth of some sort (feces, urine, eggs, etc.), or its lower, private parts may be exposed or elevated, as in the typical anecdote in which some rogue rigs a priest's vestments so that his backside is revealed precisely at the moment of consecration during the Mass (tale 7).[2] There are numerous tales in the work that fall into this corporeal, and perhaps even *scatological* category. There are six *nouvelles* in which an unmarked fictional body is marked with *ordures*. In one of the episodes of tale 20, a tanner's hands and face are covered in feces when a rogue defecates in his can of leather polish. A servant succumbs to a similar fate in tale 23 when a peasant defecates in his helmet. In tale 24, a beggar woman who is crying outside of a window where a party is being held is chased away by one of the guests, who strikes her with frozen feces. In tale 27, a gentleman buys eggs and hides them in his hat; a rogue named Growes, "who was a fine fly," sees his opportunity and smashes the hat down on the gentleman's head. In tale 48, a chaplain who is trying to seduce a nun mistakenly serves her fecal matter in the place of pâté. Finally, the fanatically clean character of tale 80 somehow covers one of his fingers in feces, upon which he asks his servant to cut it off. The clever servant strikes the finger with the back end of his ax, producing an intense pain which causes the master to bring the finger into his mouth. Most of these tales describe actions that interrupt or overturn the logical procedure of production and consumption, provoking nonproductive expenditure: the tanner's leathers are ruined; the beggar woman goes hungry; the gentleman's eggs are wasted; the nun eats feces instead of food. In this comic context, one is not far removed from the pie-in-the-face mentality of burlesque and vaudeville, in which the human intermixture with waste products is assumed to be amusing.

Some of these anecdotes, however, represent a genuine resistance to an implicitly defined order of rank. Tale 81 is perhaps the best example of a corporeal sequence that describes a female resistance to the usual male appropriation of her body, and in which she condemns her frustrated seducer to be befouled by fecal matter. During a pilgrimage to the shrine of St. James in Santiago de Compostela, a husband and wife from Rouen spend the night in the residence of a priest in Poitiers. Following the logic of corporeal substitution that is typical of the *nouvelle*, the priest formulates a plan that will allow him to act as her husband's substitute in bed during the night: he will treat the couple to a hearty supper, during which he has instructed his valet to slip a laxative into the husband's soup. There is no bathroom in the guest room, so the husband will have to leave the house in order to relieve himself; at this point, the valet will lock the door, leaving the husband outside. The priest then plans to take the husband's place in the dark room. The wife, however, "who was a clever woman [*fine femme estoit*]," is aware of every detail of this plan, and decides to take her revenge.

Many of Philippe's tales unfold within a logic dictated by the necessity of marking a character's body with some kind of filth. If the entirety of the body cannot be touched in this way, then a valorized part of it seems to suffice: the head, hands, mouth, etc. Philippe's comic technique is grotesque, in Bakhtin's sense of the term,[3] and the bodies it describes are open to their environment—especially to contact with the filth that issues from other bodies. While the syntax of the *Cent nouvelles* was seemingly generated by a will to violate the legal and sexual limits of the represented body—its seduction, unveiling, rape—Philippe's tales are often structured around the necessity that the body be covered in its own refuse, for the sake of its comic effect. The development of tale 81 is thus a kind of mapping out of its imaginary space in accord with this corporeal necessity. The covering of the priest's body occurs in four settings: the wife tells her afflicted husband to defecate in the fireplace, in a washbasin, in the priest's hat, and finally in the priest's guest bed, where they are supposed to sleep. They escape with the wife on her husband's shoulders, so that it will seem to the valet in waiting as though the husband has left alone. The valet locks the door, and the anxious priest sheds his clothes and jumps into the guest bed, where he is covered from head to toe in filth. Surprised by the odor, he instructs his valet to light a candle. The valet goes to the fire, and while scattering the ashes in search of a hot coal, his hands are covered in fecal matter; he goes to the washbasin to cleanse himself, but manages only to cover his face in feces. The priest tells him to light the candle at the church altar, but it is raining outside, so the valet decides to put on the priest's hat, at which point even his teeth are dripping in the refuse of the grotesque body.

The tale thus stakes out its represented space using the final products of a procedure of expenditure as markers, leading from the acquisition of goods by the pilgrims—eating and drinking, described at the beginning of the tale—to their consumption and rejection, their defecation and urination. The goal of the anecdote is a saturation of the represented body in the final products of this sequence. The narrator chooses the particular places that will carry out this plan: the washbasin because it is a place in which one bathes the hands and face, the hat because it is put over one's head, the bed because it "contains" the entire body. In the typical tale of seduction from the *Cent nouvelles*, an unwitting (or downright stupid) female character is tricked into offering her body to a rapacious male figure, often without her knowledge of her indiscretion. Philippe's eighty-first tale inverts this sequence of events, overturning the economic procedure that culminates in the sexual usage of the female body, which is often traded for a trifling merchandise offered to her or to her husband/lover. In tale 38, the transaction that transferred the rights to the fabric merchant's body from one man to another was the heart of the story. In contrast, tale 81 describes a resounding refusal of this kind of deal. The clever wife of this anecdote disrupts the normal course of events that would have led to her possession by another male character, whom she places at the undesirable end of an economic process presumably controlled by the male—i.e., the homosocial commerce of the female body. In this sense, this story is about the (female) resistance to a given (male) power structure, and about the ways in which certain female figures, who cannot be contained within the boundaries assigned to them by male institutions, offer comic relief from the stifling confines of male desire's phantasmic economy. The most important iconographic image of this tale is undoubtedly that of the *curé*, who jumps naked into a bed full of feces. While this type of seductive figure was the icon that signified a prototypical social order in the *Cent nouvelles*, Philippe's tale might be considered a kind of blasphemous defacement of the image that was "sacred" to the male homosocial power structure of the earlier collection. In this sense, Philippe's text is quintessentially parodic, since it subjects consecrated models to grotesque variations. Here the image of the usurping male as a "sacred" icon of the reigning order is debased to the level of a grotesque figure, stripped of the insignias that signify its social stature, and marked with the ultimate sign of degradation. Like the simultaneous elevation of the host and revelation of the priest's buttocks, here the lover is defiled precisely at the supposed moment of his sexual apotheosis. In this sense, the image of the wife escaping on the shoulders of her husband/collaborator may be an icon of a different kind of (bourgeois) social order, which resists the aristocratic privilege that assured the nobleman's (and the *curé*'s) right to appropriate the female body at will.

The extent of the economic activity described in the *nouvelles* of Vigneulles reveals an essential difference between these tales and their French predecessors. In contrast to the *Cent nouvelles nouvelles*, which were little more than the inscription of a male homosocial order, Philippe's collection inscribes a multiplicity of conflicting forces—rich versus poor, male versus female, individual versus collective, cleric versus lay, merchant versus aristocrat, professional versus peasant. His narratives concentrate these conflicts on an economic activity comprising the exchange of general merchandise, and not merely on the control of a patrimony accomplished by a fetishization of the female body. The earlier collection concentrated upon the institutionalized transactions that configured the homosocial order. In contrast, Philippe's work explores the possibilities of a social order in which every individual participates in an explosion of economic activity, which is freed from its restriction to the domain of patrimony. Characters such as rogues, charlatans, thieves, pardoners, and seducers are extremely important in this undermining of an imaginary social order. For example, the rogue protagonist of tale 20 is a certain Mannis, who "was a tricky and jolly fellow who played lots of practical jokes on people in order to make them laugh, for which he was often invited to parties in good company [*pour lesquelles choses estoit souvent mandez en bonne compaignie*]" (113). Mannis is one of a long tradition of characters that includes the Spanish *picaro* and the great Panurge. According to Livingston, he was drawn directly from the *Roman de Renart* (p. 112). In two other tales devoted to the antics of jesters (83 and 84), Livingston goes on to describe the numerous analogs in European literature in which this type of fool appears, from Poggio Bracciolini's *Facetiae*, to the *Shakespearean Jest Books*, to the *Autobiography of Benvenuto Cellini* (pp. 326 and 330). It is not surprising, therefore, that this type of character occupies such an important place in Philippe's *nouvelles*. Mannis is one of a long list of characters in the collection who ramble about the environs of Metz, trying to take advantage of others. Beneath the surface of these stories, there is almost always an economic transaction that is accomplished by means of the characters' actions. The economic sequences of Philippe's tales are thus intimately linked to the figures of the rogue, the charlatan, and the trickster.

During a party in "good company" (in the sense of "composed of *bons compagnons*"), Mannis hears that one can sell almost anything at the market in Metz. The trick he undertakes after leaving the party is difficult to categorize:

> The said Mannis, of whom we are speaking, hearing that one could sell anything in Metz, concluded that he'd take something there to sell it the first chance he could get. At his house the said Mannis had many hens and capons, which were attacked once by a bird of prey that we call a *mirru*, which strangled one of his young chickens, making him very upset. By means of some trick, Mannis captured this bird of prey alive without killing it, then he gouged out its eyes and hung a little pouch around its neck, with a written note inside the said little pouch. After that, he took a basket on his back and went to Metz, and as he was passing through a village, he found a pile of eggshells with which he filled his basket, since he had heard among his aforementioned companions that anything could be sold in Metz. After stuffing his basket full, he thought that he would go to the city to try to sell his eggshells. (113)

The trick that Mannis undertakes unfolds according to the "world-upside-down" logic of carnival. Instead of trying to sell one of his domesticated birds, he captures a wild bird of prey, which he deprives of one of its defining characteristics, its keen eyesight. Moreover, he tags the bird with a marker of domestication: a purse around its neck bearing a written message. Finally, Mannis inverts the usual sequence of production and consumption when he attempts to sell that which is thrown in the garbage after its contents have been consumed. In other words, much like the wife of tale 81, Mannis inverts the order of an economic sequence, inserting the end products of expenditure at its beginning. The text proceeds by continuously offering the reader images whose essential attributes it immediately negates or effaces, as in the bird of prey that is blind and flightless. The rogue himself incarnates this procedure, since he is defined by his will to efface, erase, degrade, undo, undermine, and overturn any situation in which he finds himself—he turns the wild bird into a domesticated, blind, and grounded being; he tries to sell garbage in the market. The following scenes of the tale confirm this character as a kind of anti-being, whose activity is much more radical and subversive than anything from the *Cent nouvelles*.

Like the other elements of this tale, causality seems to work in reverse. The detail of the *mirru* is striking: if the character's intention is merely to sell eggshells in the marketplace, why does he go to the trouble of first capturing the bird alive, then blinding it, then writing the message that it carries around its neck? The preliminary conditions of the narrative offer nothing in response. The possibility that he is going to sell the bird is immediately negated by the appearance of Mannis's "merchandise," the eggshells. The enigma is soon resolved: as soon as Mannis arrives in Metz, a policemen recognizes him and buys his eggshells at a low price in order to get rid of the rogue. By doing so, the policeman undertakes a ruse of his own: he wants Mannis to deliver the shells to his home, where some of his men will be waiting in order to arrest the charlatan. Since he is an expert in deception, Mannis is not fooled:

Mannis, who was a clever man, recognized the intentions of the officer and saw that the said officer had his eye on him, and that he would be forced to play some kind of trick [*finesse*] in order to escape, otherwise he would be in hot water [*mal logiez*]. For this reason, he suddenly came up with a rather subtle prank, to wit, he took his bird of prey with its gouged-out eyes and the note in its little pouch around its neck, and he pushed his way through the biggest crowd he could find, letting the bird flap around above people's heads, and since the bird couldn't see a thing, it started smashing into people left and right, without knowing where it was going. The people who were there were stunned to see this bird with a little pouch around its neck come out of nowhere. ... The pouch was opened, but the only thing they found inside it was a little note that read, "Alas! I'm a poor buzzard, and I used to hang around Mannis's place in Abouez. For a little chick that I took from him, he gouged my eyes out like this." (114)

The character's baffling actions ultimately allow him to escape, once he has fulfilled the prophetic statement that opens the tale ("anything could be sold in Metz"). All of the complex details included in the *mirru* section of the tale are oriented toward the success of an improbable deal, in which one character buys eggshells from another. The notion of economic exchange assumes an importance that supersedes all of the text's other details. Moreover, the tale develops a symbolic subtext that pits a representative of power (the policeman) against a marginalized figure (Mannis) in a contest that results ultimately in the transfer of money from a character who stands for legitimate order to one who signifies disorderly expenditure. May one understand from these implications that Philippe's tale is *about* the valorization of figures who undermine a standard configuration of power? Or could it be that the value that the narrator and most of the characters in the text accord to this disruptive figure is merely a comic *topos* of a literary universe that is full of confidence men, rogues, dishonest priests, seducers, and thieves? Whatever the case may be, it is clear that the nature of such characters as Mannis is to disrupt the normal functioning of a social order based largely on economic exchange, or to construct an alternative order in which the normal definitive characteristics of beings and situations are inverted. By provoking a transfer of wealth from the empowered domains of this imaginary culture to its lowest levels, this character represents the force of an alternative economic model that undermines the kind of male homosocial authority depicted in the *Cent nouvelles*, as well as in some of Philippe's other tales.

The third trick described in tale 20 highlights the inverted economy that is the basis of Mannis's character. Moreover, it valorizes a procedure of expenditure that is provoked by the character, resulting in the appropriation and consumption of goods belonging to other characters. The entirety of the anecdote brings about a transaction in which Mannis "*fait bonne chère*" at another's expense, which is a theme that is quite common in the work (cf. tales 36, 53, 91). Escaping from Metz, Mannis encounters two wagon or cart drivers (the medieval equivalent of truckers, perhaps) who have just come from the market with provisions for a good meal. Mannis plans to steal these, and the rest of the anecdote is devoted to the transfer of these goods from the *charretiers* to Mannis. The rogue disguises himself as a dead man, and lies on the road where the charioteers must pass. Seeing the body lying in their path, one of the drivers says to the other: "Truly, . . . he's our Christian brother. Let's put him on the back of our wagon so that wild animals don't devour him" (117). Once he is on the back of the wagon, Mannis takes the provisions and flees in the night, reaching the town before the drivers. When they arrive, he treats them to a sumptuous meal, prepared, of course, with their own goods. The piquancy of the typical situation in which one character knows something that the others do not is coupled here with the satisfaction of dining at another's expense, which is always cause for laughter in this collection: "Thus you have heard how Mannis prepared a feast for these men using their own goods, which they laughed about many times afterward when the truth finally come out among them" (118). As is usually the case in this type of comedy, however, the apparently frivolous surface of the narrative parodies the rather serious story of Christ's death and resurrection (one of the resurrected Christ's first acts is to join his disciples at supper), which Mannis pulls off in a characteristic fashion, by assuming the form of a being whose apparent attributes prove to be empty (he becomes a wounded body that is not hurt at all). Mannis also recalls the mythic and quasimythic beings, from Proteus to the semidemonic Panurge, who were able to assume diverse forms in order to accomplish their ends.

This type of anecdote apparently would not have held the attention of the noble members of the court of Philippe le Bon, duke of Burgundy, since there are relatively few rogue tales in the *Cent nouvelles nouvelles* (tales 63 and 64 are unusual additions to the collection). Why should this story be of enough interest that such a cultivated and wealthy man as Philippe de Vigneulles took the time to write it down? The development from the first collection of French tales to Philippe's work implies a shift in perspective from an economy based on the rigid control of a feudal patrimony (about sixty of the *Cent nouvelles* are about adultery and cuckoldry, which means that they are about marriage) to one in which exchanges of all kinds, instituted by characters from the entire spectrum of this imaginary society, are recounted with evident pleasure and satisfaction. The last part of Mannis's tale closes with the final stages of a process of production and consumption: Mannis brings his "goods" to market, sells them, procures others, and consumes them in the company of the drivers. This somewhat marginal figure—it should be remembered that he lives in a house, owns farm animals, and so on—forces members who are similar in rank to himself to consume their goods. Far from causing any kind of displeasure to these other characters, this story of expenditure, retold countless times afterward, provokes peals of carnivalesque laughter.

The story that circulates from narrator to narratees in this work is radically different from the typical story of women that delighted the knights and soldiers of the *Cent nouvelles*. The story that enthralled the collective imaginary of the earlier text catalogued the more or less severe infractions of a paradoxical social structure: in order for this structure to exist as such, the constitutive restrictions of marriage were necessary; in order for the male homosocial economy to exist, the violation of these restrictions was necessary. In contrast, the story that dominates the collective imaginary of the second volume is one of excess, disorder, the breaking of boundaries, and the *seemingly* indiscriminate transfer of goods from character to character (in point of fact, these transfers almost always take place from rich to poor). Does this perspectival shift parallel an *actual* shift in power from a feudal hierarchy to a new kind of individualist, capitalist, mercantile, and bourgeois hierarchy? This kind of global appreciation of late medieval and early Renaissance culture in France is well beyond the scope of my argument. Within the restricted narrative domains that are my focus, the clever bourgeois described in tale 1 of the *Cent nouvelles,* who uses his wealth to enter into relationships with lords and nobles by seducing their wives, gives way to a bizarre rogue and individualist such as Mannis, who is more interested in the acqusition of material wealth than in the symbolic procedure of seduction. The shift in the collective imaginary embodied by these two texts and by these two characters is, perhaps, a minute but significant part of more general historical developments.

Philippe's tales bear many of the traits that one would expect them to have, given the fact that their author was a merchant. In this work, even rogues like Mannis are occupied in bringing their goods to market. As gratuitous as it may seem, the *bon tour* itself often has the character of the economic exchange carried off by a cunning merchant. At the extreme end of this perspective, the sequence in which a wife who tricks a priest into jumping naked into a bed full of excrement (tale 81) still has the marks of a successful deal: the priest goes to her bed thinking that he will possess her body as a result of his wheeling and dealing. Convinced that he has procured her body, he finds the "goods" that she has craftily substituted for it. She clearly resists an economic activity that entails her possession by a series of male characters, who enter into relationships with one another via the intermediary of her body. Similarly, the rogue who sells eggshells in the marketplace refuses to belong to a social order that entails his imprisonment, or the restriction of his characteristic activity, which is the inversion of normal economic exchanges. The best of Philippe's tales are thus composed of a dexterous mixture of the elements that I have examined to this point, which work together in order to bring about a redistribution of wealth. For example, the longest story of the collection, tale 91, combines *bons tours* or *finesses* with scatology, *mottos*, and economic swindling to produce one of the most satisfying narratives in the work. In the opening scene, a German named Hannes and his wife are forbidden to drink because they spend all of their money on alcohol and are unable to pay their debts. The authorities grant one concession to the dissolute couple:

> [The mayor] restricted the German from going to the tavern, along with his wife, and prohibited him from drinking wine at home or anywhere else, unless it was to propose a toast in honor of some transactions that were carried out, for the sake of which they would be allowed to drink; otherwise they couldn't drink. (351)

These two characters are disciplined at first because they are unable to fulfill the economic contracts into which they enter; afterward, they are allowed to continue as before as long as they do so in the context of an exchange of goods. In the world of Vigneulles, anything is possible within the boundaries of business, and the couple finds a solution to their problem that incarnates this activity in its most basic form: they continually sell their prized goat to one another and celebrate each transaction in the tavern, the *lieu par excellence* of expenditure, which is celebrated in a number of tales of this collection. Moreover, the tavern is a place saturated by empty expenditures, to which Hannes and his wife gain entrance by means of institutionalized economic activity that has no real material base. As we have seen repeatedly in this text, then, the goal of the tale is apparently to inscribe a narrative image whose attributes it immediately effaces: the buying and selling of the two main characters is a mere empty surface phenomenon.

In the same village, there is a miser who opposes Hannes, and is constituted in the text strictly in reference to the notion of economy: Hannes represents the idea of uncontrolled expenditure, with the miser depicting its converse, obsessive thrift. In the context of Philippe's collection, there can be no doubt as to the outcome of their situation. Undoubtedly, the wealth of the latter will be transferred to the former, accompanied by the narrator's comic approbation of this economic redistribution. The tale pits the two sides of this opposition against one another, in a contest in which the winner is decided by the quality of a *bon tour*. As is often the case in comic literature, the trick is triplicated, being performed by three female characters who engage in a procedure of expenditure that culminates in the transfer of goods from one side of the opposition to the other. Three wives, one of whom is married to Hannes, all of them named as *commères* ("gossips" or "busybodies"), leave the town in order to spend the day in Metz, where part of their time will be employed in buying and selling: "so that they wouldn't waste any time, each one of the women brought along something to sell. One of them brought a block of cheese or two; another one brought a tub of butter, and the third one brought along some eggs. All of these goods were sold immediately, producing some profit [*lesquelles marchandises furent incontinant vendues et refeirent argent*]" (353–54). After selling their dairy products, they have enough money to tempt them into the tavern, where they order a feast that is well beyond their means. The forward movement of the tale is transfixed by this scene of expenditure:

> Then the three busybodies sat down at the table and lit into the leg of lamb with such gusto that, before the chickens and the partridges were even half cooked, there was nothing left of the lamb but the bones. The hostess, seeing their good appetite, hurried along the meat and put three of the said chickens in front of the women while they were waiting for the others to cook, but in a moment they had stripped them to the bone. And if they ate a lot, they drank

just as much. The hostess was astonished by the looks on their faces, and seeing their good appetites, she put everything in front of them, and the good women, feeling the vapors of the wine rise to their heads, started talking and chattering to such an extent that it was like setting foot in a jail. While they were talking and cackling, these ladies dismembered the partridges, and without any more ceremony than if they were eating lard, they ate and devoured the birds without offering even a claw or a wing to their hostess. (354–55)

The feast of the three wives is described in meticulous detail that tends toward the hyperbolic. They eat not one but three different kinds of meat; the adverb *"tellement"*—to such an extent—is repeated twice, to increase the intensity of their actions; the text insists upon the absolute stripping of the cooked animals to their bones; the chattering of the women is so intense that the metaphoric jail that the passage refers to is more like a bird cage, given all the bird references that it contains. One has the feeling that these women will consume anything that comes before them— they leave nothing for their hostess, while the narrator implies that they should have. Rogue figures such as these wives are often defined by semes of animality in the *nouvelle* literature: the three female protagonists of this tale are themselves cackling birds who devour other birds. Here as elsewhere, this type of comedy is about insatiable and long-constrained appetites that explode beyond the limits that have been imposed upon them.

The narrator is fascinated by this moment of expenditure, which the tale seems largely to be about. There is nothing in the story that would lead one to believe that the wives are authorized to spend what must have been the considerable sum of money needed to pay for their meal. When the three wives are faced with the necessity of paying their bill, they formulate the idea of the *bon tour*, which is completely illogical. Among the three of them, the wives do not have a third of the money they need; the winner of their contest will have even less money than that. The competition thus unfolds according to a "world-upside-down" logic: they decide that the winner will pay the bill, which is not much of an incentive to win. Furthermore, it is clear from the tricks themselves that they are not intended to get money from the men, one of whom, Hannes, has no money in the first place. The story is organized, however, around a central economic concept that governs the kinds of transformations that it may represent. In this world, goods have to be consumed, and money has to be spent; this means that the initial situations of each tale may be changed ultimately in only one way—objects in the possession of one or more characters have to be transferred to one or more other characters. The *bons tours* that the wives play on their husbands are part of the sequence that accomplishes the transfer of wealth from those who have it to those who do not. Any kind of action is justifiable if it is performed in the context of an economic exchange, especially if it precipitates the circulation of wealth from those who possess it to those who cleverly appropriate that which does not belong to them.

The contest of the three wives brings about such a transaction in this tale. The first wife, who is married to the miser, convinces her tired husband, after his return from his work in the fields, that he has already eaten his supper, when in fact he has eaten nothing at all. The second wife convinces her husband that he is sick by covering his body with paint, and then she drugs him so that he falls into an abnormally deep sleep, at which point she wraps him in a funeral shroud. The third wife, who is married to Hannes, makes him believe that the friend with whom he was drinking the night before has died. This friend is, of course, the husband of the second wife. Hannes's wife hurries him out of bed so that he may make it in time for the funeral, and makes him believe that he is dressed when in reality he is naked. Hannes arrives naked at the funeral and is the laughing stock of the town.

All three of these tricks are related to the functioning of the body, which is appropriate if one considers that the economy represented in Vigneulles's collection concentrates on the role of corporeal activities in spurious economic exchanges. The first wife interrupts the normal course of consumption aimed at maintaining her husband's body. The second wife covers her husband's body in an undesirable substance, wraps it in a death shroud, and essentially represents the ultimate interruption of the life cycle, with the consumptions and expenditures that it entails. The third wife reveals her husband's body, opening it to public inspection and ridicule. The three wives are thus acting as rogues much in the same manner as Mannis and as the wife who resisted the priest's advances during her pilgrimage to Santiago. They disrupt the normal functioning of an economy, appropriate merchandise (which usually means *food* in this collection, as in the case of Mannis) for themselves that does not belong to them, and take control of the movements and transformations of the represented body. In the *Cent nouvelles*, this last kind of activity was reserved for male characters, who prompted the circulation, exchange, violation, fetishization, and unveiling of the female body in an economic process that favored the relation of man to man. Philippe's tale explodes and inverts this schema and represents an appropriation of power by characters who have no real access to its exercise.

When the three tricks have been played, the wives ask the opinion of those who have witnessed the events in order to determine who is the winner of the contest:

And then the aforementioned busybodies asked the opinion of all those present, in order to know which one of their husbands had been hoodwinked the best. The general opinion expressed by the loudest voices was that he who had gone to bed without his supper was the one who had been the most deceived, for the following reason: to wit, he could never return to his supper, and it was judged that he should pay the bar bill of the three gossips, and it turns out that he was the husband who was so cheap, of whom we spoke before. (359)

In his essay on chronotopes, Bakhtin noted that the arena in which rogues, clowns, and fools operated in Renaissance narrative was the marketplace.[4] Here, the actions of the three rogue *commères* or busybodies in a public contest force the only person in the story who is described as having any money ("he had many goods in abundance"), the miser, to pay the bill of the three wives, who clearly have no money of their own. This, then, is the main *tour* that is accomplished by the unfolding of the tale, which frames the three others. The anecdotes that describe how three wives get their husbands to "buy" three spurious stories run parallel to the larger story of how the other characters get a miser to buy a feast for the three women. The tale thus traverses the entirety of an economic spectrum, moving from the prohibition of prodigality to its justification by means of a transfer of wealth. The tale of the *bon tour* is always about this same subject. Its essential transformation is always of the same type and accomplishes the movement of wealth from a somewhat privileged group to one that is marginalized or deprived of power. This redistribution of wealth is tantamount to a momentary reconfiguration of power relations in the tale, authorized for a time by the special circumstances of carnival humor.

The subtext of this economic activity is an unleashed bodily activity, which distinguishes Philippe's collection from the *Cent nouvelles*. The male characters of the earlier stories used food as a means of establishing two different kinds of relationships: illicit, *sexual* relations between male and female characters as the symbolic basis for *social* relations among males. In contrast, the purpose of the *bons tours* perpetrated by Philippe's characters is the exacerbation or exasperation of bodily activities associated with food (eating, drinking, urination, defecation) for their own sake. Furthermore, the kinds of exchange provoked by the marginal figures of the text undermine the restriction of merchandise to a privileged group: the three wives eat a hyperbolic feast, the tavern owners are paid, and the nameless spectators have a good laugh at the expense of others. Finally, as is so often the case in the parodic literature of this period, the symbolic ground that supports all of these developments is the parody of the life of Christ, signified by the spurious death and resurrection of one of the characters, which was authorized by carnival. Moreover, the parody of the sacred that signifies the carnival register is reinforced in the busybodies' feast. While the number 3 is typical of comic anecdotes, it is also an ineluctably messianic number (Jesus was supposed to have lain in the tomb for three days; he was crucified at the age of thirty-three; his mission lasted three years; there were three women at his feet when he died, etc.). Moreover, the exaggerated amount of meat that the wives eat during their feast—incidentally, they eat three kinds of meat, partridge, chicken, and lamb (*gigot*)—is the quintessential marker of the time of feasting that precedes Lent, itself defined by abstinence from meat, from which carnival derives its name (*carnelevare*).[5] The images of this tale are thus truly iconographic in that they may all be interpreted against the prototypical backdrop of Christian mythology. In this sense, Philippe's text is perhaps more "primitive" or more "primordial" than the *Cent nouvelles nouvelles*, whose prototype is markedly the secular domain of marriage and its transgressions. The socially multifarious work of Philippe de Vigneulles fragments and fractures the neurotic male perspective of the *Cent nouvelles*, obsessed with the maintenance of its untenable position, and celebrates the momentary, carnivalesque release from hierarchies, hunger, and the threat of disease and death that were the daily "realities" that structured the lives of ordinary people at the beginning of the sixteenth century.

Another high point of Philippe's art evinces a similar combination of distinct elements. By far the best example of what Hermann Wetzel calls a *motto*-type tale is *nouvelle* 59 of the collection.[6] According to Charles Livingston, the tale has deep roots, which stretch from the Orient to sixteenth-century France via the twelfth-century collection of *exempla*, the *Disciplina Clericalis*.[7] Philippe's version of the story begins with the narrator's moral commentary on his subject matter: "Although I want to judge neither them nor anyone else, since I'm the worst of all men, one could say that there are many among them in the world, as one sees every day, who are unruly rather far beyond what the rules of their order dictate [*qui sont fort desreiglez et plus assés que à la reigle de leur ordre n'apartient*]" (246–47). This statement establishes the general conditions of the monks' lives, which are devoted to general dissipation. The concepts of order and of its transgression are inextricably linked here, much as the typical story of marriage entails or includes adultery, which is its own abrogation. The essential characteristic that defines the status of the monks—their obedience to the rules of the monastic order—is not applicable to them (in general, this paradoxical situation is true of all of the religious orders described in the *Cent nouvelles nouvelles* and in Philippe's collection), and their peculiar situation becomes evident in iconographic details that signify debauchery. In other words, the text performs its usual maneuver by saying to its readers, "These men were monks who had none of the defining attributes of monks." The paradox of medieval comedy was that its public apparently always already understood that monks were inherently comic figures. The abbot of the monastery is unhappy with the conduct of his charges, since they haunt "taverns and bordellos and other dissolute places" (247). Thus, both the rule of the monastic order and a carnivalesque counter-rule are in force in this confined and supposedly sacred space, which opens to a multiplicity of debauched public spaces in which the monks, as rogues, perpetrate their *bons tours*.

The abbot asserts the necessity of the monks' return to the norms that should define their condition, concentrating mainly on their eating habits—food, again, is the point at which the contradictory forces of the sacred and the profane converge, come into conflict, and are resolved by laughter. As we have already seen, eating and drinking play fundamental roles in this work and will serve as raw material for the final *motto*, which is preceded by a preliminary *motto* in the middle of the tale. Moreover, it emphasizes the focus of these tales on the grotesque body, which transcends the confines of gender and social stature, reducing individuals from different social categories and groups to the common denominator of hunger and thirst and the seemingly limitless desire on the part of these characters to ingest and digest. The abbot's call for a return to order takes the form of a rhetorical comparison expressed in alimentary terms:

> It's no longer enough if everything is completely disorderly, and it's no longer a question of fasting and living simply on bread and soup, as our forefathers did, who at most, on a good day, had some fish or some herring without ever eating meat. But now it's no longer enough for one to eat lots of meat all at once in the convent. . . . No, today this isn't enough for them, but they want to go to taverns, bath houses, and, after that, to bordellos. . . . And I'm telling you, a monk should be satisfied with what one puts in front of him without grumbling about it, since, as the wise man said, *panis et aqua est vita sancta*, and one should satisfy one's nature with very little substance. (247)

The abbot distinguishes the profane present from the sacred past in descriptions of different foodstuffs as icons that signify either holiness or dissipation. Abstinence from eating meat had a symbolic importance for the late-medieval mind that is difficult for us to gauge in the age of

McDonald's and Burger King. A highly significant period of the religious calendar, Lent, was defined by the virtual illegality of eating meat, illustrated in the case of Clément Marot, who was imprisoned for eating lard during this time of abstinence (the allegory from the *Roman de la rose* of the hypocrite *Papelardie*, who eats lard in secret during Lent, is also significant here).[8] The eating of fish signified religious austerity and the ritual purification of body and soul before the most sacred holy day of the year, while eating meat signified the bodily abandon of carnival, a feast whose name derives from the elimination of meat from one's diet, as we have seen. The abbot thus expresses his disapproval in terms of a symbolic code that was clearly understood by a medieval audience, via the medium of meat and fish as narrative icons, much like the visual icons that dominate the painting and sculpture of the period. The conclusion of his argument is expressed in the authoritative Latin phrase, "The good life is [lived on] bread and water," which serves as a discourse that will be undermined by the actions of the other characters.

The abbot demands a verbal response and threatens the monks with punishment. The brothers reply that they are not going to obey his wishes, and their response manipulates and degrades the Latin phrase, in the name of the expenditure that they represent. This first half of the tale reaches a comic climax with this anti-*motto*:

> "Sir Abbot, we have all heard your sermon and your doctrine that you've repeated to us several times; and this time, like the others, you said that *panis et aqua est vita sancta*, as if to tell us what we should be satisfied with. Well then, your monks say and respond to that all with one voice in this regard as follows: that *aqua [et] panis est vita canis*, and . . . thus [your monks] will live as it pleases them." (248)

The mutation of the Latin *motto* introduces another motif that is common to carnivalesque literature, adding semes of animality to the semantic contents of the tale. The grotesque body is essentially an animal body, and dogs are perhaps its supreme incarnation (consider, for example, the importance of dogs in the notorious trick that Panurge plays on the *Dame de Paris*). In canine fashion, the grotesque body is always on the prowl for sex and food. Such is certainly the case of these monks, who continue their life of dissipation. It is clear that the drama of transgression that unfolds in this introductory section, and on which a Todorovian critique would have to concentrate, is secondary to the comic effect of the *motto*, which reveals the possibilities for an alternative order based on the logic of the upside-down world in which the represented body is allowed free reign.

The first half of the tale, including the abbot's alimentary speech, prepares the way for the bet that is the heart of its second half.[9] The monks retire to a tavern where they are recognized as regular customers. A group of merchants and a group of gendarmes arrive later on. The text identifies these characters only in terms of the names that evoke their professional roles, and none of them belong to the noble class that dominates the *Cent nouvelles nouvelles*. By means of these names, the text configures a narrative space whose meaning derives from the recognition of a social code. The identity of each character in this scene is determined by his inclusion within a group that is defined by the specific function that it performs within the whole of an imagined society. The reader's recognition of these iconographic labels that serve as a kind of sign language for sets of attributes is important in the development of the culminating *motto*, as we will see in a moment. When the soldiers arrive late at the tavern, they find that there is not enough food for the three groups. There are only three or four small birds or chicks (*poussins*) to be divided among the nine men. In order to decide which of them will receive the chicks, the soldiers propose a contest:

> Let's make a deal: let whichever member of the three groups that comes up with the best saying have the three chicks, which they won't share with the others, and the advantage will fall to him and his companions. I myself will be happy to propose the first statement or the first riddle, after which, if one of you is able to come up with a better proposition than mine, he will have the three chicks, and he and his companions will take the advantage, otherwise they will fall to me. (249)

The struggle for power in this case takes the form of a manipulation of language, which will result in a particular configuration of "wealth," so to speak, meaning a restricted distribution of the available food, one of the major goods that appears throughout the work. This confrontation of socially diverse groups of male characters vying for food as the focus of their encounter presents a striking contrast to the homosocial procedures of the *Cent nouvelles*. In the tale of adultery, the triangle made up of husband, wife, and stranger was transformed into a second triangle comprising the cuckold, lover, and adulteress. The merchandise that was transferred by the development of the tale was the female character, resulting in a relationship between the two male characters that took the female body as its medium, arena, and material base. In Philippe's tale, in contrast, the relationships that define the characters in reference to one another remain unchanged throughout the development of the story, while the essential transformation accomplished by the narrative is a redistribution of material goods that has no consequences whatsoever for the rapport between the characters. The tavern is a meeting point at which different social "classes" or "professions" meet and struggle for material goods that are devoid of the fetishized and phantasmatic properties of the female body. The dispute over merchandise at the heart of the story suspends the hierarchical difference that served as a prototype for the earlier tales, much in the way that the unbounded consumption and expenditure of carnival suspended the enormous social differences that defined medieval culture, at least according to Bakhtin's conception of this feast. In contrast, the struggle between males for the female body as commodity affirmed a gender-specific order of rank in the adultery tales of the *Cent nouvelles*. The usurping lovers had to be adept at manipulating appearances, situations, and even kinds of knowledge, in the service of affirming their identities as male subjects. In Philippe's *motto* tales, on the other hand, the characters manipulate, mutate, and even mutilate language as a means of securing a position for themselves on a social grid whose material goods are, apparently, equally available to all classes.

In the best examples of *motto* tales, the language of the characters is one of a set of elements that they must transform by their actions, in order to secure for themselves positions of power or privilege within an imaginary social hierarchy that is in suspense, to an extent, during the carnivalesque moment of the narrative. We have already seen the mutation of a saintly maxim by which the monks rejected the reprimand of their superior. The second *motto* sequence reaches its climax with a similar "transubstantiation" of language, this time of a vulgar phrase. The leader of the gendarmes suggests that each of the contending groups present a distinct variation of a sentence that he will pronounce. The final response, which falls to the monks, has been carefully prepared by the rest of the story.

> Then the soldier said, "Now listen to the proposition that I'm going to put forward. I say that today there is nowhere beneath the skies a better shade than that of a military standard, or a better pillow than a beautiful horse, or better trinkets than a harness. Now, merchant, say yours, since you are worthy of having the chicks and winning the contest, either you or we are, since monks know nothing about such things." One of the merchants replied, "I will say what I mean for myself and for my companions concerning what you said. You say that there is no shelter like that of a military standard, nor pillows as soft as beautiful horses, nor baubles as nice as a horse's harness. I say, on the other hand, that in my opinion there is no more beautiful shade than that of a nice house, nor a better pillow than a well-set table, nor trinkets as beautiful as coins." . . . "Alright," said the monk, "Since I have to speak, I

will do so for myself and my companions." He started hemming and hawing and then, as shamefully as a cat who has stolen a piece of cheese, he said, "I have heard your propositions concerning the beauty of your shades, and the softness of your pillows, and the value of your trinkets, and each of you has said what I heard. As for me, I say that today there is nowhere in the world nicer shade than that of a curtain [around a bed], nor a softer pillow than a woman's breast, nor trinkets nicer than a man's balls. (250)

Each of the three speakers provides a variation of the basic sentence that accords with his profession. Thus the class names or markers that introduce the other characters as merchants and gendarmes are significant. The reader understands the response of each group according to his or her knowledge of codes that describe these groups, which are represented in the text by means of iconographic details. The interpretation of the third response is markedly different from the first two, if only because it depends for its effect upon knowledge that may be had only by reading the first part of the tale (though, of course, the idea of profligate monks was a commonplace of the Middle Ages). In other words, the first two versions of the phrase have significance within a linguistic code that is available to the reader from his or her experience of language, while the third variation makes sense within the "code" that the story develops for its readers. "Horse," "harness," and "standard" establish a preliminary field that signifies "gendarme"; the "house," "table," and "coins" constitute the first transformation and in turn signify "merchant"; but the dissonance produced by the three terms of the third phrase—a bed curtain, a woman's breast, and a man's testicles cannot signify "monks"—breaks the coherence of the procedure. The *motto* brings about a fragmentation of the represented body, which figuratively "exposes" its private parts to the gaze of the reader, resulting in a comic effect. Moreover, two of the parts that it exposes—*tétine, couillons* (breast and testicles)—are markers that signify sexual difference. The tale also complements the alimentary excess of the monks with an intimation of the sexual excess that is its logical partner (the excess of carnival encompasses the entire spectrum of bodily activity). In more concrete terms, the manipulation of language brings about a distribution of goods that favors one group over another, perhaps simply because the winning group is defined by connotations of expenditure, which is the guiding principle of the work.

In essence, this example of Vigneulles's narrative art would be incomprehensible beyond the context of a specific mode of defining individual identity by means of significant details that signify social status and function. The humor of this tale resides precisely in the narrator's manipulation of icons—the iconographic dissonance of this joke's punch line highlights and unmasks the procedures of representation that are the heart of the French *nouvelle* at the beginning of the sixteenth century. During the period in which this text was written, the pleasure of going to bed on a full stomach was probably reserved for periods of feasting. In Philippe's tale 59, the rogue characters who are virtually representatives of the feast win the right to enjoy this pleasure by manipulating language to the point at which it is on the verge of being incomprehensible. Like Mannis and the *commères*, the monks are amusing and important characters because they dance at the edge of the abyss that separates a codified narrative language from its dissolution in the real. In other words, narrative, which is essentially organized, coherent, and predictable, is nothing like "real" life, just as the apparent alimentary abundance of these tales probably had nothing in common with the "reality" of the time. The text plays on its readers' understanding and knowledge of the external world at the same time that it educates them in its own internal codes and processes. The rogue figures I have examined in this chapter skirt the boundaries between these two domains. An attention to narrative icons is the key to understanding the various manipulations and permutations that result in the rather peculiar type of humor that is characteristic of the *nouvelle*. In this quintessential example of his narrative art, Philippe de Vigneulles transforms the icons by which he defines his characters—the standard, harness, and stallion of his soldiers, for example—into linguistic objects that are subject to a series of variations. His work thus highlights the emptiness of the procedure by which metonyms that signified class, stature, and gender generated the identity of individuals, in the sense that these iconographic signs have to be actively invested and reinvested with value in order to function as such, as was the case in the numerous retellings of the same abstract story in the *Cent nouvelles nouvelles*. In this way, perhaps Philippe reveals the truth of this period as well as any conception of its reality that we might formulate from reading other extant texts in which it is represented.

A comparison of the typical tale of adultery that one might find in the *Cent nouvelles* with a similar anecdote from the tales of Philippe de Vigneulles will demonstrate the essential differences that constitute the shift from one narrative universe to the other. In contrast to the simple schemes of the cuckold tale—one knows that the seduction of the wife will be accomplished with more or less drastic consequences—the multiplicity of semic elements put into "play" by *motto* tales complicates the task of determining which ones will be manipulated at the tale's end. This multiplicity is indicative, perhaps, of the manner in which

Vigneulles problematizes the model of male homosocial domination by manipulating narrative iconography. *Nouvelle* 42 of Philippe's collection is a case in point. Its opening description of an adulterous wife develops a semantic field in which terms of corporeal "heat" prepare the way for wordplay:

> I think that because of her hot complexion she must have been born a half a mile away from the rising sun, and for that reason she was always in the bath houses [*estuves*].... And since she was so hot that the Saille river, which was nearby, couldn't cool her off, she went around looking for men to provide for her needs and took on all comers. (190)

In this description, the semes of concupiscence and heat are interwoven to such an extent that virtually any term from one series implies any term from the other. The seme of humidity is also linked to the notion of promiscuity in this passage: the image of the *étuves* completes this procedure, since it is consistently defined in the tales as a place of dissipation, and since an *étuve* in itself is both hot and humid, much like the traditional female characters who crowd the popular literature of the fifteenth to sixteenth centuries.[10] Accordingly, the text transposes its focus to the metaphorical process that joins the sexual with the humid.

The procedure of semantic displacement begun in the opening sentences continues as the tale develops. The wife invents a ruse so that she may meet with one of her partners:

> One day a Carmelite, who was one of the "lieutenants" of her husband, made it known to the bourgeoise by a secret messenger that at such and such a time the baths with their beautiful banquet would be held in his room and that she should get there early. She was delighted with this news and was determined not to miss the party, so she got herself ready and made her husband believe that she was going on a pilgrimage to see Our Lady of Rabay, but, as you have heard, she went to do her devotion with the Carmelites. (190)

In this passage, the set of terms centered on heat disappears, and the text signifies the sexual meeting place as "a bath with a beautiful banquet." At this point the text has been initiated in a metaphorical procedure that continues at a vertiginous pace until the concluding *motto*, which makes it almost impossible for the reader to decide which set of terms will define the semantic context for the final linguistic maneuver. At the end of the citation, the text shifts to a religious register that will perform this function. The wife makes it appear as though she is returning home from her pilgrimage, and it is during this brief description that the material for the final *motto* is first described: "At that moment the

French woman (*la galloise*) left the convent and went from there via the entrance of the Rengmont Bridge through the gardens, where she got busy and dirtied everything, running her shoes through the mud as if she had walked a long way" (190). When the wife undertakes a second "pilgrimage" to visit her monk, the husband follows her and witnesses her activity through a chink in the wall of the monastery. The *motto* is enunciated when the husband inflicts a trivial punishment on his wife by calling his neighbors to see the event: "'Look, fellows,' he said, 'How thrifty my wife is in looking after my own profit, since she had to go to Saint Barbara on foot, she is walking and doing her pilgrimage on her back, so that she doesn't wear out her shoes. Truly, she's a good woman'" (191). The dynamics of transgression and punishment that dominate the usual cuckold tale are subordinated here to the semiotic procedure by which the text displaces its linguistic focus, culminating in the final *motto*. Moreover, the husband ironically describes a fear of expenditure—she is afraid of wearing out her shoes—that results in its absolute opposite in the sexual domain, that is, the excessive adulterous relation of the wife with her Carmelite.

The most important feature of this anecdote, however, is the indifference of the husband to his wife's amorous adventures, since he himself was involved in a process of expenditure: he was on his way to the tavern, and his witnesses were his drinking partners. Moreover, the linguistic procedure of the *motto* that equates adultery with a religious pilgrimage is a standard degradation of the sacred that is typical of the period's parodic literature. In the context of an act that is meant to demonstrate reverence for the symbols of a religious hierarchy, the text inscribes an absolute irreverence for both the sacred practice of the pilgrimage and the sexual exclusivity that constituted the institution of marriage, itself the basis of male homosocial economies. The atmosphere of consumption and expenditure that pervades this tale, as well as the carnivalesque itself, authorizes this disregard for the conventions that defined the social order at this time.

Are we to assume that this image from the "everyday life" of the period represents a kind of absolute decadence of social institutions? As I have already indicated, this type of question is well beyond the scope of my inquiry, since it would require extensive research into the *actual* state of affairs in France at the beginning of the sixteenth century. Moreover, since the historical materials at our disposal for depicting such a state of affairs (chronicles, criminal registers, literary texts, civil and ecclesiastical law books, etc.) are far from coherent, it is doubtful that one could develop a definitive description of the social mores in effect at this incredibly multifarious time. Reading the *nouvelle* literature, for example, one would be led to believe that adultery was a common occurrence in early modern Europe, while the severity of the penalties reserved for adulterers, and especially for adulteresses, in legal texts of the period might lead one to the opposite conclusion.[11] On the other hand, the exactitude of the penances for different types of adultery could lead one to assume that it was a common and perhaps even banal infraction of church law, and as such its varieties were completely codified.[12] I would argue in favor of several points, however, on the basis of a close reading of Philippe's text: first, that these tales emphasize the (perhaps momentary and carnivalesque) undermining of social institutions much more than do their narrative predecessors; second, that they favor and represent an opening and liberation of an economic activity, centered on the body and its needs, that was rigorously controlled and gender contingent in the *Cent nouvelles*; finally, this anecdote, and the others I have examined in this chapter, empower those characters—merchants, members of a protoworking class (millers, farmers, artisans), women—who were, for the most part, ridiculed, marginalized, and relegated to subordinate positions in the earlier collection (it should be noted that tale 3 of the *Cent nouvelles* already envisioned this possibility by allowing for a relationship of virtual equality between a miller and a knight via the medium of the female body). Philippe's collection concentrates on the linguistic and corporeal elements of narrative representation, while the *Cent nouvelles* was preoccupied with the relations that obtained among its limited cast of characters. Moreover, Philippe's text takes a much more radical step away from what one may conceive of as the "reality" of the time, since many of its tales seem to be concentrated on the seemingly inevitable developments of their own narrative procedures. Their linguistic manipulations are far removed from the obsessive attention that the *Cent nouvelles* paid to intersubjective relations, which was indicative, perhaps, of the overwhelming force of a real homosocial economy that weighed upon the text. Philippe's work is preoccupied with what may be termed the *emptiness* of the narrative sign. Just as the linguistic variations of the *motto* may lead the text into the realm of the incomprehensible, so the empty figures who populate the work may be occupied by virtually nonsensical attributes: an alcoholic husband and wife can sell each other their own goat as a pretext for drinking to its health in the local tavern; monks can be gluttonous and concupiscent; a miser can give away his riches; a "*bonne femme*" can do her "pilgrimage" on her back; a dead man can come to life and prepare a feast; a man who has not eaten can be convinced that he is full, and so on. Vigneulles's narrative realm was thus much more *fictional* than that of its predecessor, since it was built squarely upon the development of its own linguistic procedures, rather than on the prototypical social hierarchy that seemingly preexisted and generated the earlier text, just as the sacred prototype of the divine realm generated the icons of the Byzantine church.

Nevertheless, it is clear that the imaginary world depicted in Philippe de Vigneulles's *Cent nouvelles nouvelles* develops a multifarious resistance to the male-dominated homosocial model that was characteristic of its model text. In contrast to the restriction of wealth to an elite group of gentlemen, who maintain their relations with one another via the telling and retelling of a phantasmatic story of women, the economic situation of Philippe's tales embodies various forces that resist homosocial power in a variety of ways. The work gives a superlative value to *expenditure*, which provides access to power to distinct classes of individuals—merchants, millers, farmers, and peasants, as well as rogues, thieves, dishonest hucksters, gluttonous priests. A mischievous and even malicious cleverness motivates the actions of the characters who provoke the hyperbolic economic activity that dominates the world represented in the work. As such, the rogue bent upon stealing the wealth of others is only the most abstract example of a character type that is found across the varied social spectrum that the text brings to life. If the tales I examined from the *Cent nouvelles nouvelles* were about the control of wealth through the surveillance and restriction of the fetishized female body taken to be a kind of primal merchandise, those of Vigneulles are about the explosion of this male homosocial constraint, which allows the characters to have access to wealth and power on the basis of their "merits," so to speak, no matter how unscrupulous these may have been.

The multiplication and intensification of economic activity in these tales is accompanied by a certain suspension of the restraints placed upon female characters. Some of the most clever individuals to appear in these tales are women, who in some cases resist the sexual advances of the male characters by inverting the normal procedure of production and consumption in which they find themselves. In these cases, the desirous male receives the refuse of this process and is denied the female body that he expects to possess. In other anecdotes, the exuberant female characters propel entire populations into the domain of expenditure, provoking the redistribution of wealth (and hence of power) from those who possess it to those who procure it by means of their wits. This recognition of an unleashed "femaleness" as a force for the liberation from socioeconomic restraints, rather than as an overflowing force of sexuality that must be contained within limits, is one of the most satisfying aspects of Philippe's collection. In general, his tales move away from a conception of the female as the *other* that is to be controlled and manipulated toward a conception of the female as one of the basic principles of the carnivalesque economy of the body and its attendant expenditures.

# 4
# Feminist Ambivalence and Feminine Virtue in the *Heptaméron*

In the literature that takes the *Decameron* as its model, Marguerite de Navarre's narrative world is quite different from that of its French predecessors. The fictional domains examined in the two preceding chapters were controlled by men. The *Cent nouvelles nouvelles* depicted noblemen for whom pleasure consisted in taking advantage of women, preferably those linked by the metonymy of marriage to other men. The resultant homosocial relations among men both within the stories and in their narrative frame were the basis of a male-dominated economy that largely determined the identity of the characters. In the tales of Philippe de Vigneulles, the dominance of an imposing male sexuality was supplanted by the hegemony of a mercantile economy that valorized subversive activities of all kinds, including those of female characters who undermined existing social orders, whether sexually or economically determined. Vigneulles's collection figured a generalized and multifarious resistance to the restricted structure of power represented in the earlier text, without concentrating specifically on the problem that gender difference and desire pose to the individual in the social hierarchy. In the *Heptaméron*, the male characters of the type found in the *Cent nouvelles nouvelles* confront female characters whose primary concern is the code of honor that defines the virtue of women. This code in itself was a strategy of male power to control what was perceived as an unbounded female desire. The image of the uncontrollable female dominated the male imaginary of the period and evidently posed a threat to a society structured by marital relations under the surveillance and control of men.[1] The strict adherence of Marguerite de Navarre's female characters to the code of feminine virtue constituted a double bind for them, since it rendered the satisfaction of their own desire impossible, while obeying the male imperative that female desire be contained within boundaries. The code of virtue in the work also enforced the detouring of male desire: in order to achieve their goal (physical possession of the female), male characters adopted the mask of virtue, which was the basis of their own strategy for controlling the desire of the female other. In this context, therefore, the functioning of an idea (virtue) intended to regulate woman as the commodity whose exchange served as a base of social relations among men ultimately developed into a strategy of power that confined and frustrated male desire itself, compelling male characters, as well as their female counterparts, to act in ways that circumvented this basic interdiction. The most important male *and* female characters of the *Heptaméron*—Amadour and Floride in tale 10, Rolandine and "the bastard of a noble house" in tale 21, Jambique in tale 43—become involved in situations that exaggerate both the positive and negative effects of power, forcing them to undertake certain actions in the face of a given and static configuration of power while prohibiting them from performing others. The ubiquity of power and its effects, and the indefatigable desire of the characters, are predicated upon the fundamental difference of male and female, which the work interrogates and critiques, restricting its characters to situations overdetermined by the double bind of moral codes and imperatives that defined identity in terms of gender difference. The following readings will describe the complexity of the narrative "system" that brings the forces of power, gender, and desire into conflict, keeping in mind the general thesis with which I began: narrative as technique or technology embodies, creates, transmits, and participates in configurations of power, from which the concept of sexual difference cannot be liberated.

The tales of the *Heptaméron* are built upon a code of virtue that combines the male homosocial prohibition of female desire with the detour of desire experienced by both genders into language, often resulting in the sublimation of love relationships. These attributes were almost completely absent from the French predecessors of the work that I have examined here. Tale 10 of the text is the most complete and important example of a story based upon the prohibition of an unauthorized male desire, within a social order structured by the distribution of wealth and power through marriage. The opening paragraphs of the story establish a conventional opposition between male and female. The former is defined by belligerent semes (meaning that the good gentleman in this context is a good warrior), while the latter adheres to a concept of feminine virtue, linked to the good management of the household.[2] The text thus associates the male with aggressive excursions outside of the household and the court, while it associates the female with a domesticated interior that sublimates primary drives. The parallel dichotomies of male/female and exterior/interior form a conceptual grid for the entirety of the story. The first portrait of Amadour, for example, ties the necessary belligerence of his character, which defines him as male, to his facility with language and his physical beauty:

> Amongst these men there was one by the name of Amador. Although he was only eighteen or nineteen years of age, he had such confidence, and such sound judgement, that you could not have failed to regard him as one of those rare men fit to govern any state. Not only was he a man of sound judgement, he was also endowed with an appearance so handsome, so open and natural, that he was a delight for all to behold. This was not all, for his handsome looks were equally matched by the fairness of his speech. Poise, good looks, eloquence—it was impossible to say with which gift he was more richly blessed. But what gained him even higher esteem was his fearlessness, which, despite his youth, was famed throughout all lands. For he had already in many different places given evidence of his great abilities. Not only throughout the kingdoms of Spain, but also in France and Italy people looked upon him with admiration. Not once during the recent wars had he shrunk from battle, and when his country had been at peace, he had gone to seek action in foreign parts, and there too had been loved and admired by friend and foe alike. (122–23)

The good sense for which Amadour is renowned throughout southern Europe is inextricably linked to his talent for making war. The skill demanded of the exceptional individual in this context of endless struggles for territory and power was a capacity that would enable him to overcome enemies. The *nouvelle* thus describes an interiorization of belligerent discourse, in the military metaphors that describe Amadour's advances toward Floride, the object of his desire.[3] Amadour is a hybrid of the virtues that are necessary in both the private and the public domains. In the exterior, beyond the focus of the text in the château of the Countess of Aranda, Amadour continuously moves from place to place, practicing his belligerent craft, which the text tells us is the foundation of his reputation. Nevertheless, he is also endowed with the characteristics necessary to a gentleman who wants to succeed in the interiors of the court: beauty, grace, refined speech. The essential development of the text will be to transpose his warlike attributes from the outside to the inside of the château.

Discursive phenomena are important throughout the text, since characters who wish to occupy a certain position in the society it depicts must be allowed access to the privileged circles of communication that include the King of Spain and the nobles. Because Amadour possesses the virtues necessary to a gentleman in this context, "there was little or nothing anyone would refuse him" (123) among the ladies of Barcelona and Perpignan; similarly, even though he was a younger son of a rich family, his wealth and position among the gentlemen of the Spanish court was assured because of his daring: "He was skilled in the arts of war, and loved by lords and princes to such an extent that he refused their riches more often than he had to ask for them" (57, my translation). The status of these gentlemen themselves is determined by their skill in the arts of war: "In the Viceroy's entourage there were not a few noblemen of outstanding valour, courageous men, who, after long service in the wars had earned such honor and such heroic reputations that there was no one in the land who was not anxious to meet them and be seen in their company" (122, modified). While Amadour has everything granted to him as a result of his talents, it soon becomes clear that they cannot give him that which he desires, i.e., a legitimate relationship with Floride. Faced with this situation, which confronts a given power structure to the desire of an individual character, Amadour is forced to undertake actions that will legitimize or authorize his communication with the object of his desire, since a discursive link between male and female characters already indicates a level of intimacy between them.

In contrast to the bellicose and exteriorized character of Amadour, who is often forced to go off to war, Floride is defined by her place in the noble house of Aranda. This domain of the major female characters of the tale is marked by the absence of the male, since Floride's mother, the Countess of Aranda, is a widow:

> In Aragon, in the province of Aranda, there once lived a lady. She was the widow of the Count of Aranda, who had died while she was still very young, and left her with a son and a daughter, who was called Floride. This noblewoman took great pains to educate her children according to the virtues and honesty appropriate to lords and gentlemen. So carefully did she school them that her house was known far and wide as the most honourable in the whole of Spain. She would often go to Toledo, which was then the seat of the King of Spain, and when she visited Saragossa, which was not far from the family home, she would spend her time at the Queen's court, where she was as highly esteemed as any lady could be. (122, modified)

The royal house of Aranda is contiguous with that of the monarchs themselves, since, as the text tells us, the Countess was related to them (55). Moreover, there is a direct link between the Countess and the maximum female embodiment of power, the Queen herself. The most important detail of this description is the implicit definition of Floride's education. The physical skills, the grace and beauty of the body, the forcefulness of character, and even the ease of speech that men derived from the long "frequentation" of war, as we saw above, constituted "the virtues and honesty appropriate to lords and gentlemen." The education of Floride is thus a kind of "domestication" or "interiorization" of a warrior's virtues, whose defining characteristics are brought into the household and made the basis of its code of honor. While the maintenance of feminine virtue is the business of female characters throughout the *Heptaméron*, it is clear that this code itself derives from a particularly male code of honor that entraps or encloses the female characters of the text. As Charpentier writes of the protagonist of *nouvelle* 24, "With Elisor, one is led to ask if the masculine world does not enclose its feminine counterpart in a projection of its own cruelty or its own phantasms."[4] The ambivalence of the code of feminine virtue, which is derived from a masculine code of honor in war, constitutes the double bind that entraps the female characters of the text, and to a certain extent its male characters as well.

Amadour sees Floride for the first time and immediately falls in love with her. The reasons for his love, and the type of feelings to which he is subject are completely different from those we have seen in the other collections:

> This young nobleman had devotedly followed his commander back home, to meet the Countess of Aranda. He could not fail to notice her daughter, Floride, who was then but twelve years of age. He thought to himself, as he contemplated her grace and beauty, that she was the most honest person that he had ever seen. If only he could win her good graces, that alone would give him more happiness than anything any other woman in the world could ever give him. And, after gazing at her for a long time, he decided that he would love her, despite whatever impossibility reason put before him because she was of far higher birth than he, and because she was not yet of an age to hear and understand the words of love. (123, modified)

The honesty and the honor of women are at the heart of the *Heptaméron*. Yet, this particularly female virtue may be a domestic "sublimation" of that which the text defines as the masculine virtue *par excellence*, that of the soldier (sublimation in the sense of a diversion of "an instinctual desire or impulse from its primitive form to one that is considered more socially or culturally acceptable").[5] Unlike his predecessors from the *Cent nouvelles* and from the tales of Philippe de Vigneulles, Amadour acts rationally: his intellect provides him both with the justification of his immediate feelings and the knowledge that his love is impossible within this social context. This rational consideration of that which the character experiences as passion is a considerable refinement of the impetuous physical drive typical of the gentlemen depicted in the earlier tales. Amadour immediately recognizes the power structure within which he must operate and, as in siege warfare, takes steps to overcome the obstacles that face him. His impetuosity is diverted from the usual direct route by which the male characters of the earlier *nouvelles* approach the female objects of their desire. This diversion or detour is ultimately a negative effect of power. The rational hesitation of a male character when faced with an obstacle would be unusual in the context of the *Cent nouvelles nouvelles*, or in the tales of Philippe de Vigneulles; here, the tale itself assumes the form of an iterative vacillation between a rationally considered need for transgression and the necessity of its prevention.

Faced with the tension created by this confrontation of desire (the domain of the male?) and its prohibition (the domain of the female?), Amadour functions by means of detours and substitutions. Generally, if a male character is unable to arrive at his goal in the *Heptaméron*, he will choose an alternate route, or he will substitute a more elevated form of activity for his more base desire, in some cases attaining the level of a religious sublimation of his primary drive (see *nouvelles* 19 and 24). Accordingly, Amadour marries Floride's confidante, Avanturade, which legitimates his public conversations with his beloved:

> There was no way in which he [Amadour] might be able to speak to her [Floride]. In order to introduce himself into the society of the Countess, he approached the daughter of an old knight, who was her neighbor. Her name was Avanturade, and she had spoken so often with Floride that she knew the innermost secrets of her heart. Because of the honesty that he found in her, and because she expected to receive three thousand ducats a year by way of dowry, Amadour made up his mind to address himself to her as a suitor, and seek her hand in marriage. She was only too willing to listen. But since he was poor and her father was rich, Amadour felt that he would never consent to the marriage unless he enlisted the aid of the Countess. (124, modified)

At every point of this alternate route, the tale reinforces the idea of prohibition, intensifying the positive and negative effects of power: Amadour has no inheritance (that is, he is denied access to power), thus he must *not* act in certain ways, or he must attempt to act in *other* ways. The concept of honesty (*honnêteté*), cited here, combines both of these effects throughout the work. Evidently, a female character's honesty prohibits her from acting against the code of (female) virtue. In contrast, it is precisely this honesty that motivates the desire of the male characters to traverse the obstacles that structure the social hierarchy in which the characters move. While Amadour's decision to marry Avanturade is reinforced by the most basic of social motivations—she has a generous dowry—it is clear that the honesty of the female character plays an important role in determining the course that he will follow, as it does in the decisive scene in which Amadour sees Floride for the first time ("[Amadour] thought to himself that [Floride] was surely the most honest person he had ever seen" [56, my translation]). The desire of male characters is unidirectional, which means that they are forced to move toward an object distinguished by its honesty. The female characters who incarnate this object, in turn, are evaluated in reference to honesty as ideal. As the central concept of the work, honesty thus conjoins the positive and negative effects of power that bring the characters into being as gendered subjects: women incarnate honesty in order to be women; men desire women who embody honesty.

The tale transforms the major barrier confronting Amadour, his status as a lesser nobleman, into a linguistic one, delineating a configuration of power whose material manifestation is a network of communication in which the Countess and Floride may operate openly and to which Amadour has no legitimate access. The text also develops this communicative aspect according to a logic of inside versus outside, interior versus exterior. Entrance into the household of the Countess is assured by justifying one's right to speak to its primary female members. From the first sentence of the tale, this interior is characterized by the absence of an authoritative male figure, as we have seen. Faced with this situation, Amadour provides himself with a contact, Avanturade, who engages regularly in conversations with Floride; moreover, Avanturade participates in Floride's education, which in itself is an interiorization of the characteristics attributed to gentlemen warriors. In other words, in order to enter the household of his beloved, Amadour usurps a place in a network of communication that supports and transmits certain belligerent male "virtues" in a sublimated, perhaps "feminized" form as the basis of an economy and configuration of power. A second act of communication is also crucial to Amadour's plan, and is likewise contingent upon the action of a female character: since he is poor, the Countess of Aranda must speak to Avanturade's father in order to authorize their marriage, as we have just seen.

Similarly, Amadour manages to marry above his social station by means of verbal requests that circulate at the highest levels of the court, especially among the subordinates of the Queen:

Before his departure [for the wars], he spoke to a brother of his, who was major-domo in the household of the Queen. He told him what an excellent match he had found in the Lady Avanturade while in the Countess's household, and asked him to do everything in his power during his absence to bring the marriage about, by drawing on the influence of the Queen, the King and all his other friends. (126)

The tale is thus about the ways in which the misfits of this social hierarchy, the younger sons such as Amadour, maneuvered around the barriers that inhibited their social advancement via marriage.[6] An integral part of these various movements is the attempt to put certain stories into circulation and to bring them to the attention of those in positions of power: Amadour implores his brother to tell the Queen the story of the "good match" he has found in Avanturade. Within the tale itself, then, narrative participates in a structure of power, while access to power is provided to those characters who are able to put appropriate stories about themselves into circulation. Furthermore, characters attempt to have access to power by soliciting stories from others that have implications for their positions on the grid of power. For example, Amadour says to Avanturade, "Tell me, Avanturade, since you are her friend and must know her closest secrets, how is it possible that she hasn't stolen the heart of every single man at court?" (125). Finally, the desire to tell stories and to listen to them within these tales is inextricably linked to desire itself. The act of storytelling always implies the exercise of power; the story of power is always one of a male character who desires a female character, or vice versa, as we will see in tale 43.

Every step of the tale's development contains an act of communication, which assumes many different forms (speeches, dialogues, declarations, letters, messages communicated to others, etc.). The first aspect of this syntax of communication obeys the logic of the first stages of sublimation, since Amadour's desire is transformed into its verbal substitutes from the moment of its appearance, in accord with the standard definition of sublimation as a "detour" of primary drives toward alternate, socially acceptable activities, which may ultimately lead to an apotheosis of those drives in a relationship with God. The word is the only instrument available to the characters as a means of satisfying their desires, yet it equally serves the purposes of the transgressors at the same time that it constitutes the restrictive structures that they wish to overcome. Moreover, language as an instrument feminizes the subject who is forced to use it, since it is the medium through which the virtue of the male is internalized in the household, the domain of the female. The text makes this point rather clearly: "After his marriage, [Amadour] made himself so familiar in the Countess's household that no one took any more notice of him than if he had been a woman. He was only twenty-two at this time, but he

## 4 / Feminist Ambivalence and Feminine Virtue

had such good sense that the Countess used to keep him informed of all her business affairs" (127). Whoever attempts to use the word in order to have access to the structure ineluctably makes use of the technique and technology whose exercise serves as its base. Amadour's linguistic assaults on the edifice of power are bound to fail, since the control of language within this structure intersects the control of bodies and of desire that constituted this imaginary aristocracy. The narrative subject who speaks is already within power, is traversed by it, and feels it emanating from his or her body through the voice.

Although it may be tempered by reason, unauthorized male desire is a disruptive element within this system. Throughout the tale, the eruption of this desire is marked by the suspension of speech at crucial moments, as in the first meeting of the two main characters:

> Then Avanturade presented Amador to Floride. As he kissed her hand, he almost fainted in rapture. He, the most eloquent man in Spain, was speechless as he stood before her. This somewhat surprised Floride, for, although she was only twelve years of age, she knew well enough that there was not a man in Spain who could express his mind more eloquently than Amador. (125)

It is evident that the story of Amadour's verbal exploits (as well as his military ones) has circulated throughout the important circles. Amadour's problem is that his visceral desire for Floride, which erupts here, is beyond the realm of discourse, since it cannot possibly be satisfied in the economic and political situation of the court. While he can put the appropriate stories of his prowess into circulation in both the interior domain controlled by the Countess, as well as in the exterior domain of warfare dominated by the absent voice of the King, he cannot translate these sublimated forms of his desire into the material fact of physical union with Floride. Every time he attempts to do so, the text exhibits the markings of death: in this crucial scene, Amadour nearly faints and becomes mute. The entirety of Amadour's actions in this story, therefore, will consist of attempts to overcome the essential impossibility of translating the verbal into the physical, and the text will figure this impossibility in images that suspend the verbal and imply the suspension of the physical (that is, images that figure or represent death).

To summarize, the tale develops a power structure that conjoins a basic prohibition of desire with language usage and semes of the feminine within the domain of the household, transubstantiating the male "virtues" of belligerence in sublimated forms. Consequently, access to power within this system is contingent upon one's ability to communicate within closed circles; a privileged position within this structure corresponds to those who are allowed to speak to others in important positions. Any character who seeks to disrupt this network will inevitably do so by taking control of the communicative media and by putting valorized stories about himself into circulation. Since language is the material base of its domination, any character who attempts to overcome the structure by manipulating the word will invariably enter the area of its influence. Every action in the tale is conditioned by the concept of communication, and its major articulations depend upon manipulations of narrative or of discourse, or of narrative and discursive situations.

Once Amadour has established his place in the household of the Countess, for example, he immediately proceeds to his objective. Inevitably, his actions take a discursive form:

> Being so fond of Amador's wife, she [Floride] hid nothing from Amadour himself, not even her most intimate thoughts, [and went so far as] to tell him about her love for the son of the Infante Fortune. Amadour's sole concern was to win her completely, and he talked to her constantly about the Infante's son. Provided he was able to converse with her, he did not care what was the topic of their conversation. (127–28)

These incessant speeches about potential love relationships sublimate the physical desire that drives Amadour. While this tactic succeeds in gaining him the affection and the confidence of Floride, it also facilitates his movement within the abstract (feminine?) half of the power structure to which he has gained access:

> There was nobody who did not make him [Amadour] welcome, and the Countess ordered that he be treated as if he were her own son. During his stay, the Countess told him all her domestic business, and asked his advice on almost every aspect of it. He enjoyed such a good reputation in this household that wherever he went in it, the doors were always opened to him. (128, modified)

The combination of beauty and linguistic ease in Amadour allows him to circulate within the closed system of privilege embodied in the household of the Countess and grants him access to restricted domains that normally would be off limits to a character such as he. The intrusiveness of this character within the household of his beloved will later be reflected in his attempts literally to violate the space of her body.

The fundamental tension that pervades the tale, however, involves the confrontation of the socioeconomic apparatus of the linguistic detour with the necessity of satisfying physical desire. Amadour is faced with the problem of converting the word into flesh. In this context, however, language functions so as to defer physical drives into the realm of the abstract. The structure of power that delimits the possibilities of communication is largely founded upon the maintenance of a given distribution of wealth through marriage, which necessitates the diversion and ultimate elimination of unauthorized desire. Amadour's growing awareness of this difficulty becomes increasingly manifest in the tale:

> When Floride came to speak to him alone, in complete innocence, the fire that burned in his breast would flare up so violently that, do what he might, the colour would mount to his cheeks and the sparks of passion would shoot from his eyes.
>
> In order that no one should guess from his intimacy with Floride that he was in love with her, he began to make approaches to an extremely attractive lady called Paulina. (129; modified)

Amadour hides the seductive nature of his discourse, which serves as a substitute for the impossible fulfillment of his physical need. It is evident here that a distinct relation to language as emotional medium separates the two major characters. While desire sublimated in discourse begins to have a visceral effect on Amadour, Floride is completely unaware of the powerful male drive that assumes the form of measured words. Given the impossibility of realizing his dream of a relation with Floride, Amadour moves toward a bodily substitute, the beautiful woman who will incite Floride's jealousy. The logic that propels the plot of this tale is thus that of the incessant displacement and diversion of desire toward a series of substitute objects and media (language is clearly the medium of desire for Amadour).

The description of Amadour's relationship with this woman reinforces the idea that the intercourse between men and women in the *Heptaméron* usually takes the form of a linguistic bond, rather than a corporeal one, at least in those tales that detail the diversion or deferral of unauthorized desire. Both the narrator and the characters describe the relation between Paulina and Amadour in terms of speech. When Floride informs Amadour that she is aware of his relation to Paulina, the text proceeds as follows:

> Amadour understood from these words that she thought he derived pleasure from talking with Paulina. So hurt was he that he could not restrain his anger: "Ah! My Lady, so you're starting already to torment your servant, by stoning him right from the beginning, since I cannot think of a task that has been more boring for me than the constraint of speaking with a woman whom I do not love. Since you take exception to tasks I undertake solely in your service,

I'll never speak to her again. And let the consequences take care of themselves! To cover up my anger, just as in the past I've hidden my joy, I shall go away to a place not far from here, and wait until your mood has passed. (133–34, modified)

The confabulation of physical displacement, linguistic transference, and the diversion of desire that rules the most interesting tales of the *Heptaméron* is nowhere more in evidence than in this passage. The narrator remarks that Amadour *believes* that Floride *assumes* he takes pleasure in *speaking* to Paulina, and this estimation of interior thoughts is indeed further along a continuum of realism than the descriptions of the earlier texts I examined. The way in which Paulina is described makes it evident that speech is not that which most attracts men to her: "[She was a woman] whose charms were highly celebrated in her day, and from whose snares few men managed to escape" (129). Language excites physical sensations in Amadour that he cannot legitimately satisfy with Floride; the diversion of desire into speech, which in essence is equivalent to its frustration, forces Amadour to react physically, spontaneously, and involuntarily to his conversations with Floride. In other words, the language of the characters, and of the tale itself, is saturated by individual desire and by the power that resides in the relationships of the characters to one another. The incompatibility of Amadour as desiring individual with a power structure that dictates the possession of the female character's body as commodity forces the male character to go beyond the boundaries of this system and to seek a substitute, who is quite different from Floride:

[Paulina] told him how deeply she pitied him for having married such an ugly wife, after all his past good fortunes in love. Amadour realized from what she said that she was ready to provide him with any consolation he might require, and replied with as encouraging words as he was able, thinking that it would be possible to cover up the truth of his real feelings by making her believe a lie. But she was shrewd, experienced in the ways of love, and not a woman to make do with mere words. (129)

There can be little doubt that Amadour's bodily reaction to his conversations with Floride is sexual in nature: the blood rushes to his face, sparks shoot from his eyes.[7] Where Floride is indifferent to these effects, since she has been strictly educated within the system, Paulina seems to operate beyond the boundaries controlled by discourse, in the domain of unregulated desire and sexuality. She is described merely in terms of her physical characteristics (i.e., in terms of her desirability as object), and of the predatory and iterative nature of her sensual activity. Her value for the power structure is precisely that she is *beyond* it, because her body does not serve as a marker of honor, value, and rank. Paulina is one of the first of many characters to appear in the *Heptaméron* who imply that there is an alternative space, beyond the court, and dominated by women, in which physical desire may be satisfied outside of the code of virtue. Floride, in contrast, remains within the domain of language and subject to its negative effects, which restrict her desire for Amadour. The numerous messages and discourses that the text's restrictions provoke—Amadour's correspondence with Avanturade, his conversations with Floride in the presence of others at the court, and finally his declaration of his devotion to her—incite and provoke Floride as subject of desire, yet they eventually force her to sublimate the desire that she feels into an idealized union with God. Discourse as power both induces and restricts Floride's actions as subject and object of desire.

From this perspective, the analysis of the passage in which Amadour declares his devotion to Floride becomes clearer. The structure of the society in which these characters live is constituted by a symbolic order that maps out the routes along which the subject as signifier of desire may circulate. One of the primary rules of this structure is that the signifier must continually be displaced. Furthermore, it is apparent that this is a closed structure: the redundancy of the tale is clear, which means that there are a limited number of slots into which the signifier may be fitted, and to which it repeatedly returns.[8] Successful functioning within such a system perhaps entails following the path that is predetermined for the circulation of the signifier. Thus when Amadour remains "within language," so to speak, as does Floride, he meets with success: he circulates freely in the household of the Countess, every door is opened to him, and he has the same access to this locus of power as a female character. When his desire causes him to pause, and to leave the realm of the spoken, it is then that he is threatened with death. In the passage in which Amadour realizes that his relationship with Paulina is discovered, for example, his reaction is expressed as physical pain: he says that Floride is "tormenting" him, even that she is "stoning" him. In these two passages the revelation of desire within the power structure threatens the position of the male subject and forces him to continue in the series of displacements: when his flushed face is about to reveal his need to Floride, Amadour seeks the company of Paulina; when the nature of this relationship is intimated, Amadour is (coincidentally?) forced to move to some other place, by the absent voice of the King, who calls him off to war. The fact that (masculine) desire must be replaced by the (feminine) displacement of the letter within a prohibitive power structure is reinforced by the following passages:

> So saying, [Amadour] went, without even waiting for her reply. Floride was left utterly dejected and downcast. And Love, pushed by its opposite, began to demonstrate its great power, to such an extent that she acknowledged that she had wronged Amadour, and wrote to him over and over again, beseeching him to come back to her. . . .
>
> No sooner had Love overcome these first suspicions and jealousies, no sooner had the two lovers begun to take more pleasure than ever from talking together, than word came that the King of Spain was sending the entire army to Salces. Amadour, who was accustomed to be the first to join the royal standards, was as eager as ever to follow the path of honour and glory. (134)

The flowering of Floride's love for Amadour is immediately accompanied by an explosion of letters. Since she is more integrated than Amadour into the structure of power that the work represents (because of her noble birth, the education she has received, etc.), her physical desire for Amadour, which increases as the tale develops, could hardly assume a form that was not authorized by this structure. Indeed, the whole of the tale seems to insist upon the necessity that her love remain in the sublimated, discursive, and scriptural form of "honest friendship" (*honnête amitié*). Once again, the text repeats the same series of procedures: the two lovers begin to take more pleasure than ever in speaking to one another; the danger that this will result in the physical consummation of their love is "accidentally" interrupted by the outbreak of war; the position of the male subject is threatened, and he is forced to follow the series of displacements that lead from the domain of sublimated love, the court, to that of death and absence, the battlefield, to which he is called by the voice of the absent monarch, who embodies and replaces the authority of Floride's absent father.

The dynamics of this system become most clear when the pretext for the communication between the two lovers is removed. With the death of Avanturade, Amadour falls into a state of despair that causes the other characters in the tale to fear for his life. Floride comes to comfort him:

> Poor Floride embraced him and held him in her arms for a long time, doing everything she could in order to console him, but the medicine that she was giving him in order to lessen his pain made him suffer all the more. And, pretending that he was half dead, and without speaking, he tried to take from her that which the honor of women prohibits. When Floride recognized the malice of his intentions, she could not believe it, because of the honest words he had always said to her; she asked him what he wanted, but fearing her response, which he knew would be chaste and honest, Amadour pursued what he was after with all of his strength. (72, my translation)

"*Ce que l'honneur des dames deffend*"—this precisely is the heart of the hierarchy of displaced desire that dominates this tale. It is only in silence, beneath the cover of dissimulation, that male desire may pursue its course in a structure that permits the expression of desire only in veiled language. Here Floride demands speech of Amadour, while the act that he wishes to undertake is performed in fear of the spoken, which, as the narrator informs us, can only be chaste and honest. Male desire has no place in this system, unless it assumes a form that is suitable to it, that is, unless it is deferred or detoured into amorous language, or unless it is authorized by the configuration of wealth. Thus the male subject who is stricken by unauthorized desire has no option but to go continuously to another place, which means that he ultimately has no option but death, since that "other place" is the void of the battlefield, dominated by images of the phantasmic others who haunted European culture from its inception (the Turks, the Moors), and by the exercise of the King's power.

The "interiorized" half of the tale's power structure is feminine (in the cultural sense of "the female" that is imposed on women), and functions on the basis of a certain instrumentality of language: this point is amply demonstrated in the second scene, in which Amadour tries to force himself upon Floride. Because of the rights that he has acquired in the household of the Countess, Amadour manages to be alone with Floride in her room. The opposition of male and female is at its most extreme at this moment:

> "If I am going to die anyway," Amadour broke in, "then the agony will be over all the sooner! Nor am I going to be deterred because you've disfigured your face! I'm quite sure you did it yourself, of your own volition. No! If all I could get were your bare bones, still I should want to hold them close."
>
> Floride could see that neither tears, nor entreaties, nor reasoning were to any avail. She could see that he was going to act out his evil desires, unmoved and merciless. Exhausted and unable to struggle any more, there was only one thing left she could do to save herself, the one thing that she had shrunk from as from death itself. In a sad and pitiful voice, she shouted out to her mother with all the strength that was in her. (148, modified)

The principle that motivates the male character throughout the story finally becomes clear: he wishes to posses the object of his desire physically at all costs, even if it means her death.[9] Before this scene, Floride disfigures herself, thinking that her deformity will discourage Amadour's desire. In the criticism devoted to *L'Heptaméron*, much has been made of Floride's self-disfiguration, which is undoubtedly the most famous scene of the text. Freccero, for example, argues that Floride's act is a "prosopopoeia," in which the repressed voice of the character's desire for Amadour "assumes mouth, eye, and finally face, a chain that is manifest in the etymology of the trope's name, *prosopon poein*, to confer a mask or face." Thus Floride's face, in this scene, "is a feminine signature of the feminine, a trope of femininity based on femininity as a trope," and "Marguerite's text stages the failure of feminine self-representation and the perpetuation of a phallocracy with a 'brutal trace' of the 'culture of gender.' Yet mutilation, the feminine signature *par excellence*, is a sign of textual and political resistance."[10] Similarly, Kritzman argues that Floride's repression of her desire for Amadour, enforced by a patriarchal culture (paradoxically mediated through a matriarch, the Countess of Aranda), results in the expression of that desire on the character's face:

> Although Floride struggles violently to preserve her honor by adhering to a concept of love desexualized through the exercise of virtue, her facial expressions, nevertheless, deceive her and represent an unspeakable female language that causes embarrassment and must be masked. The multiple references in the text to Floride's 'visaige' function as figures of the silence out of which female repression speaks: they express the inexpressible. The face is the *locus* on which is inscribed the enigma of female desire.[11]

While it may be true that Floride's desperate act is a manifestation of her repressed desire, her self-disfigurement is also the mark of a feminine assimilation of a masculine code of honor predicated on the mastery of controlled violence. Floride's disfigured face thus becomes the ultimate icon of the power structure in which these characters are trapped: she enacts this kind of controlled violence on herself, "interiorizes" it, makes it her own, all for the sake of defending an idea of honor and virtue.[12]

Floride does not recognize that desire and death are complementary for the male subject: the desire of a male character in Amadour's devalorized position inevitably forces him to move toward the domain of absence and war, while the sublimated form of his desire may be authorized only by proofs of his "virtues" and his "honor," that is, by his skills as a warrior. Not reason, religion, or the threat of death can stop the demon that possesses the male spirit; rather, the virtue of the male character defined as masculine in this context is founded precisely upon his adept ability to kill and to face the threat of being killed, while the code of feminine virtue, in which Floride participates by disfiguring herself, is a "domesticated" manifestation of this death drive, i.e., its displacement from the battlefield (associated with the male) to the domicile (associated with the female). For the female character, the possibility that another woman, especially a woman in a position of authority, might recognize her subjection to male desire, is much more to be feared than male desire itself, since her position in this hierarchy is contingent upon her communication with other female subjects. The power linked to the voice and to the role of the mother is that which alone can defer or detour the death-drive of the male character. Thus, the call of one woman to another results in a prohibitive structure that breaks the force of male desire. In the final analysis, Floride's desperate act transforms her into an icon of power's inscription upon the individual body.

The power structure that the work depicts is built upon a (feminine) transcription of a (masculine) code of honor: the code of feminine virtue "interiorizes" or "domesticates" a dominant masculine code derived from the practices of warfare. In the tale we have just examined, the Countess of Aranda is the ultimate figure of authority, through whom all of the circulations of the word must pass.[13] In opposition to many readings of these tales, I would argue that the work is about the procedures of feminine or feminized power both in conflict and in collaboration with the demands of male desire. Patricia Cholakian, for example, construes the power structure in the work as explicitly male, in which the female characters attempt to become subjects, i.e., "generator[s] of signs."[14] Rather than viewing the fictional hierarchy as a linguistic economy to which male characters attempt to gain access by means of phatic contacts with their female counterparts, Cholakian understands its dynamics as a feminist struggle for self-expression (especially the expression of female desire) in a male system that leaves virtually no place for women:

> In my view, this incoherent behavior [of Floride] signifies the inability of the female characters to achieve status as subjects within the narrative. Fictional plots are moved forward by desire (what the subject wants), but since there is no room in this sexual economy for female desire, there is no way for Floride to pursue her plot or formulate a coherent counterplot. The conventional plot is the linear narrative of masculine desire. . . . But here, the female protagonist's behavior seems to have no logical goal.[15]

In essence, therefore, Cholakian reads this tale as an incarnation of the problem for women formulated by psychoanalysis: "Floride . . . finds herself completely isolated in a system that simultaneously arouses and thwarts female desire. . . . The story thus illustrates the cogency of Freud's celebrated question, 'What do women want?'"[16] While Cholakian's point is well taken, the tale's end explicitly describes the ideal relationship that Floride (a female character engendered as a woman) desired, i.e., a completely sublimated one, in which the male object of female desire is converted into the Divine Word:

> The news of [Amadour's] death reached Floride, who was at Barcelona, where her husband had expressed his wish to be buried. She conducted the obsequies with due honour. Then, saying not a word either to her own mother or to the mother of her dead husband, she entered the Convent of Jesus. Thus she took Him as lover and as spouse who had delivered her from the violent love of Amadour and from the misery of her life with her earthly husband. All her affections henceforth were bent on the perfect love of God. As a nun she lived for many long years, until at last she commended her soul to God with the joy of the bride who goes to meet her bridegroom. (152)

The sign of male desire is present in Floride's decision to become a nun: she does not speak to the tale's female figures of authority, and she goes to another place to consummate her relationship with her divine lover in death, like a bride going to her marriage bed. What Floride wants in this context is quite clear: the synthesis, in a mystical relation with God, of the opposition that confronts physical desire and its "courtly" diversion into endless linguistic displacements.[17] As Stone writes: "a woman's unswerving commitment to God brings her to marry the one true spouse. Both Floride and Paulina, the heroine of story 19, take the veil. From Marguerite's poetry it is clear that such a mystical union had great appeal for the queen."[18] Moreover, Floride's apotheosis is an eroticized union with God. In other words, the culmination of her exemplary life is a relationship with a male figure that is perfectly sensual (her "*joie*") and perfectly sublimated.[19] The problem of this authoritative structure is thus much more complex than the simple repression of one gender by another. The female characters of these stories are involved in the careful suppression of the vehement desires of their male counterparts. In doing so, however, these women enforce the prohibition of their own amorous activity beyond the bounds of a male-dominated order of rank. The place of the female subject in the text cannot be simplified to that of an individual repressed by those of the opposite gender. There is a specific space within the represented male hierarchy that is reserved for women and that subtends and supports the paradox of male supremacy: the domain of language, discourse, and communication. Beyond the linguistic domain of *honesty*, there are two possible domains in which feminine desire may be satisfied: first, that of the ultimate sublimation, a sexualized union with God in the convent; second, the more earthly realm suggested by the character of Paulina, a region located beyond language, and devoted to hidden satisfaction, which is explored by characters such as Jambique and the Duchess of Burgundy of *nouvelle* 70.

Like tale 10, the twenty-first tale of the *Heptaméron* recounts the familiar story of an amorous relationship that is prohibited by social factors. Rolandine occupies a position of privilege, since she is a cousin of the Queen who lives in the sovereign's court. Several factors combine, however, to prohibit her marriage to any of its eligible gentlemen:

> Since she bore some grudge against Rolandine's father, the Queen did not treat her at all kindly. The young lady herself, although neither particularly beautiful not particularly ugly, was so virtuous and chaste that several men of rank asked for her hand in marriage—only to receive a cold reply. The reason was that Rolandine's father was so fond of his money that he neglected the interests of his daughter. Also, her mistress, as I've already said, was so ill-disposed towards her that no one who wanted to win the Queen's favour would ever ask for Rolandine's hand in marriage. Consequently, through her father's negligence and her mistress's dislike the poor girl remained unmarried. (236)

This passage depicts the protagonist in conflict with numerous forces: the apparent displeasure with which the Queen perceives her; the insufficiency of her physical appearance; the parsimony of her father. Rolandine opposes her exemplary virtue to this overdetermined opposition, in which the figures of the Queen and of the father interact to suspend the incorporation of the female into the prevailing order. In this context, in fact, the Queen is the ultimate "father figure" for all of the unmarried, eligible young women, in the sense that she is the medium through which the patriarchal imperatives of marriage are imposed upon the young women of the court. The proof of Rolandine's (feminine) virtue, which constitutes the entirety of the story, serves only to recuperate this "revolutionary" female character back into a social hierarchy based upon suitable marriages. Although the father's refusal to transfer the ultimate marker of nobility to his daughter would be enough to make her problem a difficult one, it seems clear that the disfavor of the highest figure of female authority succeeds in isolating her completely at the tale's beginning. Thus, while this emblematic story depicts a feminine resistance to masculine hierarchies of power, it also inscribes a socioeconomic order of rank that is maintained by the actions of both male and female authority figures. Far from being an exclusively feminist text, therefore, the *Heptaméron* is an irreducibly ambivalent work, which interrogates and problematizes male-dominated power structures while it justifies analogous hierarchies that strong female characters support and sustain by their surveillance of communication.

Rolandine's isolation facilitates the relationship that will develop between her and a male character who is also denied a position in the social hierarchy. Throughout the story, this character is referred to as "the bastard son of a noble house," an epithet that defines his situation well enough. He is, however, further burdened by the insufficiency of his physical appearance, just as Rolandine is: "[He was] so ill-endowed with good looks that no lady, whoever she might have been, would have chosen him for her pleasure" (236). Even if he is high born, a bastard cannot hope to maintain legitimate relations with a relative of the Queen. The interdiction established here is one that forbids the transgression of the laws of legitimacy, which maintain a strict order of rank in the society. Since the purpose of the story is apparently to legitimize the authority of this order, it emphasizes the distinction between the motives of the Bastard and those of Rolandine (i.e., the distinction between a character who represents a transgression of the order and another who is linked metonymically to its highest-ranking member). The first moments of their relationship, which inevitably take the form of conversations, are interrupted when their verbal intercourse becomes known in the society: "Everyone . . . was scandalized at the way she spent so much time talking with a man who was neither rich enough to marry her nor handsome enough to be her lover [*amy*]" (237). Thus Rolandine's governess advises her: "Since people are talking about you in a way that concerns your honour, you must give up speaking to him" (237). The first of these citations implies that a female character of this imaginary court could choose a gentleman for "her pleasure," and that this "friend" would be selected on the basis of his physical appearance. In other words, as in the "Paulina" sequence of tale 10, the *Heptaméron's* order of rank seems to include a sector in which its members could satisfy their physical desires without threatening the integrity of the order. From this point of view, Rolandine's story is about a character's attempt to legitimize this realm of the illegitimate, incarnated by the Bastard, much as Amadour's task was to legitimize his unauthorized relationship with Floride. In doing so, the protagonist encounters a power that resists this fundamental reorganization of its structure. Power in this context manifests itself in the positive and negative effects that it has on the characters, forcing them to interrupt their conversations, to detour their meetings to different sites, to give their amorous discourse different forms, to adopt disguises, engage in subterfuges, and so on. All of the plot developments in the tale are generated, therefore, by a certain relationship of its protagonists to a restricted conception of power and its organization.

The contrasting motives and statuses of the two main characters, defined by their respective relationships to the locus of power, are evident in their distinct reactions to the first interruption of their amorous discourse:

She spent her time in constant prayer, on pilgrimages, in fasting and in acts of abstinence. For her love, of which she was as yet unaware, caused her an anxiety that gave her not even an hour's repose. The bastard of high birth was no less afflicted by the assaults of Love, but he had already resolved in his heart to love Rolandine and to endeavour to marry her. He considered too the honour that would redound to him if he could but win her, and concluded that he must find a way of declaring his desire to her, and above all of winning over the gouvernante. (238)

Rolandine engages in activities that are proper to the authoritative structure. The effect of her desire is a continuous discourse with the ultimate, abstract figure of authority. In this context, the iconographic image of the abstinent virgin in prayer is a sublimated form of female desire, much like that of Floride. Rolandine's movements figure the unending displacements of language in the text, provoked by the exercise of power. On the other hand, like Amadour before him, the Bastard thinks only of a way in which he may gain entrance to the closed system of legitimate marriages from which he is excluded by his birth; moreover, his attempt to enter this exclusive hierarchy is figured in precisely the same way as that of Amadour. The parallel that unites these two male characters implies that power configures language in the same way that it structures the relations between male and female characters, prohibiting certain kinds of conversation, and fomenting others. In other words, in the *Heptaméron*, power stratifies the language of desire into acceptable and unacceptable forms of discourse. In doing so, it also structures the relationships between male and female characters. In *nouvelle* 10, the relationship of a male character to power was determined by the types of discourse in which he could engage and by the rank of his female interlocutor. Here the Bastard undertakes the same maneuver as Amadour, attempting to constitute himself as a legitimate male subject. The story is dominated by a feminine resistance to this attempt, in collaboration with a patriarchal hierarchy (as the tale's end reveals), which assumes the form of a repeated negation of the amorous conversations between Rolandine and the Bastard.

A series of repetitions follows in which the two characters attempt to communicate with one another, which the delegates of the Queen continually interrupt. There are nine scenes in which the two protagonists communicate with one another by violating a prohibition that subtends a code of legitimacy. Each of these variations is more complex than the preceding one. In the first, Rolandine pretends to have migraine headaches so that she may close herself in her room, where the Governess admits the Bastard so that he may speak with his beloved. The

Queen restores the disturbed order of this situation by cutting off the transfer of information between the two: "[The Queen] forbade her ever to speak to the bastard again, unless it was in the Queen's own chamber or in the great hall" (238). In the second ruse, the Bastard enters Rolandine's room during her days of fasting. Again, the Queen intervenes to restore order: "They were unable to keep the affair completely secret, and some servant or other who saw the bastard going in on Rolandine's fast days passed on what he had seen until it reached quarters where it was not concealed from the Queen. So angry was the Queen that the bastard no longer dared go near the ladies' chamber" (239). The image of the Bastard, who represents illegitimate (male) desire, seeking to enter a place where virgins await their legitimate mates, incarnates the configuration of power that is at issue in the text. While the negative effect of the Queen's actions is the interruption of the conversation between the two characters, the exercise of her power also causes the lovers to *create* ever new variations on the same kind of discursive activity.

The scene of the third ruse is perhaps the most important in the series, since within it the two lovers contract an unauthorized marriage that will be annulled by the authority figures of the tale.[20] Every detail of this scene overdetermines the notion of illegality and transgression: "In order not to lose completely the joy of talking with Rolandine, he would often pretend to go away on some journey, coming back in the evening dressed as a Franciscan [*Cordelier*] or Dominican [*Jacobin*] friar. . . . He would then go to the church or to the castle chapel, where Rolandine would come to talk to him accompanied by her gouvernante" (239). The church or chapel is not an appropriate place for the lovers' amorous discourse, even if the fact of their desire is sublimated into the discussion of religious matters, as it is here (and even if amorous conversations in churches would later become a commonplace of love literature). Secondly, the kind of disguise that the Bastard adopts is rich in connotations: the *Cordeliers* were notorious hypocrites and seducers of women throughout the narrative literature of the fifteenth to sixteenth centuries. It is clear that the marriage vows exchanged by the two lovers could not be validated if the social structure based on the prohibition of such marriages were to remain in effect. As part of the ceremony, Rolandine demands a promise from her husband: "You will promise me that if I agree to this marriage, you will not seek to consummate it until my father is dead or until I have found some way to obtain his consent" (240). Even in the context of this affront to authority, Rolandine remains loyal to its principles. Though they are now married, even in the eyes of canon law at this period, their relation may never be consummated without the word

## 4 / Feminist Ambivalence and Feminine Virtue 135

of consent from the female character's father. While Rolandine imposes this restriction on the male character, it is clear that the code of female virtue to which she remains faithful derives from the patriarchal imperative that the sexual activity of the female body be subservient to the father's will, and that the female body serve as a medium through which wealth was transferred from man to man. As I indicated earlier, this fact is perhaps the ultimate feminine transcription of the controlled violence that defines many of the male characters of this text.

The following sequences repeat the motif of religious transgression. For example, in the fourth ruse, Rolandine pretends to go to confession, where she speaks to her husband. At this point, the interdiction of the Queen reaches its highest level of intensity: "The Queen had forbidden them on pain of death ever to speak to one another, unless they were in the company of other people" (241). As Foucault noted, the authority of the sovereign physically marks the body of his or her subjects when they transgress the limits of legitimacy. Foucault's conception of the "political technology of the body" in *Discipline and Punish* elucidates the kind of power structure that prohibits Rolandine and the Bastard from consummating their marriage. Foucault understands the modern "soul" as the effect of the exercise of power upon individual bodies that are placed under surveillance and disciplined within physical and psychological structures from the moment of their birth.[21] The power relations of the *Heptaméron* represent an earlier stage in this technology of power, in which the necessity that the monarch rule over his (or in this case, her) subjects was made manifest in the spectacle of public surveillance and punishment:

> There must be, in this liturgy of pain, an emphatic affirmation of power and of its intrinsic superiority. And this superiority is not simply one of right, it is rather one of the physical force of the sovereign who masters the body of his adversary by striking it. By breaking the law, the criminal has touched the very person of the Prince—it is he, or at least those to whom he has delegated his force, who take hold of the condemned person's body in order to display it as marked, defeated, broken. The punitive ceremony is thus completely "terrorizing" [*terrorisante*].[22]

The structure of surveillance and punishment of the *Heptaméron* operates in exactly this fashion, as in the scene of Rolandine's public humiliation when she refuses to obey the King and Queen and to renounce her clandestine marriage to the Bastard: "The King's deputies brought this constant response back [to the Queen]; and when they saw that there was no way of making her renounce her husband, they sent her back to her father in such a pitiful state that wherever she passed by people began crying. And although she had done nothing wrong, her punishment was so great and her constancy was such that it made her fault seem to be a virtue" (172, my translation).

The story is thus about two characters who attempt to undermine the authority of the sovereign by disguising their illicit acts (at least from the point of view of the authorities) in the form of sanctioned and sacred activities: fasting, pilgrimages, confession. All of Rolandine's actions are written in a corporeal register: she has migraine headaches, she deprives herself of food, and, later in the tale, she claims that she is indisposed in order to close herself in her room. At this point, the relationship between the two characters assumes its most sublimated form in the verbal realm. The Bastard pretends to read a romance about the Knights of the Round Table in a room adjoining that of Rolandine. The two lovers converse across the open space that separates the windows of the two rooms, until their trick is discovered by another female authority figure, the mother of a prince, who threatens to reveal the ruse to the Queen. The ironic detail of the book highlights the sharp contrast of the heroic figures of the Round Table, who endure pain and suffering in order to serve their ladies, and the Bastard, whose only possible action, that of speech, is continually impeded by the force of female authority. The scene of the discovery of this ruse uncovers the network of communication that is at the base of this power structure:

> As the lady who was the young prince's mother turned back into the room, she glanced at the big book about the Round Table, remarking to the valet de chambre: "It amazes me that young people waste so much time reading such nonsense!" To which the valet de chambre replied that it amazed him even more that persons who were supposed to be older and wiser were even more given to it, and went on to tell her how astonished he had been to find her kinsman, the bastard, spending four or five hours a day with her son's book—a fine thing for him to be reading! Instantly, the explanation bore itself into the lady's mind. . . . In the evening she spoke to Rolandine, warning her that if she persisted in this foolish and wicked attachment [*folle amityé*], she would inform the Queen of her deceitfulness. (242–43)

The Queen's "agents" are omnipresent in this tale, and the position of her authority is constituted by this network of subjects who continually report back to her. She herself is at the center of a kind of "panopticon" that functions by means of verbal reports. The mere threat of a message delivered to the Queen is enough to interrupt the carefully arranged strategy that unites the would-be lovers. It is not surprising that the Queen's delegate in this passage declares tales of chivalry to be foolish.

Chrétien de Troyes's Lancelot, for example, in *Le Chevalier de la charrette,* would be entirely out of place in the context evoked by Marguerite de Navarre. Whereas desire must be indefinitely deferred for her major characters, Chrétien inscribes a trajectory in which desire overcomes insurmountable obstacles in order to reach its objective, which is an unauthorized sexual union with the Queen, described in sacred (and sacrilegious) terms. In tales 10 and 21 of the *Heptaméron,* in contrast, the sexual act is continually deferred within the endless manipulations of the court, comprised of a network of communication saturated by the power of the King and Queen at the same time that it virtually constitutes their power.

The last three ruses of the tale equally confine desire to the realm of discourse and writing. The Bastard is forced to leave the court, due to the threats of the Queen, yet he still manages to communicate with his beloved: "So ingenious was he in this respect that, however careful a watch the Queen kept on Rolandine, never a week went by without her hearing from him twice" (243). Just as the spoken word is scrupulously monitored by the Queen, so the written word is subject to her omnipresent observation. Despite his subtlety, the Bastard is unable to escape her ubiquitous gaze, as in the case of his last two maneuvers. A page receives the Bastard's letters and passes them to Rolandine on a crowded street. Even here, among the populace, the Queen's emissaries track down these communications, and the page is forced to burn the letters. Similarly, an old servant of the Bastard is caught in the crowd by the authorities and tears up the letters while pretending to urinate against a wall. The scraps are recovered and pasted back together. Thus, even in the most vulgar circumstances, amidst the people, far removed from the court, the Queen's absolute control over every act of communication is made clear in the tale. This domination of the word is translated into a domination of the flesh: when the final letter reveals the secret of the illegitimate marriage, the Bastard is forced to flee the country, while Rolandine is severely beaten and sent back to the house of her father, a symbolic gesture that indicates the annulment of the clandestine marriage—as we have seen, marriage in this context was instituted by the literal delivery of the female body from her father's house to that of her husband. Rolandine's private transgression is transformed into the public spectacle of punishment, which incarnates royal authority in the pitiful condition of the transgressor. Moreover, her punishment consists of her complete isolation from the avenues of communication: "The Queen, beside herself with rage, ordered Rolandine to be taken out of her sight and shut up alone in a room where it would be impossible for her to speak to anyone" (249).

According to Lyons, both this tale and the complementary text (tale 40) that tells the story of Rolandine's aunt concern "men who try to prevent women from speaking and thus turn them into characters who are spoken about."[23] While it is true that Rolandine's aunt is shut up in a castle in the woods by her brother, so that she may not speak to anyone, it is clear that Rolandine's nemesis in the preceding tale is the Queen, who controls every avenue of communication. Lyons's enthusiasm for the interpretation in which men dominate and silence the women of these stories is apparent in his reading of the scene in which the fateful letter is torn up and reassembled: "Only the king's confessor, cleverly reassembling the fragments of a letter, is able to bring the proof of the marriage."[24] This is the only instance in which the King's agents act to silence the amorous discourse that unites the two characters; in the other cases, the numerous agents of the Queen are those who interrupt this dialogue.[25] An overzealous reading of the major tales of the *Heptaméron* as instances of men silencing women misses the paradox of female characters who demand that women maintain their subordinate position in the strategy of power constituted by marriage, such as the Queen in the following citation:

> Seeing that Rolandine was resolute and that she meant every word she said, the Queen was quite incapable of making a reasonable reply. She burst into tears and went on raging at Rolandine, making accusations and hurling insults at her.
>
> "Miserable wretch that you are! Instead of being humble and sorry for the serious offence you have committed, you dare to speak in this outrageous fashion with never a tear in your eye! . . . But if the King and your father heed my words, they'll put you where you'll be obliged to speak a different kind of language!" (247–48, modified)

Here the Queen is the primary agent of power, and the domain of her activity is linguistic, even though one could argue that her authority is subordinate to that of the patriarchal figures, the King and the Father, whom she names. Rolandine's attempt to enunciate a different kind of discourse within this context—that is, to follow the course of her own desire in her own way—can only be reduced to failure, and is accompanied by the public spectacle of her submission to power's inexorable effects, which are both positive and negative. She is restricted from speaking one kind of language and forced to speak another kind. By imprinting itself within and upon her body, power transforms Rolandine into an icon of its functioning. Moreover, this icon is a decidedly Christian one, in the sense that the display of the broken body of Christ is at the heart of many Christian rituals. Here the suffering body of the female figure is contemplated by a horrified public, fascinated by the spectacle of power.

The painstaking reduction of Rolandine to a state that is not suited to her social condition is eliminated in an instant. After fleeing to Germany, the Bastard falls in love with another woman and marries her. Rolandine is rehabilitated completely into the society: her father accords her a generous dowry, and she marries a legitimate gentleman. Surprisingly, the attitude of the Queen to this marriage is passed over in complete silence by the text. The tale's end leaves little doubt, however, as to its approval of her inclusion within the established order: "Thus she became heir to a fine large house, and there she lived a devout and respectable life in the company of her husband, whom she loved dearly, and by whom she too was much beloved" (253). This passage of wealth from one generation to another is accompanied by the highest approbation, while the body of the female character, which had been brutally marked by the exercise of power, becomes a medium through which wealth is maintained in the *maison*.[26]

Tale 21 of the *Heptaméron* is an exemplary manifestation of power strategies that saturate the text's amorous relations. Several factors control the representation of desire. In the first instance, desire must be converted into discourse—the lover declares his will to his beloved—and this first conversion is the beginning of a redundant process in which a longed-for but unrealized union of the characters is repeatedly restricted to discourse. The networks in which this transfer of information may take place are carefully controlled by a female authority figure, whose power derives from, or is exercised as, her regulation of communicative media (public and private conversations, letters, even the secret exchange of marriage vows). The legitimacy and illegitimacy of the characters' actions is also determined by the extent of their access to the network of communication. Illegitimate desire, for example, will be denied entry to the network, or will be indefinitely deferred, while legitimate desire will be authorized, ensuring that the economy of power remains constant: Rolandine ultimately inherits the riches of a noble house, which she will pass on to her sons and daughters, because of the Queen's persistent surveillance of her discursive relationship with the Bastard. Unauthorized male desire can only be deferred within this system; the Bastard's trajectory is restricted to the stage at which the lover seeks to communicate with the object of his desire. Even minor female figures collaborate in the maintenance of this order of desire and discourse, in a strategy or configuration of power that traverses this imaginary society from top to bottom.

Similarly, the "sisterhood" of communication that upholds the social order founded upon the idea of feminine virtue appears in miniature in tale 61. A married woman falls in love with an ecclesiastical dignitary known as a canon (*chanoine*), who invents various pretexts in order to enjoy her favors. When the husband discovers the affair, he hides his wife, but to no avail: the woman escapes and goes to live with the canon for sixteen years, during which period she bears him a son. The wife's punishment for this extreme indiscretion is rather mild: she is forced to return to her original husband. The network of communication among women brings the matter to the attention of the Queen, resulting in the reestablishment of what Todorov would call an initial state of equilibrium:

> Now it was around this time that Queen Claude, the consort of King Francis, was passing through Auntun in the company of the Regent, the King's mother, and of her daughter, the Duchess of Alençon. One of the Queen's chamber women, a person by the name of Perrette, came to the Duchess and said: "Madame, I beg you, listen to me, and you will perform a far greater work than going to hear all the services of the day." The Duchess willingly agreed to listen, knowing that nothing but good counsel could come from her. Perrette went on to explain how she had engaged a small girl to help soap the Queen's washing. When she had asked the girl for news of the town, she had been told how upset the respectable ladies living there had been at the way the canon's wife took precedence over them. She had also been told something of the woman's past history. The Duchess went at once and told this story to Madame the Regent and the Queen. Without further formality they had the unfortunate woman sent for. She made no attempt to conceal herself. Far from being ashamed, she had become proud of the distinction of being mistress in such a rich man's household. (481–82)

The story of the wife's disgraceful behavior traverses the entire spectrum of female society, from helpers of washerwomen to the Queen herself. Moreover, the named characters of this scene provide it with a remarkable aura of authority, since the narrator names the most powerful women in France at the time: Queen Claude, Louise de Savoie, who would rule France during François I's captivity in Spain, and Marguerite de Navarre herself, known at the time as the Duchess of Alençon. The means by which female figures of authority maintain their power saturate the everyday lives of even the most humble women of this fictional world, whose domestic tasks are carried out in the framework of narratives that tell and retell the story of legitimacy and its transgressions. Narrative is thus the technique (or the technology) by which power is disseminated in this context.

Tale 43 is the most intriguing inscription of the paradoxical feminine power at work in this context. Its main character, a woman in a position of legitimacy and authority, manages to enjoy illegitimate desire without being punished (at least in the story itself).[27] The story begins with the evocation of feminine power within the closed confines of a royal house: "In a beautiful château there once lived a great and powerful princess. In her retinue she had a young lady called Jambique, a rather haughty girl by whom she was so taken in that she did nothing without first consulting her, for she regarded her as the most sensible and virtuous lady of her day" (392). The markers of nobility and authority are exaggerated in this passage in order to confer greater value upon the character of Jambique, who maintains her position by manipulating appearances. As one would expect, this manipulation includes a strict control of language and the conduits of its dissemination within the house. Jambique's function is to keep her mistress informed; by exercising this communicative duty, she accrues power to herself: "This Jambique was always condemning illicit love, and if she came across any men enamoured of her companions she used to reproach the lovers sharply and make such a damning report to the princess that often they would receive a severe reprimand" (392). The character's control of this network of communication extends equally to herself: "She herself never spoke to men at all, except in a loud, arrogant voice" (ibid.).

By means of this skillful management of information in the château, Jambique maintains the appearance of an authoritative woman who opposes the follies of love. Nevertheless, this appearance dissimulates the truth of a female character who dares to satisfy her physical desire. Her entrance into this illegitimate domain, usually reserved for male characters, is marked by an effacement of the visual register:

[Jambique] saw the object of her affections taking a walk in the garden. And after having watched him for so long that evening fell and it became too dark to see, she called one of her little page-boys and pointed the gentleman out to him.

"Do you see that gentleman," she said, "with the crimson satin doublet and the robe edged with lynx fur? Go and tell him that there's a friend of his who wants to speak to him in the arcade in the garden."

While the page did this, she went out through her mistress's private room into the garden, with a mask covering her eyes and her cap pulled down over her face. (392–93, modified)

Jambique's unwillingness to present herself as the visual object of male desire figures an important resistance to the male-dominated social hierarchy of the work, which is supported and maintained by a public, female surveillance and control of discourse, in which she herself participates. Much like the scene in which Floride disfigures herself, Jambique's self-effacement places the female character in a problematic and ambivalent situation. Like the desire of illegitimate male characters, Jambique's passion for this gentleman must be satisfied in a private domain, and the narrative of this passion can circulate among the legitimate members of the court only at the expense of her reputation. In other words, if the discourse of her desire were enunciated in public, her body would be subjected to the negative effects of power (as in the case of Rolandine), just as the story of her transgression would have to be reduced to silence. Thus the individual inclination of this character, like those of Amadour and the Bastard, may be satisfied only within a space that is completely separated from the realm of legitimacy that punishes transgressions such as that of Jambique. She is thus a figure who is hopelessly divided against herself, at once devoted to the enforcement of legitimacy and to the satisfaction of her own desire.

Could it be, then, that Jambique plays a decidedly *masculine* role in this tale, since she embodies the kind of duplicitous existence represented by Amadour in tale 10? We recall that Parlamente pronounced the following judgment on Jambique: "Women who are dominated by pleasure have no right to call themselves women. They might as well call themselves men, since it is men who regard violence and lust as something honourable" (396–97). Similarly, Glidden claims that "by sighting her lover in a transfixing gaze, Jambicque assumes the libidinous male role in defiance of the presumed chastity of her sex."[28] While from one perspective these judgments are correct—that is, from the point of view of the official, public persona that Parlamente must adopt before her husband, and that Jambique must assume at court—from another perspective it may be that Jambique is not a masculine character at all. It has often been remarked that male desire is essentially visual in nature, as Glidden's comment on Jambique's "gaze" implies.[29] In the *Heptaméron*, male desire is motivated by the vision of the beautiful object (tale 10), as well as by the perception of the symbolic social value that the object represents (tale 21).[30] In either case, the desire of the male character is motivated by the gaze, and in this context male desire cannot be satisfied in the absence of visual stimuli. The basic tension of tale 43 is thus the necessity that the tactile sensations experienced by the gentleman in his relation with Jambique be confirmed by visual perception. Consequently, the kind of relationship instituted by Jambique is, perhaps, *beyond* the feminine in this context, in the sense that female characters in these tales are entrapped by the male-generated and male-imposed code of virtue that defines the feminine as such and that demands that relations between men and women be based on a desire that is motivated by the gaze. Jambique is willing to confine her pleasures to the private and the tactile sphere, despite the apparent pleasure with which she herself gazes at the object of her desire at the beginning of the tale. Her case presents a stark contrast to the male characters whom we have examined, who demanded a public and visual component in their relations: Amadour proclaimed that Floride's marriage to the Duke of Cardona served as a legitimating, public "*couverture*" for their carnal relationship;[31] the Bastard asks the King for a public legitimation of his private marriage to Rolandine. Jambique's maneuver is quintessentially *feminist*, therefore, in that she tries to create an alternative space in which she may satisfy her forbidden desire and that would be completely divorced from the structure of power in which she is a quite conscious feminine participant.[32]

In his relationship with Jambique, the gentleman enters an alien world of tactile signs that he tries to decipher. He touches her dress in the darkness and recognizes it as a marker of feminine nobility: "As he touched her clothes, [the gentleman] found they were of velvet—and in those days it was not every day one wore velvet, unless one was of high birth and had an important position" (393). His first contact with this unidentified female object is marked by his attempts to translate his tactile stimuli into the judgments of value that are typical of the male visual capture of the female image: "And as he felt what lay beneath, he found that there too everything was of high quality, firm and generally in good shape! So he made it his business to give her of his best" (393). As in the *Cent nouvelles*, this male appreciation of the female body is saturated by assessments of its use-value for the male and of its social function in the establishment of relationships among men: "And so the gentleman also learned that the lady was married" (393). While the gentleman's attempts are decidedly masculine, they are also essentially iconographic in the sense that they intend to interpret beyond the material being of the object, converting it into a sign that signifies hierarchical relationships. Perhaps, then, the practice of distilling power relations into images that require the interpretation and participation of the viewer is a fundamentally masculine activity—this would be a possible conclusion drawn from my own chapter on the *Cent nouvelles*. In contrast, what Marguerite de Navarre offers us here is a feminist desire that is outside of language, that refuses to present the feminine body as the symbolic object of a narcissistic masculine desire, and that concentrates its satisfaction within the tactile realm.[33]

Discouraged by his inability to identify this royal lady, the gentleman decides to mark her body with a piece of chalk while they are making love, so that he may recognize her in public. This masculine reconfiguration of a feminine space of satisfaction results in disgrace for both characters. Jambique denies her lover's allegations when he confronts her in public, and has him banished from the kingdom. As one would expect, this punishment takes the form of a denial of access to language, which is accomplished through a report made to the highest representative of feminine authority. When the space of her own pleasure is rejected by the male, Jambique resumes her role as a woman in a position of authority, to which she is relegated in a male-dominated social hierarchy. In other words, she is entrusted with the surveillance and control of narratives that depict love relationships, including her own, which she will treat no differently than the others:

> [The gentleman] knew that Jambique had great credit with the princess, and was anxious to appease her. But in vain. In a fury Jambique left him standing there and ran straight to her mistress. The princess, who loved Jambique as she loved herself, left her entourage to come to talk to her, and seeing that she was angry about something, asked her what the matter was. Jambique had no intention of hiding it, and told her everything the gentleman had said, presenting the poor man in such a bad light that the princess ordered him that very evening to return home immediately without speaking to anyone. (395–96)

It seems, therefore, that a woman who is enmeshed in the structure of power may enjoy the carnal pleasures that it prohibits only if she is able to maintain an absolute separation of the word and the flesh. The desire of the type that Jambique exhibits in private has no place in the public system of power. This idea is repeated in Marguerite's retelling of the *Châtelaine de Vergy* (tale 70), in which an honest widow maintains the appearance of legitimacy by making her lover promise to keep their affair a secret, in the utopian space of her private garden. The entirety of this latter tale operates as a means of pressuring this secret out into the open, at which point the widow is dishonored and literally dies of shame. In tale 43, however, Jambique is much more adroit in her manipulation of the system. She imposes an abyss between the illegitimacy of her desire and the legitimacy of her position. The moment desire attempts to intrude into the linguistic realm of her authority, she cuts it off completely and denies it any access to the agency of speech. The space of feminist desire in the *Heptaméron* is thus an alternative one, which has no place in the patriarchal social scheme structured by marriage. The *Heptaméron* remains squarely within the domain of feminine authority, at the same time that it depicts the tragic ends of women who persist in their attempts to escape from a social system that leaves no place for their desire.

In conclusion, the *Heptaméron* delineates the problematic position that was determined for women by men in a certain imaginary that comes to us from sixteenth-century France. The power that pervades the relations between the genders in this text comes to bear on the amorous activity of its characters, establishing an almost impassable barrier between their physical desires and the acceptable forms of love. The place for physical desire is beyond the courtly focus of these tales, in a realm characterized by silence, darkness, invisibility, and death, while sublimated love relationships offer those characters involved in them the promise of success in the public domain. While the "beyond" of sexual satisfaction in this text is equivalent to an outside that belongs to its male characters, its most remarkable female characters attempt to create an alternative zone in which they may define and enjoy their own kind of sexuality. At its most radical, desire in this feminist realm resists visibility, the obsessive gaze of the male, and the endless diversion of desire into discourse. The progression that I have examined in this chapter thus leads from a female character who is completely immersed in the configuration of power that the work represents, and who ultimately becomes its apotheosis (Floride), to a female character who attempts to construct a parallel order of rank that would obey the discursive imperatives of honest friendship (*l'honnête amitié*), only to be recuperated back into the prevailing order (Rolandine), to a female character who takes the most radical step of all in her attempt to configure a feminist space of satisfaction that simply has no models in a patriarchy that imposes a conception of feminine virtue upon women (Jambique). The complexity of Marguerite de Navarre's negotiations with this entire range of issues makes the *Heptaméron* a more challenging text than those of her predecessors and constitutes a powerful feminist response to a narrative genre that had existed almost exclusively for the pleasure of male readers and listeners. Remarkably, Marguerite remained sympathetic to the plight of her male characters, who in the long run appear to be the victims of the same patriarchal code that denied her female characters the possibility of defining and satisfying their desires. Given these characteristics, the *Heptaméron* is the culmination and the summit of the new narrative tradition that developed in France during the second half of the fifteenth century and the first half of the sixteenth, and offers icons that both support and undermine the iconography of power inscribed in the texts that precede it.

# Conclusion

Narrative at the end of the Middle Ages functions according to representational rules and codes that are quite different from our own and that were derived from medieval Christian iconography, as Auerbach recognized. In medieval painting and sculpture, objects and gestures signify the identity of sacred persons and their place in the hierarchy of heaven. Similarly, narrative at the end of the Middle Ages signifies the social stations and occupations of its characters by depicting them in reference to value-laden objects and names. Medieval iconography was crucial in the dissemination and maintenance of a Christian conception of the metaphysical realm, which itself supported, anchored, and structured the social world of the period. In the same way, narrative representation disseminated, supported, and ultimately embodied a social world that was rigidly hierarchical. In this context, individual identity was thus determined by its inscription or encryption upon two conceptual grids. The first was the configuration of the metaphysical universe provided by Christianity (or that *was* Christianity), which forced the individual to conceive of his or her own life and being in eschatological terms. This meant that every action on the part of the individual could be codified according to preexisting sets of value judgments (the Seven Deadly Sins, the Ten Commandments, the dictates of Canon Law, etc.). Identity was also structured by a system of castes and professions or trades, which fixed one's being virtually from the moment of birth: except in extremely rare cases, a cobbler could not expect to become a knight, and vice versa, which perhaps explains the medieval fascination for stories of the type, "lost infant son of a king raised by shepherds discovers his true heritage." As it develops throughout the fifteenth and sixteenth centuries, the French *nouvelle* explores both the secular and the sacred domains, while the importance of these conceptual paradigms for the identity of the individual subject becomes increasingly the focus of narrative as the genre develops in France, reaching its apogee in the tales of Marguerite de Navarre.

*Les Cent nouvelles nouvelles* project the type of male subjectivity that was generated by a hierarchical social structure organized into strict caste divisions. Moreover, the collection underscores the importance of gender difference in the configuration of a society whose distribution of wealth was regulated by marriage. Within this type of society, gendered subject positions are determined by phantasmic conceptions of sexual identity. The masculine position is that of characters who attempt to appropriate the wealth of other male characters via the exchange and commerce of the female body. The feminine position, largely imposed upon its representatives, is that of characters whose exaggerated eagerness for and submission to sexual advances by males serves as the basis for the bodily commerce that unites men in a social economy. The *Cent nouvelles* thus literally incarnate the series of relationships that constituted the social world of a certain caste of men. Narrative in this context is involved in the maintenance and dissemination of an abstract ideology that becomes materially manifest in or as these relations themselves. In other words, a particular narrative form, used repeatedly in a certain context by a specific category of individuals, is a technique or "technology" that supports a configuration of power on which the identity of these individuals is based.

The tales of Philippe de Vigneulles depict quite a different social space, characterized by the activity of a caste of merchants who would eventually come to dominate Europe. Vigneulles's world is ruled by usurping, predatory characters who attempt to accomplish illicit transfers of wealth across caste boundaries. It also details the activity of a roving, carnivalesque underclass who appropriate goods to which they would ordinarily have no access in a distribution of wealth that favored the noble class. In a sense, Philippe's text figures a suspension of the diverse interdictions that constituted the society that it describes. At times, it even appears to resist or to invert, whether intentionally or unintentionally, the standard order of rank, determined by marriage, whose corollary is the hyperbolic willingness of women and female characters to engage in sex beyond marriage, which is the basis of homosocial relationships among men. While they are undoubtedly derived from the traditions of the medieval fabliaux, Philippe's grotesque bodies, his transmutations of language, and his scatological farces nonetheless seem to participate in an incipient transfer of power from a knightly ruling caste to one composed of merchants and burghers, especially when these textual characteristics are seen against the backdrop of *Les Cent nouvelles nouvelles*. While this is a possible conclusion from my argument, it also could be that the apparent suspension of hierarchies and rules that dominates the work of Vigneulles is merely a depiction of the momentary release from restrictions provided by carnival, which itself is authorized and interdicted by the prevailing order of power. Nevertheless, for Vigneulles, narrative was, perhaps, a means of propagating and disseminating the subversion of a rising merchant caste. His work explores social realms—those of the nascent bourgeoisie and of the underclass, for example—that had largely been absent from the work of his French predecessors (the work of Villon provides a somewhat earlier example of a similar phenomenon). As such, it provides us with social icons from which we may interpret the prototype of a shift in the power relations that confronted the different castes of the period.

Finally, the *Heptaméron* enlarges the field of vision of the genre to include the realm of the sacred, which was present only in parodical terms in the earlier collections. The undercurrent that dominates the work is that of the Reformation, characterized by a reevaluation of the individual's relation to the conceptual universe of Christianity. The conflicting interpretations of the means to salvation that dominated and decimated the sixteenth century brought into being a new conception of the individual as one who was responsible for his or her own soul in an intimate relationship with God, via a reading of the Holy Scriptures: this is essentially the position personified in the character of Oisille, who is undoubtedly one of the alter egos of Marguerite herself. Similarly, Parlamente's problematic relationship with her husband, Hircan, dramatizes well enough the extent to which the idea of the individual generated by the Reformation intersected with the critique of traditional social institutions, such as marriage, which was a salient feature of the Renaissance. Marguerite de Navarre thus inverts the narrative schema that was initiated in France in the *Cent nouvelles nouvelles*. She puts a multitude of voices and points of view, both male and female, masculine and feminine, in the place of an exclusively male or masculine club of narrators. These multiple characters resist the limitations of subjective identity within social and religious hierarchies and within the traditional systems of gender relations regulated by marriage. For Marguerite, narrative was a means of putting into play another voice, a *differently gendered* voice, from that of the male voices that had previously dominated the genre of the *nouvelle*. It was her paradoxical means of both resisting and affirming an identity that was imposed upon her by her birth as a woman within a certain caste and by the marriages that were arranged for her (who is the Queen of Navarre but the wife of Henri de Navarre?). The *Heptaméron* combines the critique of marriage that was typical of the *Querelle des femmes* with the inchoate individualism of the Reformation, effectively

# Conclusion 149

undoing the consolidation of male power that had been accomplished in the narrative realm by the *Cent nouvelles nouvelles*. The work disseminates a new configuration of discourses, in which a feminine and perhaps feminist voice spoke with the conviction of the religious reformers. This is the ultimate meaning of the female characters who serve as narrative icons in her text.

From being a technique that supported a given order of power, the French *nouvelle* at the end of the Middle Ages became a complex and polyphonic discourse that participated in the revision, inversion, and eventual transformation of social institutions. To put it in Foucaldian terms, a specific type of narrative discourse was colonized and cannibalized by diverse forces (the bourgeois seeks to supplant the feudal, the feminine seeks to infiltrate the masculine), resulting in a multiplicity of discursive strategies that struggled within narrative for dominance. Reading these tales from a distance of nearly five hundred years, one begins much like an observer who sees for the first time an allegorical tapestry from the Middle Ages (such as the representation of the Lady and the Unicorn in *La dame à la licorne*) with a bemused curiosity that takes the form of numerous questions. What do these symbols signify? Who are these opaque and mysterious beings? What is the key that will enable me to unlock the message of these "icons"? By reading these tales and images, we reenact the play of forces that constituted a given state of power at a given time, which has been superseded and replaced by historical and technological developments. At the end of the twentieth century, we are traversed by power, we are subject to it, and we become subjects who act in accordance with its disembodied dictates when we contemplate the constant images that enfold our bodies and that come to us from television, the cinema, newspapers and magazines, advertisements, and the Internet. Now more than ever, power maintains and feeds itself by constituting bodies via the medium of images and stories that call them into being as subjects who will maintain and foster a given order of rank. This has always been the case in Western Europe, as the Christian images that dominated the Continent demonstrate. The particular moment in the history of Western narrative that I have examined is perhaps a privileged one in the sense that it was characterized by new technologies and by the sudden eruption of a new set of images that would soon dominate modern consciousness: the images of Christ on the Cross and of the Virgin and Child are replaced on the ceilings of Versailles by paintings of Greek and Roman gods, for example. It is also a key period in that the invention of the printing press made possible the rapid dissemination of dozens of new and newly rediscovered discourses, which had drastic social consequences. The *nouvelle* was one type of discourse among many, yet it was an important element in the social revolutions that were taking place. The examination of this genre at that time and in that place is a small but vital part of what would have to be a more comprehensive iconography of power.

# Notes

## Introduction

1. Lionello Sozzi, ed., *La Nouvelle française à la Renaissance* (Geneva: Slatkine, 1981), vii.
2. Cf. Erich Auerbach's discussion of "Franco-Burgundian realism," in *Mimesis: The Representation of Reality in Western Literature,* trans. Willard Trask (Garden City: Doubleday Anchor Books, 1957), as well as the following declaration by Pierre Jourda in *Marguerite d'Angoulême, Duchesse d'Alençon, Reine de Navarre (1492–1549). Étude biographique et littéraire* (Paris: Champion, 1930): "It is by means of the depiction of social mores that the *Heptaméron* proves to be a realist work. In this respect, no doubt would be able to resist, and no analysis would be able to efface an attentive reading of the tales, from which one could derive at least an infinitely varied portrait of French life in the 16th Century, if not a complete one" (799; my translation).
3. Friedrich Nietzsche, *The Birth of Tragedy and the Genealogy of Morals* trans. Francis Golffing (Garden City: Doubleday, 1956), 208.
4. Marguerite de Navarre, *The Heptameron,* trans. Paul A. Chilton (London: Penguin, 1984), 68. All parenthetical page references in the text will be to this edition. My modifications of this translation will be based on Marguerite de Navarre, *L'Heptaméron,* ed. Michel François (Paris: Bordas, 1991).
5. See Philippe de Lajarte, "The Voice of the Narrators in Marguerite de Navarre's Tales," in John Lyons and Mary McKinley, eds., *Critical Tales: New Studies of the* Heptameron *and Early Modern Culture* (Philadelphia: University of Pennsylvania Press, 1993). "To conclude . . . that narrators do not exist in the semiotic reality of sixteenth-century narrative texts would be as absurd as to deny the presence of the unconscious in the works of Racine because the concept of the unconscious did not exist in the seventeenth century, or to argue that the distinction between *langue* and *parole* cannot be applied to old French texts because Saussure's *Cours* dates only from the twentieth century" (185).
6. Cf. Mary McKinley, "Telling Secrets: Sacramental Confession and Narrative Authority in the *Heptameron,*" in Lyons and McKinley, *Critical Tales*, 152: "As is generally true in the *Heptameron*, the story [tale 72] gives us practically no detail that would help us discuss the woman's character development. Indeed, the very

notion of character development, as modern readers understand that concept, can be applied to Renaissance texts only at great risk of anachronism."

7. Robert Ousterhout and Leslie Brubaker. *The Sacred Image East and West* (Urbana: University of Illinois Press, 1995), 5.

8. See Leonid Ouspensky and Vladimir Lossky, *The Meaning of Icons*, trans. G. E. H. Palmer and E. Kadloubovsky (Boston: Boston Book and Art Shop, 1969). According to Ouspensky, the position of the hand with the ring and small fingers touching the thumb, and the other fingers curled or extended, represents "the gesture of benediction" (73), whereas icons in which only the ring finger touches the thumb represent "the gesture of the preacher" (108). Similarly, the Virgin Mary often appears in icons in a characteristic pose: "This image with characteristically upraised hands belongs to the type of the Mother of God Orans. . . . The gesture of prayer, with upraised hands characteristic of the Orans, is not specifically Christian. It was known both in the Old Testament and in the ancient Greco-roman world" (78). For a fascinating catalogue, in Latin, of different systems of sign language used in medieval monasteries, see G. Van Rijnberk, *Le Langage par signes chez les moines* (Amsterdam: North-Holland Publishing Company, 1953).

9. See Gerald Prince, *A Dictionary of Narratology* (Lincoln: University of Nebraska Press, 1987). In other words, iconographic details are completely different from what Prince defined as a "reality effect": "A seemingly functionless detail presumably reported just 'because it is there (in the world of the NARRATED),' a detail presumably mentioned for no other reason than the fact that it is part of the reality represented. Reality effects (*effets de réel*) are exemplary connotators of the real (they signify 'this is real'), and an abundance of them characterizes realistic narrative" (80).

10. Erwin Panofsky, *Meaning in the Visual Arts* (Garden City: Doubleday, 1955), 28–29.

11. See Claude Lévi-Strauss, *The Elementary Structures of Kinship,* trans. James Harle Bell et al. (Boston: Beacon Press, 1969), 12–25.

12. I will use the terms "social" and "society" in the following pages to refer to the sets of intersubjective relations, saturated by power, that determine the identities of individual characters. I will employ the term "social hierarchy" to designate the stratified character roles that constitute these relations (the position of the miller is subordinate to that of the knight in the *Cent nouvelles nouvelles*, tale 3, while Amadour's position as a younger son in *Heptaméron* 10 is subordinate to that of the Duke of Cardona, who is a wealthy, firstborn son).

13. "There was such sympathy among the men and women [of the abbey] that they were dressed in the same way every day. In order to ensure that this was the case, there were certain men who had been instructed to tell the other men every morning what clothing the women wanted to wear that day, since everything was organized according to the judgment of the ladies." François Rabelais, *Oeuvres complètes*, ed. Guy Demerson (Paris: Éditions du Seuil, 1973), 202; my translation.

## 1: Realism and the *Nouvelle*

1. In the appendix of his *Conteurs français du XVIème siècle* (Paris: Gallimard, 1956), Pierre Jourda lists thirty-one different collections of *nouvelles* published in the sixteenth century in France (some of them translations from Italian and German), many of which ran into eight or more editions. See pp. 1449–53.
2. "Although there is no doubt that the relationship between men and women in the *Heptameron* reflects to some degree the social environment in which the text was produced, that relationship is reduced so obsessively, so repetitively, so *phantasmatically*, to what Scripture calls 'lust of the flesh' (I John 2:16, King James version) that surely it is—to use the psychoanalytic term—overdetermined. Surely the 'meaning' of the relationship between men and women in the *Heptameron* exceeds any meaning that can be secured in sixteenth-century social conventions." Robert Cottrell, "Inmost Cravings: The Logic of Desire in the *Heptameron*," in Lyons and McKinley, *Critical Tales*, 7.
3. "Power must be analyzed as something which circulates, or rather as something which only functions in the form of a chain. It is never localized here or there, never in anybody's hands, never appropriated as a commodity or piece of wealth. Power is employed and exercised through a net-like organization. And not only do individuals circulate between its threads; they are always in the position of simultaneously undergoing and exercising this power. They are not only its inert or consenting target; they are always also the elements of its articulation." Michel Foucault, *Power/Knowledge: Selected Interviews & Other Writings 1972–1977*, ed. Colin Gordon, trans. Colin Gordon et al. (New York: Pantheon Books, 1980), 98.
4. See Daniel Russell, "Some Ways of Structuring Character in the *Heptameron*," in Lyons and McKinley, *Critical Tales*, 203–17. "[In the sixteenth century,] characters were still types to a certain extent; not pure types as we think of them appearing alongside personifications in medieval allegories, but hybrid, social types like the wicked and lecherous priest, the handsome, dashing, and brave young hero, or the clever, deceiving wife, types that need to be described by a combination of epithets rather than by a single one as was often the case for earlier types. As such, many characters followed certain relatively fixed models one might encounter in the theater or in woodcuts. So once again the audience could be expected to have a sufficiently clear theatrical or iconographical model in mind to conjure an image distinct enough that it could serve to unite the character and his actions into a more or less coherent entity" (205). Russell defends the thesis that the characterization techniques of the *Heptaméron* are more modern than their typological predecessors because the major characters of the text—Amadour, Floride, Rolandine, Jambique—*resist* being placed into neat, predefined categories that define social types. While this argument is quite convincing, I will maintain here that the characters of Marguerite de Navarre's text make better sense when read against the backdrop of "typecast" characters that Russell describes so well.
5. Gyorgy Lukács, *Studies in European Realism,* trans. Edith Bone (London: Hillway Publishing Co., 1958), 7–8.
6. Joseph Bédier, *Les Fabliaux. Etudes de littérature populaire et d'histoire littéraire du Moyen Age,* 6th ed. (Paris: Champion, 1969), 7, my translation.

7. Werner Söderhjelm, *La Nouvelle française au XVe siècle* (Geneva: Slatkine Reprints, 1973), 1. Further references to this text will appear parenthetically using my own translations.
8. Here, for example, Söderhjelm evidently has in mind the *exempla* of the *Disciplina Clericalis,* in which a husband who returns home from a trip is fooled by his wife and her mother, who literally spreads a sheet in front of his eyes so that he cannot see the wife's lover escape. See Petrus Alfonsi, *Disciplina Clericalis,* ed. and trans. Angel Gonzalez Palencia (Madrid-Granada: Consejo superior de investigaciones científicas, 1948), *exempla* IX and X.
9. Similarly, Pierre Jourda's reading of the genre's origins emphasized the difficulty of determining the exact sources of the short narrative forms that appeared in France in the late Middle Ages, such as the *fabliau*: "72 known *fabliaux* were written to the north of the Seine, from Normandy to Flanders, in Picardy, Champagne, and the Ile de France. It is not our intention to summarize the theses, which strongly oppose one another, related to the origin of these tales that constitute the treasure of popular wisdom: do they come from Aryan solar myths, as Jacob Grimm and Max Müller argued? Should one explain them according to sociological methods, seeing in them the slowly evolved myths of wild tribes? Or do they find their origins in the Orient and in Buddhism, as Gaston Paris claimed, only to be contested by Joseph Bédier? We haven't the time here to address or even to discuss simply this obscure and delicate problem. The *fabliaux* themselves constitute a genre that is quintessentially French" (Jourda, *Conteurs,* xiii–xiv, my translation).
10. The conviction that the *exemplum* was a genre that originated in the Orient was echoed by Dubuis: "The subjects [of the *exempla*] may be borrowed either from the real life that is known and lived by the author's contemporaries, or from fashionable collections of tales, among which one most often finds the oriental tales of the *Romance of the Seven Sages,* or the Arabian tales of the *Disciplina Clericalis.*" Roger Dubuis, "La Genèse de la nouvelle en France au Moyen Age." *Cahiers de l'Association Internationale des Etudes Françaises* 18 (1966): 13–14, my translation. On the French translations of the *Disciplina Clericalis,* see Jourda, *Conteurs,* xii: "Petrus Alfonsi composed his *Disciplina Clericalis* in Latin in Spain toward the end of the 12th century. The text was translated into French twice, using different titles: *La Discipline de Clergie* [The discipline of the clergy] and *Le Castoiement d'un père à son fils* [The warnings (or punishment) of a father to his son]."
11. The problem of tracing the *nouvelle*'s origins is further complicated by the difficulty of defining its supposed sources, such as the *exemplum,* which has become an issue in recent scholarship devoted to the subject. "Frequently invoked in studies of medieval and particularly of Renaissance literary texts, *exemplum* seems to be used with progressively greater assurance of generic consistency as the user of the term describes a period further from Latin and Neo-Latin literature. *Exemplum* in this dominant vernacular usage denotes a 'short narrative used to illustrate a moral point.' In this sense the word is often said to denote a literary genre or 'subgenre,' recognizable to all readers of medieval and Renaissance texts. Recently, however, one scholar [Robert Cotrell] has broken with this critical consensus to indicate, albeit tentatively, that *exemplum* (in the sense of narrative example) is not a genre but a 'device.'" John Lyons, *Exemplum: The Rhetoric of Example in Early Modern France and Italy* (Princeton: Princeton University Press, 1989), 9. See Lyons's

note 16 to his introduction, which appears on pp. 243–45 and which discusses the problems of defining *exemplum*.
12. Gaston Paris, "La Nouvelle française au XVe et XVIe siècles," in *Mélanges de littérature française du moyen âge*, ed. Mario Roques (Paris: Champion, 1912), 644, my translation.
13. For the text of this *fabliau*, see Raymond Eichmann and John Duval, eds. and trans., *The French Fabliau, B. N. MS. 837*, 2 vols. (New York: Garland Publishing, 1985), 1:28–43.
14. "Let's examine the ways in which diverse genres prepare the way for the *nouvelle*.... The most interesting genres for our purposes coexist and almost all of them flourish between the middle of the 12th century and the end of the 13th century, whether we are speaking of the *exemplum*, the *fabliau*, the *lai*, or the tales themselves." Dubuis, "La Genèse," 12–13, my translation.
15. Auerbach, *Mimesis*, 261.
16. Eichmann and Duval, *The French Fabliau*, 2:44–47.
17. Auerbach, *Mimesis*, 212.
18. It should be noted that many of Boccaccio's tales use an iconographic code that is far from realistic, as in the tragic tales of the *Decameron*'s fourth day. The images of Ghismunda repeatedly kissing the disembodied heart of her lover in tale 41, or of Lisabetta showering the head of her lover (whom she has decapitated herself) with tears in tale 45, are written in the code of the "sacred body dismembered" (which for example gave rise to Catholic images of the disembodied sacred heart of Christ) rather than in the code of realism.
19. Auerbach, *Mimesis*, 213.
20. Karl Vossler, "Zu den anfängen der französischen Novelle," *Studien zur vergleichenden Literaturgeschichte* 2 (1902): 7–8, my translation.
21. Janet Ferrier, *Forerunners of the French Novel: An Essay on the Development of the Novella in the Late Middle Ages* (Manchester: Manchester University Press, 1954), 1–2.
22. In general, the movement away from a concern with sources and historical origins toward more formal analyses was fueled by work in folklore, which included Propp's seminal study of the Russian fairy tale as well as the tale typologies of Aarne and Thompson. A folklorist working during the height of structuralism characterized the history of this movement as follows: "Our precursors elaborated large theoretical structures about the origin and the diffusion of folk tales, deriving them from Indo-European myths, or tying them to a presumed astral mythology by examining the motifs on which popular fantasy had constructed them. Later on, they opposed other no less grandiose constructions to these, based upon the Indian origin of the tales and their diffusion by the expansion of this cultural source material throughout the world. They also tried to explain the appearance of genre by polygenesis, due to similar psychological reactions on the part of men [living in different places] who found themselves at the same stage of social development, or by dream origins, or by ethno-psychological considerations.... In contrast to these grandiose constructions (a kind of enthusiasm for anthropological or archaeological discoveries had succeeded the excesses of Romanticism), positivist research, which was closely tied to concrete facts and to texts, attempted a first systemization and a typology of the tales, and, by means of comparative studies, the determination of archetypes or at least of ecotypes. This first systemization, which we

owe to the Finnish school, and which was developed by Nordic folklorists and lately by Professor Stith Thompson, has given rise to a taxonomy of stories which is an important stage in the scientific study of narrative." Mihai Pop, "La Poétique du conte populaire," *Semiotica* 2(2) (1970): 117–18, my translation.

23. Ferrier, *Forerunners,* 4.
24. See Tzvetan Todorov, *Grammaire du Décaméron* (The Hague: Mouton, 1969). Todorov makes verbs or narrative propositions that "modify the situation" (or, in his terms, "propositions of type A") one of the foundations of his narrative theory.
25. Ferrier, *Forerunners,* 10.
26. See Lionello Sozzi, "La Nouvelle française au XVe siècle," *Cahiers de l'Association Internationale des Etudes Françaises* 23 (1971). Sozzi tries to establish a critical distance between the *nouvelle* and other medieval genres based on the notion of irony. According to his subtle argument, the *nouvelles* represent a step backward from their Italian models, such as the *Facetiae* of Poggio, because they concentrate more on crass scatological humor than do their predecessors. Nevertheless, Sozzi claims that the consistent irony of the narrator of the *Cent nouvelles nouvelles*, for example, is part of a movement that would culminate in the social satire of the humanists: "In relation to a tradition of this type, the *Cent nouvelles nouvelles* demonstrate an important change of attitude. Far from being 'primarily intended to make the reader laugh, in the best tradition of the Gallic spirit,' these tales try above all to express a disenchanted and lucid attitude when faced with the real, beyond any form of abstract mythification, and beyond any reverential fear vis-à-vis values that [the author of the work] took pleasure in degrading and deteriorating. Critics have already highlighted this bourgeois, anti-courtly, demythifying spirit, which confers a quite typical atmosphere upon the collection. As for myself, I would underline the correspondence of this new taste for anti-sublime prose with the spirit that animated the *facetiae* of the humanists" (80, my translation).
27. "In this regard, one has spoken a great deal about realism.... As far as I know, only Miss Janet Ferrier has disputed the presence of a genuine realist tendency in the *nouvelle* of the 15th century" (ibid., 74).
28. "'Formal analysis' in Wölffin's sense is largely an analysis of motifs and combinations of motifs (compositions); for a formal analysis in the strict sense of the word would even have to avoid such expressions as 'man', 'horse', or 'column', let alone such evaluations as 'the ugly triangle between the legs of Michelangelo's David.'" Panofsky, *Meaning in the Visual Arts,* 30.
29. According to Jourda, psychological observation constitutes one of the "truths" of the *Heptaméron*: "One could almost write that Marguerite is a classical author who is unaware of her own procedures: the truth of the text that she wants to compose is not only, to her eyes, in the exactitude of the events that she reports; it is also to be found in psychological observation." Jourda, *Marguerite d'Angoulême,* 823, my translation.
30. Rouse remarks, with respect to medieval wall paintings in village churches: "The village congregation needed help. So a complete code of signs, attitudes, attributes and gestures was introduced, simply for ease of recognition.... Apostles, saints and martyrs carry objects or emblems, usually associated with their martyrdom or some prominent episode in their lives, purely for recognition purposes and as a reminder of their lives and deaths. Another convention decreed that the soul should

always be represented by a small naked figure, rank or status being indicated (somewhat incongruously) by the wearing of crowns, mitres or tonsure." E. Clive Rouse, *Medieval Wall Paintings* (Buckinghamshire: Shire Press Ltd., 1991), 16–17.

31. Pavel has taken issue with the notion that proper names in fiction are constituted by clusters of attributes taken to exist in its "possible world": "According to a widespread account, proper names are abbreviations of sets or clusters of definite descriptions. Criticizing [this] 'abbreviation' theory of proper names, Kripke showed that these do not denote sets of properties but are rigid designators attached to individuals. A name imposed on a being refers to him even if the properties of this being are unknown, variable, or different from what one believes they are. 'Shakespeare' is not the name of 'whoever wrote *Hamlet* and *Othello*,' since if one day irrefutable evidence is brought to light according to which these plays were written by, say, Francis Bacon, this discovery would not entail that Bacon *was* Shakespeare or that Shakespeare ceases to have been Shakespeare. Consequently, 'Bacon' and 'Shakespeare,' and any other proper name, are linguistic labels pegged to individuals, independently of the properties displayed by these individuals." Thomas Pavel, *Fictional Worlds* (Cambridge: Harvard University Press, 1986), 32–33. In the *nouvelle*, however, since the proper names of the characters are most often suppressed by the narrator, presumably because of the scandalous nature of most of these anecdotes, the names "knight," "merchant," "miller," and so on do indeed function as abbreviations for sets of attributes or descriptions.

32. *The One Hundred New Tales (Les Cent nouvelles nouvelles)*, trans. Judith Bruskin DIner (New York: Garland Publishing, 1990), 331.

33. Honoré de Balzac, *Eugénie Grandet* (Paris: Garnier Frères, 1965), 19, my translation.

34. "[In tale 41 of the *Heptaméron*,] the cord linguistically as well as literally represents the priest's attempt to secure the woman in sexual bondage (*corde + lier*). It also evokes metonymically the priest's sexual organs. Finally the cord reminds the reader that the offending confessor is a Franciscan, or Cordelier." McKinley, "Telling Secrets," 148.

35. Vigneulles's version of this tale, number 39 of his *Cent nouvelles nouvelles*, provides a humorous answer to this question. A husband who is impotent in bed with his wife tries to seduce his chambermaid, who reveals the plan to her mistress. When the husband arrives at the maid's bed and tries to make love to his own wife (who has taken the maid's place) without realizing it, he is unable to perform, upon which his wife begins to berate him for his desire to sleep with a young girl when he is unable to perform with his own wife. His reply implies that even the fictional body is involved in the process of recognition and misrecognition crucial to the *nouvelle*'s development: "'My God, woman,' he said, 'my member is smarter than I am, since it recognized you immediately, and that's why it doesn't want to get hard. I, on the other hand, didn't recognize you at all.'" Philippe de Vigneulles, *Les Cent nouvelles nouvelles*, ed. Charles Livingston et al. (Geneva: Droz, 1972), 181–82, my translation. All further references are to this edition, my translations.

36. The kind of fictional identity of which I am speaking here is related to, but quite different from, the "identities" that European noblemen and noblewomen defined for themselves in the emblems, mottos, and symbols that were extraordinarily popular during the Renaissance. According to Daniel Russell, *Emblematic Structures*

in *Renaissance French Culture* (Toronto: University of Toronto Press, 1995), "the emblem was a highly self-conscious enactment of a particular kind of rhetorical image, which lay somewhere between late medieval allegory and the Romantic metaphor as they were understood in the modernist lexicon of rhetoric and poetics" (3). While these "rhetorical images" revealed something essential and *individual* about those who developed emblems and mottos for themselves—Montaigne's "Que sais-je?"—the iconography that I am examining here is far from being self-conscious and concerns the definition of individuals as types who belong to a collective social structure. Thus, although the signifying images and objects that were crucial to the emblem have much in common with the narrative techniques of the *nouvelle*, the earlier genre uses them in a much less individualistic manner. I wish to thank Gary Ferguson for suggesting to me the possible relation between narrative iconography and the emblems of the period.

37. Auerbach, *Mimesis,* 260–61.

## 2: Male Homosocial Domination

1. All citations from *Les Cent nouvelles nouvelles* are given in English from *The One Hundred New Tales (Les Cent nouvelles nouvelles),* trans. Judith Bruskin Diner (New York: Garland Publishing, 1990). At times I modify the translation in order to make it fit the sense of the original more exactly, indicating when I do so in the body of the text. The original source that I consult for my own translations is found in Pierre Jourda, ed., *Conteurs français du XVIe siècle* (Paris: Gallimard, 1965). Bruskin Diner's translation of the first *nouvelle* is missing several pages in the Garland edition; I supplement these by my own translations.
2. In contrast, Dubuis argues that "the homage rendered to the Duke is a classic mixture of flattery and an expression of respect that, by itself, has little interest. We may note, however, that it was at the request of the Duke that the work was completed." Roger Dubuis, *Les Cent nouvelles nouvelles et la tradition de la nouvelle en France au Moyen Age* (Grenoble: Presses Universitaires de Grenoble, 1973), 11, my translation.
3. See Auerbach, *Mimesis,* 242: "The stable class-determined order of life, in which everything has and keeps its place and its form, is reflected in this solemn and circumstantial rhetoric, with its abundance of formulas, its superabundance of conventional gestures and invocations."
4. In two portraits that are preserved from the court of Philippe le Bon, two different scribes are shown on their knees offering books of chronicles to the Duke. Writers in the Burgundian court were minor functionaries, in a context in which practically the entire population was devoted (or enslaved) to the satisfaction of the Duke's personal needs. See Emmanuel Bourassin, *Philippe le Bon : Le Grand lion des Flandres* (Paris: Éditions Tallandier, 1983), chap. 7.
5. Prince defines the contractual relationship that is an intrinsic part of narrative as follows: "Narrative contract. The agreement between the NARRATOR and the NARRATEE, the teller and his or her audience, underlying the very existence of a NARRATIVE and affecting its very shape: an act of narration supplies something which is (to be) exchanged for something else (I will tell you a story if you

promise to be good; I will listen to you if you make it valuable)." Prince, *Dictionary*, 61.

6. "Male homosocial desire" is the term adopted by Sedgwick to describe the "stuff" of male-dominated social structures: "'Homosocial' is a word occasionally used in history and the social sciences, where it describes social bonds between persons of the same sex; it is a neologism, obviously formed by analogy with 'homosexual,' and just as obviously meant to be distinguished from 'homosexual.' In fact, it is applied to such activities as 'male bonding,' which may, as in our society, be characterized by intense homophobia, fear and hatred of homosexuality. To draw the 'homosocial' back into the orbit of 'desire,' of the potentially erotic, then, is to hypothesize the potential unbrokenness of a continuum between homosocial and homosexual—a continuum whose visibility, for men, in our society, is radically disrupted." Eve Kosofsky Sedgwick, *Between Men: English Literature and Male Homosocial Desire* (New York: Columbia University Press, 1985), 1–2. I will argue throughout this chapter that for the imaginary males of the *Cent nouvelles*, there is no continuum uniting homosocial and homosexual behaviors, homosexuality being a non-issue in this text. Sedgwick also quotes Heidi Hartmann's succinct definition of patriarchy, which is crucial to my reading of the *Cent nouvelles nouvelles*: patriarchy consists of "relations between men, which have a material base, and which, though hierarchical, establish or create interdependence and solidarity among men that enable them to dominate women" (3). Similarly, MacKinnon argues that men dominate women by constituting the latter as the objects of male desire, which is inevitably a collective and political affair that concentrates on sexuality: "Sexuality, then, is a form of power. Gender, as socially constructed, embodies it, not the reverse. Women and men are divided by gender, made into the sexes as we know them, by the social requirements of heterosexuality, which institutionalize male sexual dominance and female sexual submission. If this is true, sexuality is the linchpin of gender inequality." Catherine A. MacKinnon, "Feminism, Marxism, Method, and the State: An Agenda for Theory," *Signs* 7(3) (spring 1982): 533.

7. See Pierre Champion, ed., *Les Cent Nouvelles nouvelles* (Geneva: Slatkine Reprints, 1977), 311–12.

8. Philippe had "twelve 'chamber-squires' who dressed their master and saw to the security of his rooms, twelve valets de chambre, as many servants, which one would later call footmen, a furrier, guardians for his jewels and his tapestries, a painter of official seals, other painters, sculptors who had the title of valets de chambre, and twelve torch valets or 'light carriers.' His corps of personal servants was completed by his Body Guards, the masters and valets of his body guards, cloth makers, shoemakers, tailors, haberdashers, hat makers, and other artisans in the employ of the château." Bourassin, *Philippe le Bon*, 112–13, my translation.

9. MacKinnon describes the male fetishization of women as follows: "Like the value of a commodity, women's sexual desirability is fetishized: it is made to appear a quality of the object itself, spontaneous and inherent, independent of the social relation which creates it, uncontrolled by the force that requires it. It helps if the object cooperates: hence, the vaginal orgasm; hence, faked orgasms altogether." MacKinnon, "Feminism, Marxism, Method," 540–41.

10. Cf. #23: "Ung procureur de la cour dudit Mons, assez sur eage et ja ancien, entre aultres ses clercs avoit ung tresbeau filz et *gentil compaignon*, du quel sa femme a chef de piece s'enamoura tres fort" [A procurator of the court of Mons, a rather

aged man, had among his other clerks a very handsome young man who was a merry companion, with whom his wife soon fell in love] (Jourda, *Conteurs,* 97, my translation); #37, the tale of a jealous husband who collects cuckold stories and rigidly controls his wife's movements: "Ung *gentil compaignon,* oyant la renommée de ce gouvernement, vint rencontrer ung jour ceste bonne damoiselle [A merry companion, hearing the renown of this treatment, went one day to meet this young lady] (Jourda, *Conteurs,* 165). Other seducers are referred to simply by using the appropriate adjective, such as the "gentil chevalier" of #9, the "gentil escuier" of #16, or the "gentil conte" of #24. Of course, the most celebrated example of the expression appears after Panurge's notorious description of the walls of Paris, when Pantagruel addresses him as follows: "Vrayement, dist Pantagruel, tu es gentil compaignon; je te veulx habiller de ma livrée" ["Truly," said Pantagruel, "you are a merry companion; I want to dress you in my colors"]. Rabelais, *Oeuvres complètes,* 299; my translation.

11. "Triangular desire" was described in detail by René Girard in *Mensonge romantique et vérité romanesque* (Paris: Éditions Bernard Grasset, 1961): "In order for a vain man to desire an object, one need only convince him that the object is already desired by a third person of a certain prestige. The mediator is here a *rival* that the man's vanity has virtually called into being, so to speak, before demanding that the rival be defeated. . . . The mediator can no longer play the role of model without equally playing, or seeming to play, the role of obstacle as well" (16, my translation).

12. "In this new matrix of history, where man engenders man in his own likeness, women, girls, and sisters serve only to foster the possibility and to define the stakes of relations among men. Their usage and their commerce suppose and support the reign of masculine hom(m)o-sexuality, at the same time that they maintain this sexuality in speculations, in the play of mirrors, in identifications and appropriations that more or less defer the real practice of homosexuality. Reigning everywhere, but forbidden in practice, this hom(m)o-sexuality is played out via women's bodies as material or sign, and heterosexuality until now has been nothing but an alibi for the smooth functioning of the relationship of man to himself, and of relations among men." Luce Irigaray, *Ce Sexe qui n'en est pas un* (Paris: Editions de Minuit, 1977), 168, my translation.

13. See Laura Mulvey, *Visual and Other Pleasures* (Bloomington: Indiana University Press, 1989), especially chap. 3, in which she discusses the "scopophilia" and the "pleasure of looking" that largely constitute male desire.

14. According to Jourda's notes, the *chaudeau* was a "hot broth that it was customary to offer to the young married couple" (Jourda, *Conteurs,* 1317, my translation) or, "the broth that one brought to the newlyweds on the night of their wedding" (1321, my translation). It is clear from the usage of the term in the text, however, that the *chaudeau* was intended as a means of verifying that the marriage had been consummated, without which it could not be considered valid: "And when the husband tried to hug her and kiss her and, beyond that, to do his duty in order to win the *chaudeau,* she [the bride] started turning from side to side in such a way that he couldn't accomplish his task, which made him extremely mad" (Jourda, *Conteurs,* 50, my translation). Tale 29 describes another wedding night: "The poor young bride screamed loudly, which was heard by several people, who thought that she had let out this scream after being deflowered, as is the custom in this kingdom. The gentlemen of the house where the young couple were staying came knocking

on their door, bringing the *chaudeau* with them. They knocked a long time without getting a response" (127, my translation).

15. Cottrell writes of marriage in the *Heptaméron*: "From the pagan point of view, sexuality was (in theory, at least) a desire that led to a *social* act. Marriage was an investment in the future of the social order. By refusing marriage, and more drastically, sexuality, Christians claimed for themselves a 'freedom' that loosened the bonds of community.... The Christian advocacy of virginity implied a new social order that was radically different from the old." Cottrell, "Inmost Cravings," 18.

16. "It is settled that a woman can be married by a man in his absence, either by letter or by messenger, if she is led to his house. But where she is absent, she cannot be married by letter or by messenger because she must be led to her husband's house, not her own, since the former is, as it were, the domicile of the marriage." Theodor Mommsen and Paul Krueger, eds., *The Digest of Justinian,* trans. Alan Watson (Philadelphia: University of Pennsylvania Press, 1985), 657–58.

17. See Hope Glidden, "Gender, Essence, and the Feminine (*Heptameron* 43)," in Lyons and McKinley, *Critical Tales,* 25–40: "Let us recall what Roland Barthes calls the 'maleness of all narrative movement,' that is, the plotting of stories as sequences wherein the protagonist's goal, explicitly acted upon, is to discover the answer to a secret.... [In numerous stories,] a male protagonist eavesdrops, spies, or physically intrudes into the space which his lady occupies. The extreme case of this is *viol*, rape, in which transgression occurs literally on the site of the female body." (29)

18. MacKinnon, "Feminism, Marxism, Method," 531.

19. MacKinnon has stated the sexual overdetermination of women's identities in much more powerful terms: "Each element of the female *gender* stereotype is revealed as, in fact, *sexual*. Vulnerability means the appearance/reality of easy sexual access; passivity means receptivity and disabled resistance, enforced by trained physical weakness; softness means pregnability by something hard. Incompetence seeks help as vulnerability seeks shelter, inviting the embrace that becomes the invasion, trading exclusive access for protection ... from the same access. Domesticity nurtures the consequent progeny, proof of potency, and ideally waits at home dressed in saran wrap." MacKinnon, "Feminism, Marxism, Method," 530.

20. Marguerite de Navarre examines in depth the problem of a female character who resists the sexual aggression of a male character in tale 10 of the *Heptaméron*, which I will discuss in chapter 4.

21. According to Todorov's narrative grammar, narrative propositions of type *a* have a syntactic function which is to "modify the situation" (34) and may be broken down into various subtypes. An agent may modify a situation by disguising it, or by unveiling the disguise that obscures it; by punning, finding a metaphor, or telling a parable or a story; by acting; by soliciting someone's aid; by moving to another place; by paying. See the *Grammaire du Décaméron*, 35–38.

22. Georges Bataille, *La Part maudite, précédé de La Notion de dépense* (Paris: Éditions de Minuit, 1967), 23–46.

23. Cf. the description of the wife that appears in Philippe de Vigneulles's tale 42, which I will examine in the following chapter: "[I] think that because of her hot complexion she must have been born in an oven or half a mile away from the rising sun, and for that reason she went often to the bath houses (*estuves*).... And since she was so hot that the Saille river, which was nearby, couldn't cool her off,

she went to look for men to satisfy her needs all over the place and took on all comers." Vigneulles, *Les Cent nouvelles nouvelles*, 190, my translation.

24. James Brundage describes the mitigating influence of canon law on the older Roman laws concerning adultery that were still in effect in the Middle Ages: "The canonists rejected in principle one of the strongest and most persistent traditions of secular law systems in dealing with adultery, namely, the right of the injured husband to avenge himself by slaying the adulterer and his unfaithful wife. The Roman law had maintained the death penalty for adultery, allowing the wronged husband the license to kill the adulterer, although the right to kill an adulterous wife was by the *Lex Julia de adulteriis* reserved to her father, rather than her husband." Vern L. Bullough and James Brundage, *Sexual Practices and the Medieval Church* (Buffalo: Prometheus Books, 1982), 132.

25. Speaking of a medieval depiction of animals ripping flesh on the Souillac trumeau, Michael Camille writes: "The ripping of animal flesh would have resonated for the monks, evoking not only the bloody meat of animals from which they were meant to abstain, but also the rite at the very center of their lives, which involved eating a body. Fasting was an especially important issue in monastic reforms and was a major structuring principle of religious experience." Brendan Cassidy, ed., *Iconography at the Crossroads* (Princeton: Princeton University Press, 1993), 47. In passing, the *Trésor de la langue française* claims that the term *"brochet"* became a slang expression for *"maquereau"* or "pimp" in the twentieth century due to the voracity of this fish, known in English as a "pike." It could be, then, that the fish signifies illicit sexuality in this scene, much as it does in the popular imaginary of our time, though the validity of this point for the late Middle Ages would have to be demonstrated.

26. "Dupin, *from the place in which he is*, cannot defend himself against the man who interrogates him in this way, and from feeling a rage that is clearly feminine in nature." Jacques Lacan, *Écrits 1* (Paris: Éditions du Seuil, 1966), 51, my translation.

27. Marguerite de Navarre highlights and problematizes this metaphorical usage in tale 10 of the *Heptaméron*. See Marcel Tetel, *Marguerite de Navarre's 'Heptaméron': Themes, Language, and Structure* (Durham: Duke University Press, 1973), 28–31.

28. Cf. tale 35, which describes an older man in bed with his chambermaid: "He turned toward this beautiful girl, and after a great effort, he managed to break a single lance, while she let him do what he was doing without even breathing half a word" (Jourda, *Conteurs,* 161, my translation). Tale 29: "When he became master of the place, he broke only one lance, and then called off the assault and put a stop to his work" (ibid., 127, my translation).

29. See Carla Freccero, "Rape's Disfiguring Figures: Marguerite de Navarre's *Heptaméron*, Day I:10," in *Rape and Representation*, ed. Lynn Higgins and Brenda Silver (New York: Columbia University Press, 1990), 227–47. François Rigolot, "Magdalen's Skull: Allegory and Iconography in *Heptameron* 32," *Renaissance Quarterly* 47(1) (spring 1994): 57–73.

30. See Livingston's comments in Vigneulles, *Les Cent nouvelles nouvelles*, 179: "The most well-known version [of this story] is the 13th *fabliau* of Enguerrant d'Oisy, *Le Meunier d'Arleux* [The Miller of Arleux]. . . . Philippe's tale [number 39] . . . is evidently an amplification of the *facezia* 85 of Poggio" (my translation). Cf. Navarre, *L'Heptaméron*, 8.

31. Cf. tale 62, in a scene that describes the meeting of two lovers: "He entered and found her all alone; she received him very well and offered him a sumptuous feast [*elle luy fist tresbonne chere*], as the table was set. . . . After supper, they romped around together, naked body against naked body" (Jourda, *Conteurs,* 244–45, my translation). Cf. tale 1, which describes a wife and her lover: "In this glorious state they spent most of that sweet and short evening, with kisses given and kisses returned for so long that each one of them desired nothing more than to go to bed. While they were entertaining each other in this way [*tandiz que ceste grande chiere se faisoit*], the good husband returned from his trip" (ibid., 22, my translation).

## 3: Philippe de Vigneulles and the Economy of Expenditure

1. Vigneulles, *Les Cent nouvelles nouvelles,* 177. Further references will be given parenthetically in the text, using my own translations.
2. This is one of the best-known anecdotes of the Late Middle Ages and is found, for example, in the *Facetiae* of Poggio Bracciolini as well as in the *Pantagruel.* See Livingston's comments on page 77 of Vigneulles's text, op cit.
3. "The grotesque body is not separated from the rest of the world. It is not a closed, completed unit; it is unfinished, outgrows itself, transgresses its own limits. The stress is laid on those parts of the body that are open to the outside world, emerge from it, or through which the body itself goes out to meet the world. This means that the emphasis is on the apertures or the convexities, or on various ramifications and offshoots: the open mouth, the genital organs, the breasts, the phallus, the potbelly, the nose. The body discloses its essence as a principle of growth which exceeds its own limits only in copulation, pregnancy, childbirth, the throes of death, eating, drinking, or defecation." Mikhail Bakhtin, *Rabelais and His World*, trans. Hélène Iswolsky (Bloomington: Indiana University Press, 1984), 26.
4. "The rogue, the clown, and the fool create around themselves their own special little world, their own chronotope. . . . These figures carry with them into literature first a vital connection with the theatrical trappings of the public square, with the mask of the public spectacle; they are connected with that highly specific, extremely important area of the square where the common people congregate." Mikhail Bakhtin, *The Dialogic Imagination,* ed. Michael Holquist, trans. Caryl Emerson and Michael Holquist (Austin: University of Texas Press, 1981), 159.
5. "Carnival *n* [It *carnevale,* alter. of earlier *carnelevare,* lit., removal of meat, fr. *carne* flesh (fr. L. *carn-caro*) + *levare* to remove, fr. L, to raise]." Henry Bosley Woolf et al., eds., *Webster's New Collegiate Dictionary* (Springfield: G & C Merriam Company, 1973), 169.
6. "The *motto* has been subject to several types of narrative elaboration. The short *Bel parlare* mentions only those elements that are absolutely necessary to the understanding of the narrative; the *facetia*, which is the erudite and humanist form of the *motto*, takes advantage of Latin's concision in order to sharpen the point of its play on words; finally, the *motto* crowns a narrative that has been diligently oriented by its characters and their actions with its final joke or pun." Hermann Wetzel,

"Éléments socio-historiques d'un genre littéraire : l'histoire de la nouvelle jusqu'à Cervantes," in Sozzi, *La Nouvelle française à la Renaissance*, 60, my translation.

7. Livingston writes: "[This tale] belongs to a branch derived from a well-known traditional theme, which was probably born in the Orient, and which penetrated into Europe via the *Disciplina Clericalis* of the 12th Century." Vigneulles, *Les Cent nouvelles nouvelles*, 246, my translation.

8. "In 1526, he [Marot] made the mistake of eating some fat during Lent. A woman, because of her tenacious jealousy or her gratuitous cruelty, denounced him. He was thrown into the Châtelet jail. This painful adventure gave him the opportunity to write a Confession of Faith full of clever ambiguities." Albert Marie Schmidt, ed., *Poètes français du seizième siècle* (Paris: Gallimard, 1953), 4, my translation.

9. Livingston writes that the motif of a bet in which different stories are compared is also typical of this tale's analogs: "In the main branch [of analogous tales], a bet is made among three people regarding a meal that will be won by the person who has described the most beautiful dream. This theme reappears several times, usually with a moral, in collections of *exempla* and in medieval stories." Vigneulles, *Les Cent nouvelles nouvelles*, 246, my translation. As we have seen, the story of the three *commères* or busybodies followed this same model.

10. Cf. the *Cent nouvelles*, tale 91: "A merry companion told me a funny story about a married man whose wife was so extravagant and so hot in her soup [*chaulde sur potage*], and so public about it that she was barely satisfied until she got humped in the middle of the street [*a paine estoit elle contente qu'on la cuignast en plaines rues avant qu'elle ne le fust*]." Jourda, *Conteurs*, 319, my translation. See Natalie Zemon Davis, *Society and Culture in Early Modern France* (Stanford: Stanford University Press, 1975), chap. 1, in which she discusses the stereotypical representations of the female as *cold* and humid.

11. According to the *Digest of Justinian*, "A woman caught in adultery is in the same position as one convicted of a criminal offense. So if she is shown to be guilty of adultery, she will be branded with *infamia* not just because she was caught in adultery but also because she has been convicted of a crime. However, if she was not caught in adultery, but was convicted of it, she will suffer *infamia* because of the conviction. If she has been caught in adultery, but not convicted, would she still suffer *infamia*? I think that even if she were acquitted after being caught, she will still suffer *infamia*, because it is clear that a woman taken in adultery suffers *infamia* automatically by statute, no judgement being required. We are not told here, as in the *lex Julia* on adultery, who must catch her or where it must be done; so it seems she will suffer *infamia* whether it is her husband or someone else who catches her. Even if she is not caught in her husband's house or her father's, she will suffer *infamia* according to the terms of the statute." Mommsen and Krueger, *The Digest of Justinian*, 662–63.

12. "Hast thou committed adultery with the wife or the betrothed of another, or defiled a virgin, whether a nun dedicated to God or an unattached woman, that is, one without a husband, or thine own maidservant? If thou hast had intercourse with another's wife or with a nun, thous shalt do penance for seven years; if with a virgin, two years; if with a widow, one year. If thou has put away thy wife and attached thyself to another, thou shalt do penance for seven years; if it is with an unattached woman, three forty-day periods and the appointed fasts; if with thine own maidservant, thou shall do penance for forty days." John T. McNeill and Helena M. Gamer, eds. and trans., *Medieval Handbooks of Penance: A Translation*

*of the Principal Libri Poenitentiales and Selections from Related Documents* (New York: Columbia University Press, 1938), 317–18.

## 4: Feminist Ambivalence and Feminine Virtue in the *Heptaméron*

1. The philosopher of the *Disciplina Clericalis*, for example, describes this male paranoia of female desire in the following manner: "I am afraid if naïve people read my story about the wiles and tricks of women, a story I have written to admonish them and instruct you and others, where you can read how these women have without the knowledge of their husbands called their lovers to them and embraced them and kissed them and fulfilled all their lusts with them, I repeat, I am afraid, if all this be so, that they will naïvely believe that I too am as immoral as those women." Petrus Alfonsi, *The* Disciplina Clericalis *of Petrus Alfonsi*, ed. and trans. Eberhard Hermes (Berkeley: University of California Press, 1970), 119.
2. The *Digest of Justinian* defined marriage in the following manner, which limited the role of the woman to the domicile of her marriage, that is, her husband's home, as we have already seen in the preceding chapter: "Marriage is the union of a man and a woman, a partnership for life involving divine as well as human law. . . . Marriage cannot take place unless everyone involved consents, that is, those who are being united and those in whose power they are. . . . It is settled that a woman can be married by a man in his absence, either by letter or by messenger, if she is led to his house. But where she is absent, she cannot be married by letter or by messenger because she must be led to her husband's house, not her own, since the former is, as it were, the domicile of the marriage." Mommsen and Krueger, *The Digest of Justinian*, 657–58.
3. "The image of war meaning the confrontation between man and woman, though it appears throughout the *Heptaméron*, is most salient and is sustained at greatest length in the tenth novella. In fact, Marguerite in this tale and others uses the verb *guerroyer* to denote the verbal and psychological combat between the two protagonists. Stripped to its essential nature, the tenth tale amounts to a series of confrontations between Floride and Amadour. . . . In this offensive and defensive climate, a military vocabulary imposes itself and transforms lady and love into mere matter, an object to be captured at all costs." Tetel, *Marguerite de Navarre's Heptaméron*, 29–30.
4. Françoise Charpentier, "A l'épreuve du miroir: Narcissisme, mélancolie et ''honneste amour' dans la XXIVe nouvelle de *L'Heptaméron*," *L'Esprit Créateur* 30(4) (winter 1990): 36, my translation.
5. Woolf, *Webster's*, 1159.
6. Duby writes: "The fear of dividing up the family heritage, and a prolonged reticence concerning the affirmation of the rights of the first-born inversely reinforce the obstacles to marrying off young men and make of the 12th Century, in the North of France, the time of the 'young men', of celibate knights, expelled from their paternal homes, going on binges, and dreaming during the stages of their errant adventures of finding young maidens who, as they say, are seeking them out [*les <<tastonnent>>*]. These men, however, search anxiously, but almost

always in vain, for a social situation that will transform them finally into lords, and for a good heiress of a household that will accept them, or, as one still says today in certain regions of France, they're looking for a place where they may 'become sons-in-law' [*faire gendre*]." Georges Duby, *Mâle moyen âge: De l'amour et autres essais* (Paris: Flammarion, 1988), 24–25, my translation.

7. As Cottrell remarks, language is inevitably erotic in the *Heptaméron*: "If in the *Heptaméron* the word 'plaisir' designates primarily sexual gratification and is sharply distinguished from 'amour', it also designates the gratification that is derived from speech. 'Le plaisir de parler' is often linked with 'le plaisir de faire bonne chere,' one of the text's euphemisms for sexual activity. In the *Heptaméron*, speaking, like eating, is eroticized." Cottrell, "Inmost Cravings," 13.

8. On the conception of a closed symbolic system that predetermines where and how consciousness as a kind of signifier may circulate, see Lacan, *Écrits 1*, 19–75 ("Le séminaire sur 'La Lettre volée'").

9. In this sense, Amadour is like most of the male characters in the text, at least according to Cottrell: "Nearly all the men in the *Heptaméron* are driven by 'la fureur de la concupiscence' (189; 269), by a peculiarly masculine 'malice' that compels them to satisfy their desire in a paroxysm of what the text calls 'jouissance' (140; 217) on the conquered and humiliated, often raped and wounded, female body." Cottrell, "Inmost Cravings," 10.

10. Carla Freccero, "Rape's Disfiguring Figures," 240–41.

11. Lawrence Kritzman, *The Rhetoric of Sexuality and the Literature of the French Renaissance* (Cambridge: Cambridge University Press, 1991), 52.

12. Moreover, Floride's disfigurement is also a sign of the *sacred*: "In the devotional and representational practices of the fifteenth and sixteenth centuries, the female body was not legible first of all as mimesis but as *sign*. To read images of the 'mortified' female body mimetically only, that is, to see in them nothing more than reflections of reified female bodies exploited by males in a patriarchal society, is to bracket out the function of desire, physicality, and *mortification* in the economy of salvation." Cottrell, "Inmost Cravings," 11. Cf. Rigolot, "Magdalen's Skull," for a discussion of the ways in which the female protagonist of tale 32 functions as an embodiment of the traditional icon of the penitent sinner, that of Saint Mary Magdalen.

13. One of the best examples of this phenomenon is the ruse by which Amadour obtains his final meeting with Floride. "Since [Amadour's] credit stood high with the governor, he was able to get himself appointed to a mission to the King for the purpose of discussing some secret campaign directed against the town of Leucate. He also managed to get himself issued with orders to inform the Countess of Aranda of the plan, and to take her advice before meeting the King. Knowing that Floride was there, he went post-haste into Aranda" (146). Entrusted with secrets that he must communicate to the King, Amadour knows that it will seem normal if he asks the council of the leading female authority figure.

14. Patricia Francis Cholakian, *Rape and Writing in the* Heptameron *of Marguerite de Navarre* (Carbondale: Southern Illinois University Press, 1991), 17.

15. Ibid., 99.

16. Ibid., 95.

17. For Charpentier, this union with God is the logical outcome of the *Heptaméron*'s code of honest love: "The apparent contents of this *nouvelle* [24] express the

simple but elevated law of 'honest love', which is, ideally, an apprenticeship, or a transitory stage toward the perfect love that is found only in a relationship with God. . . . The logic of this kind of doctrine leads lovers to transcend their human love at some point in order to elevate themselves toward divine love, or at least to renounce their human love in the name of 'virtue'. This scenario is made possible only by means of extreme abstention from human love and an asceticism that allows the lovers merely to contemplate each other's beauty, and to engage in beautiful conversations (sight and hearing being the only senses permitted): this is the scenario of numerous novellas in the *Heptaméron*." Charpentier, "A l'épreuve du miroir," 23–24, my translation.

18. Donald Stone, "'La Malice des hommes': 'L'Histoire des satyres' and the *Heptaméron*," in Lyons and McKinley, *Critical Tales*, 58–59.

19. Cottrell writes: "Around 1200, women mystics began to articulate with increasing frequency their experience of Christ in the register of erotic desire and sexual fulfillment. They stressed their joy at feeling their body pressed against Christ's body, their ecstasy at pressing their lips against his wound, often figured as a mouth that uttered ineffably beautiful sounds." Cottrell, "Inmost Cravings," 13.

20. While this marriage may not be to the liking of the King and Queen in the text, de Reyff notes that it was legal from an ecclesiastical perspective: "Canon law admitted the validity of a marriage contracted *de praesenti* by the two partners without the authorization of their parents. In some cases, the presence of the priest was not considered indispensable. This theory, which generated innumerable abuses, was opposed by Erasmus, Rabelais, Calvin, and others, before giving rise to several juridical ordinances under Henry II that supported civil law." Marguerite de Navarre, *L'Heptaméron*, ed. and trans. Simone de Reyff (Paris: Flammarion, 1982) 508 n. 2, my translation. See Émile Telle, *L'Oeuvre de Marguerite d'Angoulême, Reine de Navarre, et la querelle des femmes* (Toulouse: Imprimerie Toulousaine Lion et Fils, 1937), chap. 1, for a discussion of marriage during the Reformation, and the relationship of this debate to Marguerite de Navarre's text.

21. "The history of this 'microphysics' of punitive power would thus be a genealogy, or part of a genealogy, of the modern 'soul'. Instead of seeing in this soul the reactivated remains of ideology, one would recognize in it the contemporary correlative of a certain technology of power exercised upon the body. One should not say that the soul is an illusion, or an ideological effect. On the contrary, one should say that it exists, that it has a reality, that it is produced continuously around the body, on its surface, and inside it by the functioning of a power exercised upon those who are punished—and, in a more general manner upon those who are subject to surveillance, who are disciplined and corrected, such as mentally ill people, children, students, the colonized, and all those who are attached to an apparatus of production and controlled by it throughout the course of their existence." Michel Foucault, *Surveiller et punir: naissance de la prison* (Paris: Gallimard, 1975), 38, my translation.

22. Ibid., 60, my translation.

23. Lyons, *Exemplum*, 93.

24. Ibid., 94.

25. In Le Hir's edition of this scene, it is the *Queen's* confessor who deciphers the letter: "The confessor of the Queen was sent for, and after assembling all the pieces of the letter, he read it, revealing the truth of the marriage, which had been

hidden for so long." Marguerite de Navarre, *Marguerite de Navarre: Nouvelles,* ed. Yves Le Hir (Paris: PUF, 1967), 146, my translation. In contrast, Lyons's reading is apparently based on the François edition.

26. Lyons identifies the symbolic interaction of the castle and the other terms of the patriarchal order: "The castle is a concrete form of the institution of the *maison* or family. Rolandine's marrying a bastard without her father's consent was a threat to his *maison*, and the castle is that form of a *maison* that can prevent further injury to its name." Lyons, *Exemplum,* 97

27. Géburon's judgment of Jambique in the frame is another matter: "So, Ladies, you see how this woman, who placed her worldly reputation higher than her conscience, lost both. For the story I've told today has revealed to everyone what she tried to keep from the eyes of her lover. She wanted to avoid being laughed at by one person, and now she is laughed at by everybody" (396).

28. Glidden, "Gender, Essence, and the Feminine," 33.

29. On the visual nature of masculine desire, see Mulvey, *Visual and Other Pleasures.*

30. See, for example, the description of the motives for the bastard's desire: "The bastard of high birth was no less afflicted by the assaults of Love, but he had already resolved in his heart to love Rolandine and to endeavour to marry her. He considered too *the honour that would redound to him if he could but win her,* and concluded that he must find a way of declaring his desire to her, and above all of winning over the gouvernante" (238, emphasis added).

31. Amadour says to Floride during the first attempted rape scene: "Before you were married I was able to overcome the desires of my heart so successfully that you knew nothing at all of my feelings. But now you are a married woman. You have a cover (*couverture*) and your honour is safe. So what wrong can I possibly be doing you in asking for what is truly mine?" (141).

32. Similarly, Hope Glidden argues: "Jambicque wears a mask to hide her identity, but the mask also frees the subject to become a locus of sexual desire. To desire is to turn herself into an active agent in defiance of all courtly ritual." "Gender, Essence, and the Feminine," 35.

33. "A return to the character of Jambicque defined not as a hypocrite, but as a resistant subject, permits other elements of the story to surface, and in particular, Jambicque's determination to escape the stigma of sexuality defined as dishonorable in a courtly setting, that is, to keep her secret. Here, the feminine resistance to male knowing reasserts itself" (ibid., 32).

# Bibliography

Alfonsi, Petrus. *Disciplina Clericalis*. Edited and translated by Angel Gonzalez Palencia. Madrid-Granada: Consejo superior de investigaciones científicas, 1948.
———. *The* Disciplina Clericalis *of Petrus Alfonsi*. Edited and translated by Eberhard Hermes. Berkeley: University of California Press, 1970.
Auerbach, Erich. *Mimesis: The Representation of Reality in Western Literature*. Translated by Willard Trask. Garden City: Doubleday Anchor Books, 1957.
———. *Zur Technik der Frührenaissancenovelle in Italien und Frankreich*. Inaugural dissertation. Heidelberg: Winters Universitätsbuchhandlung, 1921.
Aulotte, Robert. "Note sur la quarante-deuxième nouvelle de L'<<Heptaméron>>." In Sozzi, *La Nouvelle française à la Renaissance*, 355–59.
Bataille, Georges. *La Part maudite, précédé de La Notion de dépense*. Paris: Minuit, 1967.
Bakhtin, Mikhail. *The Dialogic Imagination*. Edited by Michael Holquist. Translated by Caryl Emerson and Michael Holquist. Austin: University of Texas Press, 1981.
———. *Rabelais and His World*. Translated by Hélène Iswolsky. Bloomington: Indiana University Press, 1984.
Balzac, Honoré de. *Eugénie Grandet*. Paris: Garnier Frères, 1965.
Barthes, Roland. *S/Z*. Paris: Éditions du Seuil, 1970.
Battaglia, Salvatore. *Contributu alla storia della novellistica*. Napoli: R. Pirouti, 1947.
Baxter, Harry. "Author's Point of View in *Les Cent Nouvelles Nouvelles*, *Le Petit Jehan de Saintré*, and *Les Quinze Joyes de Mariage*." Ph.D. dissertation, University of Michigan, 1970.
Bédier, Joseph. *Les Fabliaux. Etudes de littérature populaire et d'histoire littéraire du Moyen Age*. 6th ed. Paris: Champion, 1969.
Beneke, August. *Das Repertoir und die Quellen der französischen Farce*. Weimar: Roltsch, 1910.
Beyer, Jürgen. *Schwank und Moral. Untersuchungen zum altfranzösischen Fabliau und verwandten Formen*. Studia Romanica, 16. Heidelberg: Winter Universitätsverlag, 1969.
Bourassin, Emmanuel. *Philippe le Bon: Le grand lion des Flandres*. Paris: Éditions Tallandier, 1983.
Bowen, Barbara C. [née Cannings]. *Les caractéristiques essentielles de la farce française et leur survivance dans les années 1550–1620*. Illinois Studies in Language and Literature, 53. Urbana: University of Illinois Press, 1964.
———. "Towards a Definition of Farce as a Literary 'Genre.'" *Modern Language Review* 56 (1961): 558–62.

Bremond, Claude. "Morphology of the French Folktale." *Semiotica* 2 (1970): 247–76.
Bullough, Vern L., and James Brundage. *Sexual Practices and the Medieval Church.* Buffalo: Prometheus Books, 1982.
Cassidy, Brendan, ed. *Iconography at the Crossroads.* Princeton: Princeton University Press, 1993.
Chambers, Ross. *Story and Situation: Narrative Seduction and the Power of Fiction.* Minneapolis: University of Minnesota Press, 1984.
Champion, Pierre, ed. *Les Cent Nouvelles nouvelles.* Geneva: Slatkine Reprints, 1977. Originally published Paris, 1928.
Charpentier, Françoise. "A l'épreuve du miroir: Narcissisme, mélancolie et 'honneste amour' dans la XXIVe nouvelle de *L'Heptaméron.*" *L'Esprit Créateur* 30(4) (winter 1990): 23–37.
Cholakian, Patricia Francis. *Rape and Writing in the* Heptameron *of Marguerite de Navarre.* Carbondale: Southern Illinois University Press, 1991.
Cholakian, Patricia Francis, and Rouben C. Cholakian. *The Early French Novella.* Albany: SUNY Press, 1972.
Clements, Robert J., and Joseph Gibaldi. *Anatomy of the Novella: The European Tale Collection from Boccaccio and Chaucer to Cervantes.* New York: NYU Press, 1977.
Cohen, Gustave. *Recueil de farces françaises inédites du XVe siècle.* Cambridge, Mass: Mediaeval Academy of America, 1949.
Cottrell, Robert. "Inmost Cravings: The Logic of Desire in the *Heptameron.*" In Lyons and McKinley, *Critical Tales,* 3–24.
Davis, Natalie Zemon. *Fiction in the Archives: Pardon Tales and Their Tellers in Sixteenth-Century France.* Stanford: Stanford University Press, 1987.
———. *Society and Culture in Early Modern France.* Stanford: Stanford University Press, 1975.
DeJongh, William F. J. *A Bibliography of the Novel and Short Story in French from the Beginning of Printing till 1600.* Albuquerque: University of New Mexico Press, 1944.
Deloffre, Frédéric. *La nouvelle en France à l'âge classique.* Paris: Marcel Didier, 1967.
Des Périers, Bonaventure. *Nouvelles récréations et joyeux devis.* in Jourda, *Conteurs français.*
Diner, Judith Bruskin, trans. *The One Hundred New Tales (Les Cent nouvelles nouvelles).* New York: Garland Publishing, 1990.
Dorner, Marie. "Philippe de Vigneulles, un chroniqueur messin des XVe et XVIe siècles." *Mémoires de l'Académie de Metz* 95 (1913–14): 45–110.
Dubuis, Roger. *Les Cent nouvelles nouvelles et la tradition de la nouvelle en France au Moyen Age.* Grenoble: Presses Universitaires de Grenoble, 1973.
———. "La genèse de la nouvelle en France au Moyen Age." *Cahiers de l'Association Internationale des Etudes Françaises* 18 (1966): 9–19.
Duby, Georges. *Mâle moyen âge: De l'amour et autres essais.* Paris: Flammarion, 1988.
Eichmann, Raymond, and John Duval, eds. and trans. *The French Fabliau, B. N. MS. 837.* 2 vols. New York: Garland Publishing, 1985.
Ferrier, Janet. *Forerunners of the French Novel: An Essay on the Development of the Novella in the Late Middle Ages.* Manchester: Manchester University Press, 1954.
Flake, Otto. *Der französische Roman und die Novelle. Ihre Geschichte von den Anfängen bis zur Gegenwart.* Leipzig: Teubner, 1912.
Foucault, Michel. *Histoire de la sexualité, I: La volonté de savoir.* Paris: Éditions Gallimard, 1976.
———. *Power/Knowledge.* Edited by Colin Gordon. Translated by Colin Gordon et al. New York: Pantheon Books, 1980.

———. *Surveiller et punir: naissance de la prison.* Paris: Éditions Gallimard, 1975.
Freccero, Carla. "Rape's Disfiguring Figures: Marguerite de Navarre's *Heptaméron*, Day 1:10." In *Rape and Representation*, edited by Lynn Higgins and Brenda Silver, 227–47. New York: Columbia University Press, 1990.
———. "Rewriting the Rhetoric of Desire in the *Heptaméron*." In *Contending Kingdoms: Historical, Psychological, and Feminist Approaches to the Literature of Sixteenth and Seventeenth Century England and France*, edited by Marie Rose Logan and Peter Rudnytsky, 454–73. Detroit: Wayne State University Press, 1991.
Gillespie, Gerald. "Novella, Nouvelle, Novella, Short Novel? A Review of Terms." *Neophilologus* 51 (1967): 117–27 and 225–30.
Girard, René. *Mensonge romantique et vérité romanesque.* Paris: Éditions Bernard Grasset, 1961.
Glidden, Hope. "Gender, Essence, and the Feminine (*Heptameron* 43)." in Lyons and McKinley, *Critical Tales*, 25–40.
Hendricks, William O. "Linguistic Models and the Study of Narration: A Critique of Todorov's *Grammaire du Décaméron*." *Semiotica* 5 (1972): 263–89.
Hernnstein-Smith, Barbara. "Narrative Versions, Narrative Theories." In *On Narrative*, edited by W. J. T. Mitchell. Chicago: University of Chicago Press, 1981.
Hoepffner, Ernest. *Aux origines de la nouvelle française.* The Taylorian Lecture, 1938. Reprint, Oxford: Clarendon Press, 1939.
Irigaray, Luce. *Ce Sexe qui n'en est pas un.* Paris: Editions de Minuit, 1977.
Jefferls, Ronald R. "The 'Conte' as a Genre in Renaissance France." *Revue de l'université d'Ottawa* 26 (1956): 435–50.
Jourda, Pierre. *Marguerite d'Angoulême, Duchesse d'Alençon, Reine de Navarre (1492–1549). Étude biographique et littéraire.* Paris: Champion, 1930.
———, ed. *Conteurs français du XVIe siècle.* Paris: Gallimard, 1965.
Kasprzyk, Krystyna. "Les Thèmes folkloriques dans la nouvelle française de la Renaissance." *Cahiers de l'Association Internationale des Etudes Françaises* 18 (1966): 21–30.
Kritzman, Lawrence D. *The Rhetoric of Sexuality and the Literature of the French Renaissance.* Cambridge: Cambridge University Press, 1991.
Küchler, Walther. "Die Cent Nouvelles nouvelles. Ein Beitrag zur Geschichte der französischen Novelle." *Zeitschrift für französische Sprache und Literatur* 30 (1906): 264–331; 31 (1907): 39–101.
Lacan, Jacques. *Écrits 1.* Paris: Éditions du Seuil, 1966.
Lajarte, Philippe de. "Modes du discours et formes d'altérité dans les 'nouvelles' de Marguerite de Navarre." *Littérature* 55 (1984): 64–73.
———. "Des *Nouvelles* de Marguerite de Navarre à *La Princesse de Clèves*: Notes sur quelques transformations de l'écriture narrative de la renaissance à l'âge classique." *Nouvelle revue du seizième siècle* 6 (1988): 45–56.
———. "The Voice of the Narrators in Marguerite de Navarre's Tales." In Lyons and McKinley, *Critical Tales*, 172–87.
Langlois, Ernest, ed. *Nouvelles françaises inédites du quinzième siècle.* Paris: Champion, 1908.
"La Nouvelle en France jusqu'au XVIIIe siècle." XVIIe Congrès de l'Association. *Cahiers de l'Association Internationale des Etudes Françaises* 18 (1966).
Larsen, Anne Rickie. "Traditional Elements in the Tales of Philippe de Vigneulles and Nicolas de Troyes." Ph.D. dissertation, Columbia University, 1975.
Lévi-Strauss, Claude. *The Elementary Structures of Kinship.* Translated by James Harle Bell et al. Boston: Beacon Press, 1969.

Livingston, Charles H. "Les Cent Nouvelles nouvelles de Philippe de Vigneulles, Chaussetier messin." *Revue du Seizième Siècle* 10 (1923): 159–203.

———. "The *Heptaméron des Nouvelles* of Marguerite de Navarre: A Study of Nouvelles 28, 34, 52, and 62." *Romanic Review* 14 (1923): 97–118.

———, ed. *Philippe de Vigneulles: Les Cent Nouvelles nouvelles*. Geneva: Droz, 1972.

Lorian, Alexandre. "Deux Cents Nouvelles Nouvelles." *The Hebrew University Studies in Literature* 2 (1974): 151–70.

Lukács, Gyorgy. *Studies in European Realism*. Translated by Edith Bone. London: Hillway Publishing Co., 1958.

Lyons, John D. *Exemplum: The Rhetoric of Example in Early Modern France and Italy*. Princeton: Princeton University Press, 1989.

———. "The *Heptaméron* and the Foundation of Critical Narrative." *Yale French Studies* 70 (1986): 150–63.

———, and Mary B. McKinley, eds. *Critical Tales: New Studies of the* Heptameron *and Early Modern Culture*. Philadelphia: University of Pennsylvania Press, 1993.

MacKinnon, Catherine A. "Feminism, Marxism, Method, and the State: An Agenda for Theory." *Signs* 7(3) (spring 1982): 515–44.

Mathieu-Castellani, Giselle. *La conversation conteuse: Les Nouvelles de Marguerite de Navarre*. Paris: Presses Universitaires de France, 1992.

McKinley, Mary B. "Telling Secrets: Sacramental Confession and Narrative Authority in the *Heptameron*." In Lyons and McKinley, *Critical Tales*, 146–71.

McNeill, John T., and Helena M. Gamer, eds. and trans. *Medieval Handbooks of Penance: A Translation of the Principal Libri Poenitentiales and Selections from Related Documents*. New York: Columbia University Press, 1938.

Mommsen, Theodor, and Paul Krueger, eds. *The Digest of Justinian*. Translated by Alan Watson. Philadelphia: University of Pennsylvania Press, 1985.

Mulvey, Laura. *Visual and Other Pleasures*. Bloomington: Indiana University Press, 1989.

Mustacchi, Marianne Mares. "Levels of Realism in the *Cent Nouvelles nouvelles*." Ph.D. dissertation, Pennsylvania State University, 1969.

Navarre, Marguerite de. *L'Heptaméron*. Edited and translated by Simone de Reyff. Paris: Flammarion, 1982.

———. *The Heptameron*. Translated by Paul A. Chilton. London: Penguin, 1984.

———. *L'Heptaméron*. Edited by M. François. Paris: Bordas, 1991.

———. *Marguerite de Navarre: Nouvelles*. Edited by Yves Le Hir. Paris: PUF, 1967.

Neuschäfer, Hans-Jörg. *Boccaccio und der Beginn der Novelle. Strukturen der Kurzerzählung auf der Schwelle zwischen Mittelalter und Neuzeit*. Theorie und Geschichte der Literatur und der schönen Künste, 8. Munich: W. Fink, 1969.

Nietzsche, Friedrich. *The Birth of Tragedy and the Genealogy of Morals*. Translated by Francis Golffing. Garden City: Doubleday, 1956.

Ouspensky, Leonid, and Vladimir Lossky. *The Meaning of Icons*. Translated by G. E. H. Palmer and E. Kadloubovsky. Boston: Boston Book and Art Shop, 1969.

Ousterhout, Robert, and Leslie Brubaker. *The Sacred Image East and West*. Urbana: University of Illinois Press, 1995.

Panofsky, Erwin. *Meaning in the Visual Arts*. Garden City: Doubleday, 1955.

Paris, Gaston. "Les contes orientaux dans la littérature française du moyen âge." In *La Poésie du Moyen Age*, 2e série, 75–108. Paris: Hachette, 1895.

———. "La nouvelle française au XVe et XVIe siècles." In *Mélanges de littérature française du moyen âge*, edited by Mario Roques, 627–67. Paris: Champion, 1912. Originally published in the *Journal des Savants* 80 (1895): 298–303, 342–61.

Weber, Henri. "La facétie et le bon mot du Pogge à Des Périers." In *Humanism in France at the End of the Middle Ages and in the Early Renaissance*, edited by A. H. T. Levi, 82–105. New York: Barnes and Noble, 1970.

Welter, J.-Th. *L'exemplum dans la littérature religieuse et didactique du moyen âge*. Paris: Occitania, 1927.

Wetzel, Hermann H. "Éléments socio-historiques d'un genre littéraire: l'histoire de la nouvelle jusqu'à Cervantes." In Sozzi, *La nouvelle française à la Renaissance*, 41–78.

Wiley, Karen F. "Communication Short-Circuited: Ambiguity and Motivation in the *Heptaméron*." In *Ambiguous Realities: Women in the Middle Ages and Renaissance*, edited by Carole Levin and Jeanie Watson, 133–44. Detroit: Wayne State University Press, 1987.

Woolf, Henry Bosley, et al., eds. *Webster's New Collegiate Dictionary*. Springfield: G & C Merriam Company, 1973.

# Index

adultery, 14, 28, 84, 104, 110; in ecclesiastical laws, 164 n. 12; punishment in civil law, 164 n. 11
Alfonsi, Petrus: *Disciplina Clericalis*, 33, 57, 101, 154 n. 10, 165 n. 1
Auerbach, Erich, 36–40, 146, 151 n. 2, 158 n. 3

Bakhtin, Mikhail, 12, 14, 22, 39, 61, 84, 89, 100, 105, 163 n. 3–4
Balzac, Honoré de: *Eugénie Grandet*, 47
Barthes, Roland, 45
Bataille, Georges, 12, 65–66, 84, 161 n. 22
Bédier, Joseph, 30
Boccaccio, Giovanni, 30, 34, 37, 43; *Decameron*, 34, 37, 155 n. 18
body, grotesque. *See* grotesque body
Bourrassin, Emmanuel, 53, 158 n. 4
Bracciolini, Poggio, 34–35, 74, 91; *Facetiae*, 34
Brubaker, Leslie, 15
Brundage, James, 162 n. 24

Camille, Michael, 162 n. 25
*Canterbury Tales* (Chaucer), 29–30, 47
carnival and the carnivalesque, 22, 78; and dissolution of hierarchies, 67; and expenditure, 95, 109; and lower body, 61; and male homosocial domination, 84–85; in *motto* sequences, 101–5; "world upside-down," 92, 103
castration complex, 79
Champion, Pierre, 53
characters: charlatan, rogue, and trickster characters, 91–107, 111; iconographic representation of, 45–50

Charpentier, Françoise, 117, 165 n. 4, 166 n. 17
Chaucer, Geoffrey, 30, 47; *Canterbury Tales*, 29–30, 47
*chaudeau*, 60, 160 n. 14
*Le Chevalier de la charrette* (Troyes), 137
Cholakian, Patricia Francis, 129, 166 n. 14
chronotope of the rogue, clown, and fool, 91, 100
circulation of the phallus. *See* phallus, circulation of
Cixous, Hélène, 12
collective imaginary. *See* narrative
Cottrell, Robert, 153 n. 2, 161 n. 15, 166 n. 7, 166 n. 9, 166 n. 12, 167 n. 19

*dame à la licorne, La,* 149
*Decameron* (Boccaccio), 34, 37, 155 n. 18
desire. *See* power, desire and
*Digest of Justinian,* 164 n. 11, 165 n. 2
*Disciplina Clericalis* (Alfonsi), 33, 57, 101, 154 n. 10, 165 n. 1
Dubuis, Roger, 35, 41, 51, 154 n. 10, 158 n. 2
Duby, Georges, 165 n. 6

*Eugénie Grandet* (Balzac), 47
*exemplum*, 27, 31–34, 36, 101, 154 n. 10, 154 n. 9, 154 n. 11, 155 n. 14
expenditure: definition of, 65–66; and female characters, 111–12; and hyperbolic exchange, 84; and lower body, 13; and marginalized characters, 93, 97–99; in *motto* sequences, 103, 105–6, 109; in scatological sequences, 89–90. *See also* Bataille, Georges

*fabliau*, 27, 31–36, 39, 74, 155 n.14
*Facetiae* (Bracciolini), 34
female body: as commodity, 14, 21–22, 29, 87, 91, 124, 143, 147; disfigurement of, 72, 74; as fetish, 60, 65, 69, 79–82, 105, 111; as medium for exchange 21, 29, 63, 77–78, 83–84, 110, 135; representation of, 111–12, 166 n.12
feminine virtue and honor: and communication in narrative, 140; and female authority figures, 29, 131; "feminist" alternatives to, 124–25, 143–45; and honesty, 118–19, 126, 130, 145, 166–67 n.17; as sublimation of male virtues, 113–14, 117–18, 128–29
feminine double bind, 29, 73, 117
feminist desire, 124–25, 144–45
Ferrier, Janet, 41–44, 156 n.27
fetishism: and castration complex, 78–82; and female body, 14, 65, 82, 87–88, 91, 105, 111; and narrative, 65, 68–69, 73–74, 77, 82
Foucault, Michel, 12, 14, 22; definition of power, 17–20; definition of soul, 135, 167 n.21; description of power as active and passive, 29, 153 n.3; and narrative, 149; and punishment, 135, 167 n.22
France, Marie de, 35
Freccero, Carla, 72, 128, 166 n.10
Freud, Sigmund, 12, 79–80, 129

gaze, 63, 66, 71, 81, 142–43, 145
gender difference, 18, 20, 69, 87; and identity, 18, 69, 73–74, 107, 113–14, 147–48; and power configurations, 82, 105; and resistance to power structures, 57, 90, 130
Girard, René, 160 n.11
Glidden, Hope, 142, 161 n.17, 168 n.28, 168 nn.32–33
grotesque body, 89–91, 100, 102–3, 147, 163 n.3

Hartmann, Heidi, 57, 159 n.6
*Heptaméron, L'* (Navarre), 29, 44, 46, 74, 77, 148–49; Prologue, 13;Tale 10, 21, 114–30; Tale 21, 18–19, 130–39; Tale 43 19, 22, 45, 141–45; Tale 61 140; Tale 70, 144
honesty. *See* feminine virtue and honor

icons: Byzantine, 15–17, 44, 111; and fetishism 81–82; fictional characters as, 16, 46, 39, 60, 62–63, 67–68, 88, 90–91, 106–7, 128–29, 138–39, 145, 148–49, 166 n.12; food as, 75–76, 102–3, 107; and marriage, 67, 87; in parody, 90–91, 100–101
iconography: definition of, 15–17; and insignia in narrative, 45–47, 66–67, 75, 77–78, 104–7; prototypes in narrative, 39, 44–46, 90, 111, 133, 146, 148; and realism, 34; sacred prototypes, 16, 44–46; and social stratification, 104, 106, 143
imaginary, collective. *See* narrative
Irigaray, Luce, 12, 59, 61, 160 n.12

Jourda, Pierre, 151 n.2, 153 n.1, 154 nn.9–10, 156 n.29, 158 n.1, 160 n.14

Kristeva, Julia, 12
Kritzman, Lawrence, 128, 166 n.11

*La dame à la licorne*, 149
Lacan, Jacques, 21, 69, 80, 125, 162. n.26, 166 n.8
*lai*, 27, 31–36, 155 n.14
Lajarte, Philippe de, 151 n.5
*Les Cent nouvelles nouvelles* (anonymous), 12, 14, 21–23, 29, 35, 37, 41–42, 44, 83, 95, 110, 147; Tale 1, 57–62; Tale 3, 47, 62–69; Tale 9, 74–78; Tale 15, 78–81, 85; Tale 33, 69–74; Tale 99, 46
*Les Cent nouvelles nouvelles* (Vigneulles), 13, 22–23, 29, 74, 113, 117, 147–48; 157 n.35; Tale 20, 91–96; Tale 38, 85–88; Tale 42, 107–9; Tale 59, 101–7; Tale 81, 89–91; Tale 91, 96–101
Lévi-Strauss, Claude, 19, 152 n.11
Livingston, Charles, 13, 86, 91, 101, 162 n.30, 164 n.7, 164 n.9
Lorris, Guillaume de: *Le Roman de la rose*, 103
love, 117

## Index

lower material bodily stratum, 61, 84
Lukács, Gyorgy, 29–30
Lyons, John, 138, 154 n.11, 167 nn.23–24, 168 n.26

MacKinnon, Catherine, 63, 68, 73, 81, 159 n.6, 161 n.18–19
Madonna and child, 39
male homosocial economy: definition of, 12–13, 21–22, 159 n.6; and male subjectivity, 29; narrative manifestations in *Les Cent nouvelles nouvelles*, 52–82, 113; as paradox, 95; resistance to, 72, 85–112, 142
marriage: definition of, 165 n.2; and exchange of women, 14, 19–20, 83, 87, 123, 147–48; and female authority figures, 131, 134; and female desire, 113–14; interdiction as basis of, 101, 120; and male homosocial economy, 95; parody of, 60; *de praesenti*,167 n.20
Marot, Clément, 103
Marx, Karl, 12, 14
McKinley, Mary, 151–52 n.6, 157 n.34
Montaigne, Michel de, 157–58 n.36
*motto* sequences, 101–9
Mulvey, Laura, 160 n.13, 168 n.29

narrative: and character representation, 46–50; and metaphoric circulation of the phallus, 68–69; as collective imaginary, 45, 146; and feminine resistance, 148; and identity, 146; as medium of male homosocial exchange, 51–57, 64–65, 71–74, 77–78, 82–83, 111; narratological accounts of, 44–45; narrators and narratees, 51–56; relation to *nouvelle* in the history of realism, 27–30, 34, 39; as technique or technology, 17, 135, 140, 149
Navarre, Marguerite de: *L'Heptaméron*, 29, 44, 46, 74, 77, 148–49; Prologue, 13;Tale 10, 21, 114–30; Tale 21, 18–19, 130–39; Tale 43 19, 22, 45, 141–45; Tale 61 140; Tale 70, 144
Nietzsche, Friedrich, 12
*nouvelle*, 11, 17, 27–29; definition of, 28; French and European sources of, 31–34, 155 n.14; orientalist account of, 30–31; origins of, 27, 30, 154 n.11; realist defense of, 32–44; scholarship concerning 27–44

Ouspensky, Leonid, 152 n.8

Panofsky, Erwin, 16, 44–45, 156 n.28
Paris, Gaston, 27, 30–31, 33–34, 43
parody, 60, 90–91, 94, 100–101, 109, 148
Pavel, Thomas, 157 n.31
Pérouse, Gabriel, 28
phallus, circulation of, as metaphor, 68–70, 79–80
Philippe le Bon, Duke of Burgundy, 51–58, 95, 158 n.4
Prince, Gerald, 45, 152 n.9, 158 n.5
Pop, Mihai, 155–56 n.22
power: and communication, 119–22, 130–31, 133, 136–37, 139–41; definition of, 17–20; and desire, 124–25, 130; and female authority figures, 22, 116, 131, 136–40, 144; historical evolution of in narrative, 85, 95; and male homosocial relations, 46–82, 83; and *motto* sequences, 104; and narrative exchange, 62–69, 120; positive and negative effects of, 18–19, 22, 114, 118–19, 125, 132, 134, 138; and punishment, 135; and redistribution of wealth, 100; resistance to, 22, 83–84, 90, 93, 99, 113
professions, representation of, 86, 104, 106
Propp, Vladimir, 42, 155 n.22
prototypes, iconographic. *See* iconography

Rabelais, François, 39, 152 n.13, 159–60 n.10; *Gargantua*, 22, 152 n.13; *Pantagruel*, 16, 91, 103
rape, 64, 70, 89
realism, 11–12, 14, 27–50, 109–10
Reformation, 148
religious orders, 78, 101–3
Reyff, Simone de, 167 n.20
Rigolot, François, 72, 162 n.29, 166 n.12
rogue characters. *See* characters
*Roman de la rose* (Lorris), 103
Rouse, E. Clive, 156–57 n.30
Russell, Daniel, 153 n.4, 157–58 n.36

Saulnier, V.L., 11

scatological sequences, 28, 84, 88–91, 96
scopic desire and scopophilia, 60, 63, 160 n.13
Sedgwick, Eve Kosofsky, 159 n.6
signifier, as metaphor for fictional characters, 125
Söderhjelm, Werner, 31–35, 38, 40, 43, 154 nn.7–8
soul, definition of in relation to power, 135, 167 n.21
Sozzi, Lionello, 27, 151 n.1, 156 nn.26–27
Stone, Donald, 130, 167 n.18
storytelling, in narrative, 64, 68–69, 71–74, 77, 83
subjectivity: female, 20, 22, 63, 73–74, 83; in relation to narrative, 149; male, 20, 28, 60–62, 76–77, 80, 83, 147
sublimation: as detour of primary drives, 120, 122; and discourse, 126; and feminine virtue, 113–14, 117–18, 121, 128–29; and union with God, 120, 125, 129

Tetel, Marcel, 162 n.27, 165 n.3
Thompson, Stith, 155–56 n.22
Todorov, Tzvetan, 32, 44–46, 64, 103, 140, 156 n.24, 161 n.21
Toldo, Pietro, 31–33
Trask, Willard, 38
triangular desire, 58–59, 160 n.11
trickster characters. *See* characters
Troyes, Chrétien de: *Le Chevalier de la charrette*, 137

Vigneulles, Philippe de: *Les Cent nouvelles nouvelles*, 13, 22–23, 29, 74, 113, 117, 147–48, 157 n.35; Tale 20, 91–96; Tale 38, 85–88; Tale 42, 107–9; Tale 59, 101–7; Tale 81, 89–91; Tale 91, 96–101
Villon, François, 148
Vossler, Karl, 40–41

war, as metaphor for amorous relations, 70, 114–15, 165 n.3
Warburg, Aby, 16
Wetzel, Hermann, 101, 163–64 n.6
"world upside-down." *See* carnival and the carnivalesque

Zemon Davis, Natalie, 164 n.10

Pavel, Thomas. *Fictional Worlds*. Cambridge: Harvard University Press, 1986.
———. *The Poetics of Plot: The Case of English Renaissance Drama*. Minneapolis: University of Minnesota Press, 1985.
Pérouse, Gabriel A. *Nouvelles françaises du XVIe siècle: Images de la vie du temps*. Geneva: Droz, 1977.
Pop, Mihai. "La poétique du conte populaire." *Semiotica* 2(2) (1970): 117–27.
Prince, Gerald. *A Dictionary of Narratology*. Lincoln: University of Nebraska Press, 1987.
———. *Narratology: The Form and Functioning of Narrative*. Berlin: Mouton, 1982.
Rabelais, François. *Oeuvres complètes*. Edited by Guy Demerson. Paris: Éditions du Seuil, 1973.
Rigolot, François. "Magdalen's Skull: Allegory and Iconography in *Heptameron* 32." *Renaissance Quarterly* 47(1) (spring 1994): 57–73.
Rouse, E. Clive. *Medieval Wall Paintings*. Buckinghamshire: Shire Press Ltd., 1991.
Russell, Daniel. *Emblematic Structures in Renaissance French Culture*. Toronto: University of Toronto Press, 1995.
———. "Some Ways of Structuring Character in the *Heptameron*." In Lyons and McKinley, *Critical Tales*, 203–17.
Schenck, Mary Jane Stearns. "Narrative Structure in the Exemplum, Fabliau, and the Nouvelle." *Romanic Review* 72(4) (November 1981): 367–82.
Schmidt, Albert Marie, ed. *Poètes français du seizième siècle*. Paris: Gallimard, 1953.
Sedgwick, Eve Kosofsky. *Between Men: English Literature and Male Homosocial Desire*. New York: Columbia University Press, 1985.
Söderhjelm, Werner. *La nouvelle française au XVe siècle*. Geneva: Slatkine Reprints, 1973. Originally published Paris, 1910.
Sozzi, Lionello. *La nouvelle française de la Renaissance*. Turin: G. Giappichelli, 1973.
———. "La nouvelle française au XVe siècle." *Cahiers de l'Association Internationale des Etudes Françaises* 23 (1971): 67–84.
———, ed. *La nouvelle française à la Renaissance*. Geneva: Slatkine, 1981.
Stone, Donald. "'La Malice des hommes': 'L'Histoire des satyres' and the *Heptameron*." In Lyons and McKinley, *Critical Tales*, 53–64.
Sweetser, Franklin P., ed. *Les Cent nouvelles nouvelles*. Geneva: Droz, 1966.
Telle, Émile. *L'Oeuvre de Marguerite d'Angoulême, Reine de Navarre, et la querelle des femmes*. Toulouse: Imprimerie Toulousaine Lion et Fils, 1937.
Tetel, Marcel. *Marguerite de Navarre's 'Heptaméron': Themes, Language, and Structure*. Durham: Duke University Press, 1973.
Tiemann, Hermann. *Die Entstehung der mittelalterlichen Novelle in Frankreich*. Hamburg: Europa-Kolleg, 1961.
Todorov, Tzvetan. *Grammaire du décaméron*. The Hague: Mouton, 1969.
———. "La grammaire du récit." *Poétique* 3 (1970): 322–33.
Troyes, Nicolas de. *Le grand parangon des nouvelles nouvelles*. Edited by Krystina Kasprzyk. Paris: Didier, 1970.
Van Rijnberk, G. *Le langage par signes chez les moines*. Amsterdam: North-Holland Publishing Company, 1953.
Vigneulles, Philippe de. *Les Cent nouvelles nouvelles*. Edited by Charles H. Livingston et al. Geneva: Droz, 1972.
Vossler, Karl. "Zu den anfängen der französischen Novelle." *Studien zur vergleichenden Literaturgeschichte* 2 (1902): 3–36.

QL